'The policing of gang activity in the West of
easy. Police Scotland has had to look at new
impact on this type of territorial and recreatioi
based academic research has been used by th
effectiveness. The work by Professor Deuchar has been central to the
development of our successful strategy and I would recommend this book
to all who have an interest in this type of law enforcement work.'

**Chief Superintendent Robert Hamilton, Head of the Licensing and Violence
Reduction Unit, Police Scotland**

'Ross Deuchar provides a textured and compelling account of youth
violence, unraveling the unique and common causes that lead impoverished
teens – White in Scotland, African American in the United States – to
victimize in lethal ways. He also shows, however, that this violence is
not intractable but, through criminologically sound and supportive
interventions, can be diminished – and the futures of troubled youngsters
rescued. Carefully researched and accessibly written, this volume is both
essential reading for scholars and ideal for classroom use.'

Professor Francis Cullen, University of Cincinnati

'Ross Deuchar tells a fascinating tale of two different cities which share a
desire to reduce the harm caused by violence. Like so many forces around
the world the Cincinnati Police Department were encouraged to look at
policing differently by a critical event. Ross's book tells the story how the
adoption of a Focused Deterrence model using a 'pulling leavers' approach
to violent crime has resulted in a changed community where, instead of
simply responding to violent crime, the police and community actively seek
to prevent it together. A strong focus on purposeful deterrent activity and
community activism was instrumental in helping to heal the fragmented
communities he explored, whilst putting an end to the suggestion of 'zero-
offend-the-community policing'. Ross carried out an ethnographic study
in both Cincinnati and Glasgow so his book brings to life the lessons
learned from a street level, clearly illustrating how a sound criminological
understanding can really aid modern-day policing. Ross's book shows
how, on both sides of the Atlantic, thinking about effective violence-harm

reduction has moved on from the 'masculinization' of a response to crime to where a truly holistic and multi-agency approach can deliver real change.'

Assistant Chief Constable Garry Shewan, Force Command, Greater Manchester Police

'Cross-national comparative research is rare in criminology. Ross Deuchar's *Policing Youth Violence*, which examines innovative initiatives in Cincinnati and Glasgow aimed at reducing youthful criminality, is therefore particularly to be welcomed. Innovative in approach and wide-ranging in scope, this book will be of huge interest to scholars of policing, youth crime, gangs, and desistance.'

Professor Tim Newburn, London School of Economics

Policing Youth Violence

IOEPress Trentham Books

Policing Youth Violence:
Transatlantic connections

Ross Deuchar

A Trentham Book
Institute of Education Press

First published in 2013 by the Institute of Education, University of London,
20 Bedford Way, London WC1H 0AL

www.ioe.ac.uk/ioepress

British Library Cataloguing in Publication Data:
A catalogue record for this publication is available from the British Library

ISBNs
978-1-85856-519-4 (paperback)
978-1-85856-540-8 (PDF eBook)
978-1-85856-541-5 (ePub eBook)
978-1-85856-542-2 (Kindle eBook)

Every effort has been made to trace copyright holders and to obtain their permission for the use of copyright material. The publisher apologizes for any errors or omissions and would be grateful if notified of any corrections that should be incorporated in future reprints or editions of this book.

The opinions expressed in this publication are those of the authors and do not necessarily reflect the views of the Institute of Education, University of London.

Typeset by Quadrant Infotech (India) Pvt Ltd
Printed by CPI Group (UK) Ltd, Croydon, CR0 4YY

Cover: Aquarium Graphic Design

Contents

List of figures and tables

Acronyms and abbreviations

ACPOS	Association of Chief Police Officers in Scotland
CAD	Computer-aided Dispatch
CBT	Cognitive Behavioural Therapy
CCTV	Closed-circuit Television
CID	Criminal Investigation Department
CIRV	Cincinnati/Community Initiative to Reduce Violence
CLD	Community Learning and Development
COMPSTAT	Computer Statistics
CPD	Cincinnati Police Department
DMI	Drug Market Intervention
EEI	Early and Effective Intervention
FARE	Family Action in Rogerfield and Easterhouse
FBI	Federal Bureau of Investigation
GCPP	Glasgow Community Planning Partnership
GCSS	Glasgow Community and Safety Services
GIRFEC	Getting It Right for Every Child
LTS	Learning and Teaching Scotland
NNSC	National Network for Safe Communities
NYPD	New York Police Department
POP	Problem-oriented Policing
SPS	Scottish Prison Service
SWAT	Special Weapons and Tactics (specialized law enforcement unit)
UCICS	University of Cincinnati Institute of Crime Sciences
UNODC	United Nations Office on Drugs and Crime
VRU	Violence Reduction Unit
WHO	World Health Organization
YOI	Young Offender Institution

Glossary of slang terms and idioms – Cincinnati

beef	an intense rivalry that can be the stimulus for a fight
Bloods	a primarily African-American gang founded in Los Angeles
bro'	brother or friend
cop	police officer
crack head	cocaine addict
Crips	a primarily African-American gang founded in Los Angeles
downtown	city centre or central business district
fed agent	federal criminal investigator
gangsta rap	a subgenre of hip hop music that celebrates violent lifestyles
homie	homeboy (male friend from the same district or gang)
hood	ghetto
mamma	mother
punked out	made fun of
rapper	rap artist
sidewalk	pavement
Tot Lot	a notorious gang in the West End neighbourhood of Cincinnati

Glossary of slang terms and idioms – Glasgow

aboot	about
aye	yes
batter	attack
blade	knife
buzz	excitement, adrenalin
cat A	category A, high tariff offender
chew the fat	to participate in idle conversation
couldnae	could not
da'	father
dae	do
dishin'	giving
fae	from
football casual	a person belonging to a football sub-culture associated with hooliganism and expensive designer clothing
game	brave
gie	give
gob-smacked	shocked
high vis	high visibility clothing
lads	young men or boys
ma'	mother
mair	more
missus	wife or female partner
motor	car
nae	no
ned	non-educated delinquent
no'	not
oot	out
polis	police
rap	quit, give up
rep	reputation
sack	quit, give up
Stone Island	an Italian designer brand, popular among football casuals
tartanize	add a Scottish focus to

wasted	drunk
wean	child
wee	small
weed	cannabis
wi'	with
yoos	you (plural)

Dedicated to Alan – I hope you enjoy reading this some day

Acknowledgements

My thanks go to all the police officers, police staff, street workers, and members of youth and community agencies who participated in the study. And to all the young men who provided me with such insight and inspiration.

Special thanks go to Robin Engel for her hospitality and encouragement during my visits to Cincinnati, for the wonderful Foreword, her support with Chapter 2, and for her feedback on earlier drafts of the book. And Sammy – I just loved your Girl Scout cookies!

I am most grateful to the Carnegie Trust for the Universities of Scotland and to the University of the West of Scotland for providing the funding that supported the research.

Thanks also to William Graham and Douglas Weir for their continued friendship and for the feedback they gave me on draft chapters of the book; to Iain Hunter, for his help with constructing the index; and to Gillian Klein and the IOE Press team for believing in this project, and for all their support throughout it.

And, as always, to Karen and Alan – thanks for putting up with me working every hour that God sent, once again!

Foreword

Robin S. Engel, PhD, University of Cincinnati

The story of the Cincinnati Initiative to Reduce Violence (CIRV, pronounced 'serve') that unfolds across the pages of Ross Deuchar's book is a very personal one for me. I arrived in the City of Cincinnati in April 2001 as part of an interview process at the School of Criminal Justice, University of Cincinnati. Just prior to my arrival for the interview, university officials changed my hotel accommodation to a neighbouring city in Northern Kentucky. The downtown area of Cincinnati was engulfed in race riots, and law enforcement officials had issued a city-wide night-time curfew to clear the streets. I eventually accepted the position at the University of Cincinnati and found myself – an academic specialist in policing and race issues – relocating to a city struggling to heal, with a well-intended but resource-limited police department trying to adapt and change. In the decade that followed, the Cincinnati Police Department (CPD) transformed itself from an agency that had been a primary factor in instigating race riots to an international award winner for excellence in policing. In 2008, the CPD won the International Association of Chiefs of Police (IACP) Webber Seavey Award for Excellence in Policing – the highest accolade given to a single law enforcement agency in the world every year – for its work with CIRV. It also won the National Criminal Justice Association's Outstanding Criminal Justice Program Award in 2008 and the International Association of Chiefs of Police West Award for Excellence in Criminal Investigations in 2009, also for its innovative work with CIRV and resulting reductions in violence.

All this was accomplished while also implementing a large-scale violence-reduction initiative that brought together groups of unlikely partners to do extraordinary things. The story of CIRV is one of hope and healing, partnerships and reform, renewal and reformation. It is also a story that transcends the City of Cincinnati, because CIRV-style interventions have been demonstrated to interrupt the type of group-related violence that is experienced in cities across America, the United Kingdom, and around the globe. Many of the lessons from CIRV that were shared and implemented in Glasgow, Scotland, are described between the covers of Deuchar's provocative book.

The Cincinnati riots in April 2001 were sparked by an officer-involved shooting of a 19 year-old black male wanted on more than a dozen misdemeanour (less serious) warrants. Timothy Thomas was the fifteenth black man to have died during contact with police in the six years up to that point (Klepal and Andrews, 2001). Although the majority of these previous incidents were deemed 'clean shootings' – necessary because the suspect posed an imminent deadly threat to officers or others – outrage in our racially divided community was readily apparent. The CPD lacked widespread legitimacy in many neighbourhoods, where poor police–community relations were the norm. In the aftermath of three straight days of civil unrest, looting, and rioting, a series of litigations were filed and compromises established that included federal oversight of the CPD by the US Department of Justice for the following six years. The CPD was required to make significant reforms in policies, procedures, and training in a number of areas including the use of force, and problem-solving became the primary agency-wide strategy for all aspects of policing (Eck and Rothman, 2006).

The years immediately following the race riots were tumultuous, as the CPD attempted to understand, define, and implement the reforms that were required. Likewise, the community was asked to come to the table and work as partners with a police agency they did not yet trust. The result was continual conflict and officer disengagement. From the police perspective, why risk life and limb for a community that did not support them? Further, why risk potential civil and criminal litigation when trying to police violent, crime-ridden areas? Some officers weighed the pros and cons and decided it was not worth the risk; as a whole, the agency did the minimum required – responded to calls for service, but little more. This slowdown did not last long, however, as the community became increasingly violent, turning to firearms. Initially these shootings involved non-fatal wounding of community members, but escalated into homicides and eventually the targeting of police. The crime rate skyrocketed, and violent crime in several Cincinnati neighbourhoods became commonplace. By 2005, the City of Cincinnati was in the midst of a crisis of violence, and 2006 ended on a record-high of 88 homicides and an average of 35 shootings per month, despite a significantly declining city population. Although five years had passed since that turbulent time between police and community that erupted in civil disobedience – and despite the major police reforms that had been implemented – violence in predominantly minority communities continued to escalate.

The initial response by the CPD was to flood the affected neighbourhoods with additional resources. A centralized, high-impact strike team was created, called Vortex. Vortex officers did not respond to calls for service, but rather were used as a proactive, aggressive enforcement presence in high-crime neighbourhoods. Their initial aggressive tactics and widespread geographical scope created more angst among minority citizens and served to further alienate the local population from the police. Later described by CPD leadership as equivalent to 'carpet bombing', these approaches resulted in significant increases in arrests, but made little impact on the level of violence. The approach failed to be effective due, in part, to the lack of focus on specific offenders, groups, gangs, and places. In addition, it failed to establish police legitimacy among the community – a necessary component for effective and equitable policing.

As the violence increased, political pressure led the CPD towards a different violence-reduction strategy. Dr Victor Garcia, a leading trauma surgeon at Cincinnati Children's Hospital and Medical Center (CCHMC), paved the way for change and was instrumental in bringing a 'focused deterrence' approach to Cincinnati. He engaged Professor David Kennedy, then at Harvard University, who had been heavily involved in the initial work in Boston in the mid-1990s that led to significant reductions in youth violence. Under the leadership of Mayor Mark Mallory, City Manager Milton Dohoney, and Council member Cecil Thomas, the City of Cincinnati hired Professor Kennedy as a consultant. He worked with me and my colleagues from the University of Cincinnati, Dr Garcia, and city leaders to initiate a focused deterrence initiative. Cincinnati Police Chief Thomas Streicher, Jr. was willing to take a risk on a theory that, at that time, had limited empirical support. The head of the police operational team, Lt. Colonel James Whalen, pledged and delivered on the law enforcement component that is critical for the success of this type of initiative. S. Gregory Baker, a civilian member of the CPD command staff, served as a much-needed project manager to coordinate the efforts across partnering agencies. The other strategy teams were formed – social services, community engagement – although leadership on these teams often changed hands.

My initial role was to engage with the CPD leadership and provide technical support along with data-collection and analyses for all partnering agencies. I was already working with the CPD to help train their crime analysts and assist with problem-solving efforts, and had become an academic whom the CPD leadership trusted – a rarity in US police–academic relationships (see Engel and Whalen, 2010). This trust afforded me an opportunity to help guide what would become an international model for violence-reduction.

It was the most challenging, exhausting, and rewarding experience of my professional career.

The focused deterrence approach to violence-reduction applied by CIRV was first used in Boston during the mid-1990s (Braga *et al.*, 2001) and has now proven successful in multiple cities (for a review, see Braga and Weisburd, 2012a). The approach uses a 'pulling levers' strategy to identify and communicate the consequences of violence to at-risk gang members. The strategy is based on the premise that a majority of offences are committed by a small number of individuals who are often organized (to some degree) in groups or gangs. The use of collective accountability is a central theme of many focused deterrence initiatives and is based on the assumption that individuals are organized in groups (McGloin, 2009). Even a loose organization of offenders in groups is necessary for the success of a focused deterrence initiative for violence-reduction. Another underlying assumption is that while violent acts are often perpetrated by individuals, they are rooted in a group dynamic. It is believed that the majority of violence associated with gang members is based on respect issues related to the norms and narratives of the street (Anderson, 1999).

The effectiveness of these strategies is based on the belief that group pressure and support, if handled properly, can be key mechanisms for reducing violence. To reduce violence effectively, consistent and sustained communication of the non-violence message to gang members by practitioners, social service providers, and community members is critical (Braga and Weisburd, 2012a). During face-to-face offender notification meetings in Cincinnati, members of violent groups were told that the violence must stop, that there would be group consequences if it did not, and that the community would support these consequences. Violent group members were told that there was social service help for all who wanted it, and that CIRV Street Advocates would be assigned to help them navigate the specially developed social service and employment programme.

In summary, our goal was to use a data-driven approach to reduce violence while helping offenders, reducing incarceration, strengthening police–community relations, fostering partnerships across law enforcement and social service agencies, and addressing racial conflict. It was a lofty goal, as no other documented initiative had achieved such outcomes and sustained the results over time. In Cincinnati, CIRV partners included law enforcement officials, political leaders, medical professionals, business leaders, community organizers, and academics. We each brought different expertise and perspectives to the collective. As a result, the story of CIRV is of an imperfect collective at best. Our team of hard-working, dedicated professionals and community members often did not agree as to the best approaches. There were continual challenges, and we struggled to maintain good relations across partnering agencies that had never before worked together in meaningful ways. We had to deal with many personality conflicts, competing interests, and limited resources.

There were successes and failures along the way – but in the end, many lives were saved. After three and a half years, our analyses demonstrated that CIRV resulted in a 42 per cent reduction in group or gang member-involved homicides and a 22 per cent reduction in all non-fatal shootings (Engel *et al.*, 2013). Now, as CIRV approaches its six-year anniversary of continuous efforts, the City of Cincinnati is still recording significant reductions in violence. The 53 homicides (30 gang member-involved) committed in 2012 constituted the lowest annual homicide total in the previous 12 years. The relationship between the CPD and minority citizens improves every year and can now fairly be described as reconciliatory. The ten-year anniversary of the April 2001 riots came and went with little fanfare; police and communities continue to move forward together. Cincinnati is clearly a different city from what it was just a decade ago.

The larger impact of CIRV on communities across the United States and the United Kingdom has been profound. Over the years, CIRV has added key components to the work that are now widely recognized as best practice. These improvements include: 1) the development of a team organizational structure and accountability mechanisms by business executives from Procter and Gamble; 2) the hiring of a full-time project manager; 3) high-level political engagement and accountability; 4) a more robust social service component; and 5) continual researcher involvement from initial implementation through evaluation (Engel *et al.,* 2013). Along the way, the CIRV team has shared its experiences with the world – what works, what doesn't, and what's promising. Many CIRV team members continue to provide training and consultancy to other cities around the world. We also host visitors to let them experience first-hand the inner workings of CIRV. Some of our first visitors have been from the United Kingdom; representatives from the London Metropolitan Police made their way to Cincinnati in 2008, followed soon after by officials from Glasgow, Scotland, and the then Strathclyde Police Department. The Scottish officials visited again the following year, and so began our efforts at international policy transfer. The Scottish delegation was particularly keen to observe and learn; while on-site, they brainstormed about the adaptations that would be necessary for a similar initiative to be effective in Glasgow.

I was quite sceptical about the possible impact that our style of violence-reduction might have in Glasgow. I always joked that it was similar to *A Tale of Two Cities*. Judging by the numbers alone, Cincinnati and Glasgow differed considerably. The City of Cincinnati has an estimated population of just under 300,000 residents, with a declining population in the urban core, but a greater metropolitan region of 2.1 million, with economic growth concentrated in the predominantly white suburban areas. When CIRV began, the CPD had approximately 1,100 sworn officers, but this has been reduced to just 970 officers with a possible reduction of up to 150 additional officers anticipated in the next fiscal cycle. In contrast, Glasgow was twice the size, with approximately 600,000 residents and approximately 3,400 police officers (Strathclyde Police had approximately 8,400 officers covering Glasgow and the west of Scotland, but in April 2013 this was consolidated into the new national police force for Scotland). Cincinnati has 49 per cent white, 45 per cent black, and 3 per cent Hispanic residents. In contrast, Glasgow is approximately 95 per cent white, with only 5 per cent non-white combined.

The violence problems across these two cities also appeared dramatically different at first. In Cincinnati, the homicide victims were predominantly black (85 per cent), male (85 per cent), killed with a firearm (90 per cent), and an average of 29 years-old; homicide suspects generally followed the same demographic patterns. Further, nearly three-quarters of our homicide incidents involved a gang member as a victim, suspect, or both, and the violence was often intertwined with illicit drug markets. Likewise, the City of Cincinnati averaged 35 non-fatal shootings per month, the victims mainly being black (89 per cent) and male (90 per cent), and an average age of 27 years-old. In contrast, the violence problem in Glasgow differed significantly. Violent incidents involved almost exclusively white males of a much younger age, and often the incidents were alcohol-related. Violence in Glasgow was also less lethal but perhaps more interpersonal (involving knifings) compared to the typical firearm violence experienced in US cities. As Ross Deuchar describes, the homicide rate in Glasgow of 4.1 per 100,000 was one of the highest in Europe. By comparison, the homicide rate in Cincinnati in 2006 was more than seven times greater, at 29.3 per 100,000.

The two police agency cultures also differ greatly. Most apparent is that all sworn Cincinnati police officers (and nearly all police officers in the USA) carry firearms; and unfortunately, circumstances involving the use of deadly force are much higher in the USA compared to the UK. More US officers are shot or killed in the line of duty by criminal suspects compared to the UK, and Scotland specifically. As a result of the higher likelihood of danger encountered by police officers in Cincinnati compared to Glasgow – along with significant differences in legal constraints, policies, procedures, and political influences – their approaches during police–citizen encounters were also dramatically different.

And so it became an empirical question – could the underlying principles of focused deterrence be adapted and implemented to address a different type of violence problem in a different culture? Yet, as Ross Deuchar so perceptively describes in this book, the violence was only superficially different – its underlying causes were actually quite similar across the two cities, even if the violence was perpetrated by individuals who looked different. Deuchar skilfully unpacks this violence problem to demonstrate that, at the core, these communities actually do share very similar problems. The global issues of disenfranchised youth, lack of opportunities, poverty, and cycles of violence and despair transcend cultures, and appear more important than the more commonly discussed issues of race and firearm access that are debated in the US. Likewise, there were more similarities than differences in the cultures of law enforcement agencies and social service providers, and interesting parallels in political and social contexts. And therefore we learned that while CIRV's exact replication might not be successful, a strategically modified version that remained true to the same underlying propositions could save lives across the Atlantic as well.

The Glasgow team used and modified our approach, and even borrowed our name CIRV (exchanging the 'C' in Cincinnati for Community). I joked with my new Scottish friends and colleagues that we were now an international franchise. It is important to recognize that this information-exchange was not a one-way street; rather, we were able to exchange with, and learn from, one another. In my opinion, the Glasgow CIRV team was much better at social service delivery compared to the Cincinnati CIRV model. Glasgow's success in this area was due in part to cultural differences, higher levels of available funding, and better social service agency preparation and commitment. As a result, many of the Scottish would-be offenders not only reduced their levels of violence, but were also able to significantly change their lives by embracing a pro-social lifestyle. Importantly, the Glasgow initiative started in communities with lower levels of violence – in short, Glasgow had less road to travel compared to Cincinnati, and therefore was able to incorporate a robust social service structure from the outset.

When I visited my CIRV partners in Glasgow in 2009, I was struck by the similarities and differences, and in awe of the effectiveness of policy transfer (Graham, 2012). While nearly all of the details were different, the core problems and solutions remained the same. I returned to Cincinnati energized, with the belief that our work could make a difference not only in Cincinnati, but in many cities around the world. I visited the UK again in 2011 and 2012. During these trips I met with organizational partners, along with former offenders who had, with CIRV's help, pulled themselves out of their violent circumstances. With each trip I found my colleagues in the midst of various successes and challenges. We continued to share stories, experiences, and expertise, often finding solace in the company of those who understood the trials and tribulations of the work.

Given the successes of CIRV in both Cincinnati and Glasgow, we have learned many important lessons about the nature of violence and, perhaps more importantly, about effective responses for its reduction. We have also learned of the many obstacles that stand in the way of the sometimes simple, low-cost solutions that often do not gain enough traction or political support to become sustainable. CIRV in both cities was imperfect, but demonstrated effectiveness at reducing violence and improving police–community relations. Now the next step in the process can begin: as violence is reduced, communities have a better chance of achieving stability and economic revitalization. Both Glasgow and Cincinnati are moving on to the next stage in the continued effort to improve public safety and quality of life for all residents. I am optimistic that the lessons learned through the CIRV partnerships on both sides of the Atlantic will continue to serve these communities and help disrupt the cycle of violence.

Finally, I note the personal side of violence. As an academic trained in quantitative methods, prior to CIRV I had little experience of dealing first-hand with suspects and victims, and family and community members affected by violence. These are the individuals our law enforcement officers, social service providers, and medical professionals encounter every day, yet academics rarely venture into the fray. In his compelling description of two communities struggling to reduce violence, Ross Deuchar has given a voice to these individuals, eloquently describing the problems of violence and its solutions from their perspective. He illustrates the complexities of lifestyles intertwined with poverty, hopelessness, and a view of violence as normal. He also describes the hopes and frustrations of those frontline professionals attempting to make our communities safer.

Despite some mistakes and missteps along the way, I am so proud of the efforts of the CIRV team, and in particular, the extraordinary commitment of the CPD. Our city no longer just responds to violence; with CIRV support,

Robin S. Engel

it actively seeks to prevent it. I have also learned the value of partnerships, and the importance of academics working with agencies to guide programme implementation, rather than simply evaluating programmes after the fact. The work is not easy, but it is well worth the investment. We are a changed community.

Introduction

My introduction to CIRV was on a cold, wet November afternoon in Glasgow in 2008. On that memorable day, I visited the offices of Glasgow Community and Safety Services (GCSS) where the core members of the CIRV team were based. I met Chief Inspector Andy McKay, who at that time headed up the team along with his colleague, Inspector William Graham. Andy and Willie talked enthusiastically and at length about the first 'self-referral' session that had recently taken place in Glasgow Sheriff Court, and described their vision of how CIRV had the potential to reduce gang violence, re-engage disadvantaged young men, and, in the long term, save lives.

During that first meeting, Andy talked to me about Cincinnati and the ideas he had brought back from his visit there. At that time, Cincinnati seemed like a glamorous and far-away place that I had only ever heard about in films. Little did I know that it would become such an important place for me over the next few years. Inspired by Chief Superintendent John Carnochan during numerous presentations he gave on behalf of the Scottish Violence Reduction Unit (VRU), I was then introduced to acting Inspector Robert Stevenson who replaced Andy in his role as CIRV coordinator in 2009. Having taken up a professorship at the University of the West of Scotland in 2010, I kept in touch with both Robert and Willie, who encouraged me to pursue my interests in CIRV and make contact with Dr Robin Engel from the University of Cincinnati. As Robin notes in the Foreword to this book, she supported and guided the CPD in adopting what became an international model for violence-reduction.

In March 2011 I arrived in Cincinnati for the first time. My immediate impressions of the city were tainted by the social stigma that dominates local people's perceptions about socially deprived neighbourhoods. In the hotel where I was staying, the young receptionist showed me a map of the city and warned me not to go into communities such as Over-the-Rhine or Walnut Hills. The next day, while walking around the central business district (or 'downtown' area of the city), I was admiring the skyscrapers and observing the young white professionals in business suits going to work in the city banks. I then visited a local store, where the young assistant gave me a strong piece of advice: 'When you leave the store, go right – that's downtown. Don't turn left and go uptown – that's a bad part of the city.' My curiosity getting the better of me, I left the store and turned left and within ten minutes I found myself in the deprived community known as Over-the-Rhine. The skyscrapers and city banks had disappeared as well as the white faces, to be replaced with young African American males hanging around on street corners selling drugs. My ethnographic research had begun.

During my visits to Cincinnati in 2011–12, I was able to uncover the challenges of the city as well as dispel some of the myths and public misconceptions. I was amazed at how the officers in CPD welcomed me and gave me unlimited access to observe and immerse myself in police practice. Thanks to the close working relationship with Robin, they provided me with some unforgettable experiences, enabling me to observe critical situations such as specialized police patrols and undercover work, car chases, narcotics investigations, and drug raids. I met some inspirational figures in American policing and gained first-hand experience of the community activism that characterizes the work of Street Advocates (reformed offenders who now devoted their lives to trying to re-engage young offenders on the streets of Cincinnati), as well as that of social service providers, and probation teams. And, most importantly, I gained an insight into the causes and impact of the violence by talking at length to both current and reformed offenders about the social pressures they experienced.

When I returned from my first visit to Cincinnati, I set about the task of meeting the equivalent members of the CIRV team in Glasgow. As well as interviewing police officers, members of social services agencies, and community teams I rode along with the Gangs Task Force officers. I was inspired by the work of these officers, who had to be creative in their responses to young men on the streets in order to build trust and rapport. My ethnographic work showed me that the violence problem differed from that of Cincinnati, but the causes were pretty much the same. Meeting both current and reformed offenders took me on a rollercoaster ride of emotions – at times I laughed with them and was inspired by them, but I also felt deep compassion for their plights.

In conducting the research on both sides of the Atlantic, I went on a long, thought-provoking, and challenging journey. This book allows me to share that journey. In Part 1, I explore the causes and impact of youth violence and the police strategies that have been put in place to try to manage the issues. Chapter 1 sets out the key criminological and sociological theories that have often been drawn on to examine what stimulates violence. I consider the contested nature of the 'gang' phenomenon and the relationship between youth violence and wider issues such as social deprivation, racism, and masculinity. Classic insights from Emile Durkheim, Robert Merton, and Albert Cohen are combined with more contemporary sociological analyses that demonstrate how crime can be seen as a social product in both the USA and Britain. The chapter explains how social and cultural oppression, set against the backdrop of 'liquid' modernity (Bauman, 2012), can often lead to defensive masculinity characterized by violence.

The question of how best to police these issues is explored in Chapter 2. I review what is known about policing research and what we have learned about the best strategies for policing young people in particular. I describe the aggressive police strategies that have been put in place and the impact they have had on public perceptions of police legitimacy and equity. And I review the recent policy initiatives that combine problem-oriented policing, multi-agency work, and focused deterrence to manage and reduce youth violence. The chapter concludes with an overview of CIRV as it was implemented in both Cincinnati and Glasgow, and illustrates the reductions in violent offending that have been achieved among young men who have engaged with the programmes attached to the CIRV initiative.

Mindful of these positive outcomes, my approach to criminological research has always been to prioritize the voices of my participants. I wanted to move beyond the positive statistics and meet the police officers and service agencies that implemented CIRV, and hear the voices of the suspects, victims, families, and community members affected by the violence. Chapter 3 provides an insight into the two cities that were the focus for the research, with their contrasting cultures and demographics, and sets out the part-time ethnographic methods I used to gather the data in both settings. I describe how I accessed the participants and interviewed senior and operational officers, youth and street workers, social service providers, and current and reformed offenders. I explain the nature of the participant observation I carried out while accompanying police officers and shadowing community teams as they engaged with the most marginalized. A general overview of the research participants is provided, and I relate how I dealt with the challenging ethical issues that arose while conducting the study.

The reality of young men's lives in the most deprived neighbourhoods in Cincinnati and Glasgow is outlined in Part 2. First, Chapter 4 explores the experiences of both current and reformed offenders in Cincinnati. The insights from those young men who are currently deeply involved in violence in the city are combined with the perspectives of Street Advocates, who have a history of violent offending but now devote their lives to helping others. In exploring the insights gleaned from interviews, I provide some illustrations of the social and cultural disadvantage these men have faced. I also explore how, and to what extent, they have dealt with these issues through violence, crime, and gang culture. Supplementary insights provided by police and probation officers are included, together with those gained from participant observation conducted during real and virtual tours of Cincinnati neighbourhoods. The chapter offers some reflections on how young men's lives are often characterized by adhering to a street code centred on drug dealing and sustaining credibility and respect through the possession and use of firearms.

In Chapter 5, a comparative perspective is adopted from which I explore the extent to which street violence among young men in Glasgow may be encouraged or shaped by the same types of socio-cultural issues as those I uncovered in Cincinnati. Drawing on the data from my life history interviews with reformed offenders in communities and with current offenders in prison, I present the reader with the biographies of four young men. I also make reference to additional illustrations from other research participants. Through presenting the biographies and interview data, I identify the causes, nature, and impact of the violence that happens on the streets of Glasgow, as well as the limited impact of the criminal justice system on deterring involvement with crime.

A key aspect of my research was to examine the role the police can play in implementing interventions that stimulate social support, and to explore the remaining challenges. In Part 3, I examine the focused deterrence principles underpinning the CIRV initiative as it was applied in both cities. I begin with Cincinnati, and in Chapter 6 I reflect on the voices of senior police officers within CPD and members of the wider CIRV team. The chapter explores the cultural reorientation that senior officers embraced to implement CIRV, the case-management process that provided young men with access to purposeful activity, and the tensions that arose between command-level police culture and frontline practice. These tensions are further explored in Chapter 7, where I examine the extent to which the focus on preventive and welfare-oriented policing influenced the practice of those officers on the streets. In examining the work of the specialized enforcement unit in Cincinnati, I use interview data and fieldnotes from police patrols to illustrate the dispositions and practice of officers. I demonstrate the cultural disparity that can be found between command-level strategy and the work of those who view themselves as traditional, aggressive street cops.

Moving across the Atlantic, Chapter 8 focuses on Glasgow's own version of CIRV and includes data from my interviews with senior officers in the city and the partners they worked with as part of the strategy. I explore the policy transfer principles that underpinned the initiative as it travelled across the Atlantic, and the personal and professional journeys officers undertook to embrace them. A key aim of the chapter is to examine the multiple inputs that social and community partners provided and the case-management process that enabled young men to access tailor-made interventions. I describe the case of one young mother who, by sharing her emotional experiences, appealed to young men to leave the violence behind – an example that illustrates the impact of the strategy on volunteers as well as clients. But, as issues of cultural disparity impacted on police practice in Cincinnati, I examine how the work of the Gangs Task Force Unit supported or undermined the wider strategic focus underpinning CIRV in Glasgow. Chapter 9 summarizes my fieldnotes, to enable readers to accompany police officers on specialized patrols and gain a deeper understanding of the work of plainclothes officers in high-crime areas. In describing the outcomes from participant observation, I present further insights from interviews with Task Force officers about how they conceptualized their frontline duties.

One of the key themes in my discussions with senior officers in both Cincinnati and Glasgow was the focus on multi-agency partnership work and community activism for preventing youth violence from escalating. In Part 4, I attempt to unravel the nature of these non-traditional partnerships and their impact on re-engaging violent young men. I begin in Chapter 10 by examining the role of Street Advocates in Cincinnati. Using data from interviews and participant observation of Advocates' practice, the chapter explores how these reformed offenders engaged young men through pre-emptive strategies in neighbourhoods with a history of high homicide rates. I illustrate how Advocates employed evangelistic, faith-based approaches to appeal to young men to leave offending behind and engage them in the wider services that CIRV provided. Chapter 11 illustrates how youth workers and community-based agencies in Glasgow used recreational sport and issues-based workshops to re-engage those on the margins. By exploring interview data and ethnographic fieldnotes, the chapter examines the subtle spiritual journeys that young men were taken on, the work placements that were arranged for them, and the intensive support that was provided for those at the extreme end of violent offending.

Mindful of the positive statistics associated with violence-reduction in both cities, in Part 5 I examine the transitions that have occurred as a result of CIRV. In Chapter 12, I re-visit some of the young men's stories that were told in previous chapters and present case studies of the journeys they have made since then. Drawing on the desistance literature, I illustrate how situational contexts, structural influences, and the opportunity to engage in generative action enabled these men to move away from violent offending. I examine the role that CIRV played in supporting them as clients or volunteers. I also identify the social and structural barriers that some young men faced when they left the programme and sought further integration.

In Chapter 13, I reflect on my journey as an ethnographic researcher collecting the data that underpin this book. I look back across the evidence from interviews and fieldnotes, summarizing the insights and the transformations that have occurred as a result of the strategies. And I conclude by looking at how the CIRV initiative itself continues to evolve. The chapter illustrates that an approach based on prevention, intervention, and inter-agency collaboration has gone on to be applied more widely across the USA, Scotland, and the UK. It also examines how the learning derived from CIRV's experiences has informed the UK Government's response to the 2011 riots in England. The book ends by considering the benefits that can be gained when researchers forge trusting partnerships with police and other service providers.

This book is not intended to be a definitive guide to what works in terms of policing, criminal justice, or community engagement. Nor is its principle purpose to provide a micro-analysis of the social problems in Cincinnati and Glasgow and the way CIRV has helped tackle these localized issues. Rather, the book provides a macro-understanding of the causes and impact of violence, from a transatlantic perspective. It analyses the potential of focused deterrence to reduce that violence and lead young men towards criminal desistance. Throughout the book, I adopt multiple perspectives to demonstrate the complexity of the issues and to examine potential solutions. And I draw on the examples of CIRV, from both Cincinnati and Glasgow, to illustrate and support my arguments about the type of strategies that international police agencies can use to enable oppressed and violent young men to become socially included.

While the book is about policing, it also illuminates the partnerships that can make policing more effective and help to repair and heal broken young lives and fragmented communities. Its scholarly focus will make it appealing to criminology researchers seeking academic knowledge about the social stimuli for youth violence, particularly academics and students with an interest in policing and those with a passion for ethnographic research methods. But it will also be of interest to police officers and their public sector partners who are in leadership roles or studying towards postgraduate qualifications. Through reading this book, academic researchers will become more informed about the complexity of the issues that stimulate youth violence in diverse settings. They will also better understand the factors that can contribute towards the success and failure of social interventions and multi-agency collaborations focused on tackling these issues. And for scholarly practitioners in leadership roles, the book's content will act as a stimulus for forming evidence-based action plans that seek to manage violence more successfully, while also addressing the related community safety priorities. Most importantly, I hope that readers will be inspired and excited by the insights uncovered in Cincinnati and Glasgow – just as I was.

Part One

Youth violence and policing:
Previous insights and new
research approaches

1

Chapter 1

The causes and effects of youth violence: Transatlantic perspectives

As we drive into East Melville Street, I am immediately struck at how quiet it is. 'At this time in the day, there tends to be mainly an afternoon crowd – but this is the most violent area of the city right now,' Dave (a senior police officer) explains, 'there have already been 20 shootings this year, and it's only May. This is where one of the largest gangs in the city is based. These guys are into high-level drug trafficking and violence ... they believe that everyone should respect them, even the police.'

Author's fieldnotes, Cincinnati

I see a group of young guys dressed in hoodies running across a busy main road and confronting an opposing gang. One of the boys holds a bottle, which he smashes on the head of his opponent, and liquid gushes out onto the street. The boys all flee and then wait until the opportunity presents itself for their next attack.

Author's fieldnotes, Glasgow

These extracts from my fieldnotes illustrate that violence among some groups of young men in socially deprived communities is an issue that spans the Atlantic. The first excerpt hints at the nature of the vibrant criminal economy that exists in the ghetto areas of Cincinnati, Ohio. The violence that takes place centres around upholding individual and group-related respect and honour. The second illustrates my first-hand observations of the type of recreational violence that can erupt on the streets of Glasgow on an average Friday or Saturday night. The young men involved are engulfed in issues of territorial rivalry. These two cities – Cincinnati and Glasgow – could hardly be more different in terms of local demographics and socio-cultural dynamics. But both have problems with violence among a minority of young men.

Focused deterrence strategies, based on problem-oriented policing (POP), have led many young men to go on powerful personal journeys in both cities. They have also taken the professionals who work with the young men on their own journeys. I examine the principles underpinning these strategies in Chapter 2, and document the journeys in later chapters. But first I explore the issues that have been at the forefront of criminological research and debate for over a century: What is it that causes some young men in deprived urban communities to become involved in the kind of violence described above?; What role do sub-cultures and gangs play in this?; How are gangs defined in both British and American settings?; And to what extent do issues related to masculine identity or racial oppression play a part in leading some men to engage in street violence? In both Cincinnati and Glasgow there have been recurring media reports about the kind of youth violence that occurs in local communities, and its impact:

> More than two dozen people are rounded up today in Cincinnati as police go after gang members and the city's most violent criminals. Twenty-seven people were indicted on federal charges including conspiracy to distribute drugs, organized possession of firearms with intent to sell and selling firearms without a license.
>
> Local 12 News, Cincinnati: 22 February 2010

> Cincinnati's top law enforcement officer had a blunt warning Thursday for would-be gang members intent on committing violent crime in the city ... The Chief's comments came as his department, the FBI and the US Attorney's Office announced federal indictments on drugs and weapons charges against five members of a street gang ... all five men were arrested and charged under Ohio law. Several weapons were recovered, including an AK-47 and numerous handguns.
>
> ABC 9 News, 30 March 2012

> A stabbing victim lies in a pool of his own blood as Scotland's streets witness another shameful episode of booze-inflamed savagery. The reveller was left writhing in agony after he was knifed twice in the chest by a drunken thug in Glasgow ... Paramedics rushed him to hospital fearing the weapon may have hit a major artery – as cops cordoned off the street and recovered a deadly lockback blade.
>
> Nelson, *The Sun*, 25 August 2010

> Glasgow is a city divided. Cut in half by one lethal weapon – the blade. There are more scarred faces in Glasgow than anywhere else in Britain and in 2002 the World Health Organization designated Glasgow the murder capital of Europe.
>
> *Daily Record*, 20 April 2013

I recognize that some of these news reports are sensationalized. As I have argued before, I believe that only a minority of young men in marginalized communities participate in violence, while many others become demonized (Deuchar, 2009a). But I also recognize the grave problem of violence that exists among some young males in urban settings such as Cincinnati and Glasgow. In this chapter I outline the key criminological and sociological theories that have been developed and explore what stimulates the type of youth violence that happens in deprived communities. In particular, I explore the principal areas of research on American and British gang culture. I analyse the relationship between violence, issues of masculinity, and social exclusion as they apply to inner-city areas on both sides of the Atlantic.

Social disorganization, anomie, and strain

Over the last century many sociologists and criminologists have attempted to examine the conditions that may stimulate crime and violence in society. I am particularly interested in those theories that suggest that crime is a social product, and that inequality often stimulates violent offending, as opposed to those theories that attribute the causes of crime to individuals (Lilly *et al.*, 2011). In this section I explore some of the themes related to social disorganization and strain as a source of violent offending and crime.

Emile Durkheim was one of the first authors to analyse how the oppressive influences of urbanization can stimulate a tendency towards crime. In the late nineteenth century he argued that a state of 'normlessness' or anomie may occur in the lives of those who become exposed to unlimited, socially generated aspirations combined with a lack of realistic opportunities for achieving these goals (Durkheim, 1897/1952). He also argued that deviation is a naturally occurring phenomenon in all forms of society (Durkheim, 1938 and see also Matza, 1969). Later, Robert Merton took these arguments further when he drew attention to how some elements of social and cultural structure exert a strain on some people to engage in non-conformist conduct. In particular, he highlighted the existence of 'culturally defined goals, purposes and interests' that provide a 'frame of aspirational reference' (Merton, 1938: 672). He argued that 'aberrant conduct' may arise where there is a disassociation between culturally defined aspirations and the 'socially structured means' of achieving these goals (Merton, 1938: 674). In Merton's view, large sections of the North American population found themselves unable to achieve their aspirations through conventional, legitimate means, and so the disjunction between means and goals led to a propensity for deviation (Lilly *et al.*, 2011).

Researchers associated with the Chicago School of Sociology attempted to learn more about why young people become deviant, using ethnographic research approaches, and their findings had a widespread influence on American criminology (Lilly *et al.*, 2011). For instance, Shaw and McKay (1942) argued that social disorganization in cities, characterized by poverty, residential mobility, and racial heterogeneity, often led to high levels of juvenile delinquency. Later, Cohen (1955) identified the particular pressures associated with the vitality of middle-class goals and the 'American dream', and the difficulties that can arise when members of deprived communities find themselves unable to achieve these goals through acceptable means:

> ... our American culture, with its strongly democratic and equalitarian emphasis, indoctrinates all social classes impartially with a desire for high social status and a sense of ignominy attaching to low social status. The symbols of high status are to an extraordinary degree the possession and the conspicuous display of economic goods. There is therefore an unusually intense desire for economic goods diffused throughout our population to a degree unprecedented in other societies. However, the means and the opportunities for the legitimate achievement of these goals are distributed most unequally among the various segments of the population. Among those segments which have the least access to the legitimate channels of 'upward mobility' there develop strong feelings of deprivation and frustration and strong incentives to find other means to the achievement of status and its symbols. Unable to attain these goals by lawful means, these disadvantaged segments of the population are under strong pressure to resort to crime, the only means available to them.
>
> Cohen, 1955: 35

Hence, Muncie (2009: 109) cites Merton's (1938) view that the very nature of American society 'generates crime', while Matza (1969) asserts that deviation is implicit in social and moral organization. The compulsion to use criminal means to achieve the social and cultural goals projected by society was illustrated by Whyte (1943) in his ethnographic account of the slum district of Cornerville in Chicago. Whyte argued that, while society placed a high value on social mobility, it was difficult for young men living in deprived communities such as Cornerville to 'get on the ladder, even at the bottom rung' (Whyte, 1943: 273). Thus, the achievement of material possessions was only possible through crime. These views were consolidated by Yablonsky (1967: 223). He identified how aspects of class, ethnicity, race, and other background factors may combine to prevent the socially excluded from achieving success, and lead some to participate in violence:

> Although the 'socially deprived' segment of the population is not fully blocked from means of achievement available to other segments, the degrees of availability are not fully equal. Among the alternatives to him in his search for 'success' are such institutionalised deviant patterns as illegal behaviour opportunities (theft, robbery, vice for profit), illusion and fantasy techniques (alcoholism, drug addiction), and contemporary, thrill-seeking kicks based on assault and violence.
>
> Yablonsky, 1967: 223–4

However, Matza (1964: 28) later argued that, even when young people do turn towards crime, they often drift between 'criminal and conventional action' and respond in turn to the demands of each. More recently, Elijah Anderson's (1999) pioneering ethnographic study of urban street life in Philadelphia finds that the inclination to violence results from the life circumstances of the ghetto poor. Their lives are characterized by unemployment, the dominance of the drug trade, and feelings of alienation and marginalization. And the most profound casualties adopt a 'code of the street', which amounts to a 'set of informal rules that direct all of their interpersonal public behaviour, particularly violence' (Anderson, 1999: 33).

The past century has seen a recurring emphasis in criminological research on aspects of social disorganization and 'strain' as the stimulus for violence and crime. In recent years Robert Agnew (2006) has built on these earlier insights, constructing his own General Strain Theory. Moving beyond Merton's views, he identifies a wider set of strains that may stimulate crime besides 'the inability to gain future economic success' (Lilly *et al.,* 2011: 74). According to Agnew, wider social strains include stressful life events (poverty, unemployment, separation, death or absence of parents, or health problems). They also include neighbourhood problems (vandalism, drug abuse, or other forms of crime); goal blockage (lack of opportunities for employment, and failure to achieve monetary success or – in young men – masculine status); and challenging relationships with adults or peers. In some cases, individuals (and, in particular, young people) may experience a complex blend of social strains. The emotionally vulnerable may interpret them as being so great in magnitude that they become compelled to cope with them in a criminal manner (Agnew, 2006). However, as far back as 1955, Albert Cohen argued that social disorganization theories fail to take account of the nonutilitarian quality of the sub-cultures that develop against the backdrop of anomic conditions. He asserted that the destructiveness and negativism that characterize these sub-cultures needed to be further explored.

Delinquent sub-cultures, gangs, and violence in America

Cohen (1955) replaced the focus on anomie that Durkheim had initiated with an alternative emphasis on 'status frustration'. He noted that the groundwork for violent behaviour includes the existence of unresolved tensions and the drifting together of individuals who experience social exclusion. Participating in delinquent sub-cultures was thus a way of dealing with the problems of adjustment by creating opportunities for gaining alternative types of status (Cohen, 1955: 121). Young people could either engage in innovation, whereby conflict and frustration are eliminated by rejecting conventional means of achieving success and by creating alternatives, or in rebellion, where extreme forms of frustration and marginalization lead to attempts to introduce a 'new social order' (Merton, 1938: 678).

Since the beginning of the last century, gangs have been commonly cited as manifestations of delinquent youth sub-cultures. Puffer (1912) was one of the earliest authors in the US to explore the nature of the gang. He described it as a 'play group', and argued that gang fighting tended to be centred around personal disputes related to the upholding of a 'code of honour' or could be about territorial disputes with other gangs (Puffer, 1912: 67–8).

Later, Thrasher (1927), in his famous study of 1,313 gangs in Chicago, argued that a gang was an 'interstitial group originally formed spontaneously, and then integrated through conflict'. He found that gang members most commonly engaged in the following types of behaviour: 'meeting face to face, milling, movement through time and space as a unit, conflict and planning' (ibid. 57). Thrasher's ethnographic research in Chicago revealed that the gang tended to occupy the poverty belt, a region characterized by 'deteriorating neighbourhoods, shifting populations and the mobility and disorganization of the slum' (ibid. 22). Further, Thrasher believed that gangs were a function of specific conditions and represented the 'spontaneous effort of boys to create a society for themselves where none adequate to their needs exists' (ibid. 37). His insights reflected the later focus on differential association put forward by Sutherland (1947), who suggests that criminal activity becomes more likely if individuals are exposed to other influences that pass on ideas about law-breaking (Newburn, 2013). They also supported the views of Durkheim, Merton, Whyte, and Cohen regarding how violence and crime evolve jointly against the backdrop of social disorganization and strain, and the rebellious and innovative nature of alternative youth sub-cultures.

In the 1960s, authors such as Cloward and Ohlin (1960) continued to use theories of social disorganization to explain the existence of gang culture. They argued that young men in socially deprived communities of the US experienced intense status frustration and that 'exploration of nonconformist alternatives may be the result' (ibid. 86). However, an alternative perspective was later put forward that looked beyond an exclusive emphasis on the social environment when attempting to explain violence-related behaviour. Jankowski (1991) suggested that scarce resources and lack of opportunity led to personal characteristics such as competitiveness, mistrust, and defiant self-reliance, while violence could be committed by individuals as well as those acting on behalf of a gang structure.

In more recent years, Hagedorn (1998, 2008) observed that the de-industrialization process across inner-city areas in the USA and the wider world has led to more violence being motivated by economic impulses. As the free market has gained influence, the state has also retreated from providing social welfare (Hagedorn, 2008). As a result, there is 'ruthless control by the illegitimate forces of violent, private groups' (ibid. 7). Wacquant (2008: 66) has also argued that the sums that can be grossed in the drug trade and through the upholding of respect through violence are 'extravagant in relation to the crushing poverty' in inner-city American ghetto communities. And to uphold respect, young men need to rely on their 'running buddies' or 'homies' to help them defend their status on the street, even more than before (Anderson, 1999: 73).

The question of what stimulates youth and gang-related violence, then, is a complex one. American sub-cultural theorists have suggested that the frustration and tension caused by poverty and social exclusion lead some young people to create alternative social organisms where they can band together and seek opportunities to gain status and identity. However, the phenomenon of the gang has always been a contested one; there is no consensus on the definition of a gang in the USA, with criteria varying across jurisdictions. That said, criminological analyses have emphasized the centrality of territorial conflict. Some academics have also pointed to the defiantly individualist nature of violent young men, who go on to engage in violence either alone or in groups or gangs. Armed young men thus seek to uphold a code of respect and gain economic security from the lucrative drug trade.

Gang culture, street violence, and Atlantic transitions

Even though the phenomenon of the gang was traditionally seen as an exclusively American entity, some claim that gang culture is now proliferating in other countries, including the UK (Hallsworth and Young, 2008). Organizations such as the Eurogang network (a group of European and American researchers who have attempted to create a generic definition of a gang) have helped to increase gang awareness internationally (Bradshaw, 2005). Two of the network's members, Van Gemert and Fleisher, provide a definition that encompasses a strong association with illegal activity as an identifying feature of a street gang in Europe:

> A street gang is any durable, street-oriented youth group whose involvement in illegal activity is part of its group identity.
>
> Van Gemert and Fleisher, 2005:12

Earlier researchers focused on a more eclectic use of the word 'gang' in a British context. Yablonsky (1967) classified the type of gangs in evidence in inner-city neighbourhoods in the UK into several categories. First, there were 'social' gangs, in which a certain degree of responsible social interaction would take place. Second, 'delinquent' gangs were primarily organized to carry out illegal acts such as burglary and assault for the purpose of profit. And third, 'violent' gangs were organized around violence as a means of 'self-protection and defence' or to 'channel aggression' (ibid., 174). Yablonsky argued that gang wars often originated over trivial issues such as a 'bad look' or an argument over a girl (ibid., 177). Insights from research carried out in the UK, as in the US, have illustrated that gang membership is often associated with socially disorganized neighbourhoods and poverty (Thornberry *et al.*, 2003; Deuchar, 2009a). Academics associated with the Eurogang network argue that, unlike the USA, youth gangs in the UK have fluid membership and flexible boundaries and are often involved in less criminally oriented activity (Klein, 2008; Aldridge *et al.*, 2008; and see also Pitts, 2011).

Other UK researchers have claimed that the activity associated with some youth gangs in England is akin to the type of violence that might be found in towns and cities across the US. For instance, Stelfox (1998) gathered information about local street gangs via a survey of all police forces in the UK and as part of the Home Office Police Award scheme. Three-quarters of gangs were found to be involved in some form of drug dealing, and 60 per cent possessed firearms (Bennett and Holloway, 2004; Pitts, 2011). Bullock and Tilley's (2002) research also revealed that Manchester gangs were involved in a great many violent incidents involving firearms. Bennett and Holloway's

(2004) research illustrated that there were some similarities between the social characteristics and problem behaviour of gang members reported in USA research and those found in England and Wales. Their study revealed that many young gang members were reported to be criminally active, often involved in robbery and drug supply offences and with a tendency to carry guns. Pitts' (2007) research in Waltham Forest (Greater London) also identified an 'articulated super gang' that involved young adolescents in street crime and drug distribution (Pitts, 2011).

Conversely, some academic studies have indicated that the focus of youth violence in the UK is quite distinct from that found in inner-city areas in the USA. In 1973, the pioneering ethnographic study by James Patrick conducted in Glasgow illustrated how violence among groups of young men often centred around territorial disputes and was motivated by a 'desire for status of any kind, won at any price' (Patrick, 1973: 94). Territoriality can be described as 'a situation where a claim is made over an identified geographical space and there is a willingness to defend that space against others' (Kintrea *et al.*, 2011: 55). For Patrick, the strong sub-cultural emphasis in Glasgow on 'self-assertion' and 'rebellious independence against authority' and the hallowing of violence as features of masculinity ensured that marginalized young men became street fighters as opposed to drug dealers or addicts.

More recently, Kintrea *et al.* (2011) illustrated how young people in inner-city communities in the UK are often aware of subjective territorial boundaries that inhibit social interaction and mobility (see also Kintrea *et al.*, 2008; Earle, 2011). This form of 'hyper place attachment' is driven by lack of opportunities for employment, social stigmatization, and oppression (Kintrea *et al.*, 2011: 68). In their research in Glasgow, they note that a recognizable territory can be as restricted as a 200-metre block, and a key motivation for violence is the desire to 'protect the home neighbourhood' (ibid. 59). Other UK research has illustrated the importance of place and territory in the activity of gang members (Young *et al.*, 2007; Deuchar, 2009a; Ralphs *et al.*, 2009; Aldridge *et al.*, 2011; Deuchar, 2010b, 2012). Aldridge *et al.*'s (2008) findings from research conducted in England suggest that violent conflict is rarely related to criminal drug markets. Although territorial behaviour can in some circumstances be an 'escalator to more organized and more violent forms of crime', Kintrea *et al.*'s (2011: 65) findings suggest that connections between territorial groups and the world of organized adult criminal networks are weak or non-existent. However, they also report that the life of a 'gangster' is often conceptualized as 'glamorous and attractive to young people' in several UK cities, including Glasgow (ibid. 67). Evidence suggests that gang culture in the USA is also becoming more associated with issues of respect and the norms and narratives of the street, as opposed to purely being linked to drug markets (R. Kennedy, 1997; Anderson, 1999).

Some academics are somewhat sceptical about whether violent youth gangs even exist in the UK at all. They argue that the current interest in gang culture is akin to the moral panics that surrounded other youth sub-cultures such as the 'mods and rockers' in the 1960s and the punks in the 1970s (Pitts, 2011). Others have argued that concerns about violent youth culture have been promoted by the state and the media to exert greater social control (see, for instance, Rose, 2000; Squires, 2008; Waiton, 2001, 2008). Hallsworth and Young (2008) argue that many of the young people typically labelled as gang members do not conceptualize the peer groups with which they associate as gangs. Further, Hallsworth (2011: 184) asserts that 'much of the violence that is often attributed to "gangs" appears not to be specifically "gang"-related', even if it is (in some cases) gang-motivated. Street violence, Hallsworth argues, can be norm-less and unregulated and often lacks a social orientation. He argues that, in focusing exclusively on American stereotypes of gang culture and violence, so-called 'gang talkers' (researchers, journalists, and politicians, among others) lose sight of the wider issues that lead to street violence.

How the phenomenon of the gang should be applied to inner-city youth culture in the UK is thus disputed. Some claim that young people in deprived communities sometimes become involved in serious organized crime within gang structures. Others claim that gang culture is more centred on hyper-place attachment and is characterized by territoriality and innocuous adolescent offending, with occasional tendencies to move on to more persistent and serious crime (Deuchar, 2009a; Kintrea *et al.*, 2011; Pitts, 2011). Still others dispute that gangs exist in the UK at all, and view the political interest and 'media hype' around the issue as symptoms of moral panic and a means of social control. In the inductive approach I adopted in my research, I sought to explore these contested issues in more depth through immersion in the empirical data I present in later chapters. I also took into account sensitizing issues that have been brought to the fore in previous research into youth violence, namely issues of race and masculinity.

Youth violence, race, and masculinity

Some international research suggests that there is a relationship between youth violence and young people's experiences and perceptions of racial prejudice (Joe and Robinson, 1980; Van Gemert *et al.*, 2008; Wottley and

Tanner, 2008). For instance, Fiori-Khayat (2008) observes how young refugees in France involve themselves in group-related violence as a response to perceptions of racial discrimination. In Canada, Wortley and Tanner's findings suggest that young immigrants in Toronto who perceive racism against their own group are 'more likely to be involved in gangs' than others (Wortely and Tanner, 2008: 194). They indicate that violence is sometimes seen as a 'cultural response to alienation and estrangement' (ibid., 203) and that involvement in gangs is often linked to feelings of racial injustice and social exclusion.

Anderson (1999: 46) demonstrates that, in many deprived inner-city black communities in America, 'the persistence of racial discrimination has engendered a deep-seated bitterness and anger in many of the most desperate and poorest blacks, especially young people' (for a wider discussion, see also Suttles, 1968; Hagedorn, 2008; Venketesh, 2008; Duran, 2009). The American ghetto has been described as an 'ethnoracial prison' that ensures the systematic social ostracism of African Americans who have been oppressed by the state policies of welfare entrenchment and urban withdrawal (Wacquant, 2009a). The socio-spatial relegation and exclusion they experience leads to 'advanced marginality', whereby conjugated segregation to ghetto communities occurs on the basis of race and class (Wacquant, 2008: 2–3). Hagedorn (2008) criticizes earlier criminologists such as Cloward and Ohlin (1960) and Cohen (1955) for the non-racial and ethnically neutral means they adopt for analysing issues of social disorganization and delinquent sub-cultures. He argues that, while personal, familial, and community problems are influential in understanding street violence, they 'lead us away from racial oppression and understanding the source of the alienation that is so fundamental to inner-city gangs and their culture' (Hagedorn, 2008: 88).

In the UK, there are conflicting reports about the ethnic profiles of recognized gang members. Stelfox's (1998) national survey findings suggested that gangs were predominantly white, with only 25 per cent described as 'black Caribbean'. Bennett and Holloway's (2004) findings also suggested that gang members in England and Wales were predominantly white. However, in some locations, such as Bethnal Green in London, they found that gang members were 'significantly more likely than non-gang members to be from an ethnic minority' (ibid. 314). More recently, Kintrea *et al.*'s (2011) research findings from a range of cities in both England and Scotland demonstrate that, although tensions between areas are sometimes 'overlaid by ethnic residential segregation', territorial divisions also exist in areas of particular ethnic group concentration. They conclude that territorial divisions take precedence over issues of race:

> Territoriality ... transgresses simplified notions of inter-racial and ethnic divisions; it exists within and between groups from similar ethnic backgrounds even if it appears to be accentuated where neighbourhood boundaries coincide with ethnic divisions.
>
> Kintrea *et al.*, 2011: 68

In addition my own research conducted in the more culturally diverse communities of Glasgow illustrates that the 'presence of mono-ethnic gangs in urban settings may not always be a reflection of conflict based around ethnicity' (Deuchar, 2011: 684). Rather, the spatial concentration of refugee families in some socially deprived areas of the city has led to the presence of both mono-ethnic and mixed-ethnic territorial gangs within their housing schemes. As a result, young, marginalized men from ethnic minority groups often find themselves in conflict both with other ethnic minorities *and* white youth.

In the most deprived neighbourhoods on both sides of the Atlantic (including Cincinnati and Glasgow), an overwhelming sense of status frustration among young men from differing cultural groups suggests an ascendency of issues of masculinity over those associated with ethnicity, as a root cause of violence. Taking a social constructionist approach, Connell (1987) argues that 'hegemonic masculinity' emphasizes a dominant ideal of heterosexual power and authority (Muncie, 2009). Young men who have become marginalized through the collapse of heavy industry and the lack of meaningful opportunities for employment may engage in a form of 'protest' or 'toxic' masculinity (McDowell, 2003: 12; Kupers, 2005: 714). In such cases, crime provides these men with a means of living their masculinity when other resources are unavailable to them (Muncie, 2009: 138). In his recent analysis of the causes underpinning the riots that erupted across English towns and cities in the summer of 2011, David Lammy blames the social liberalism of the 1960s combined with the free-market, liberal revolution of the 1980s. Although together they made the UK into a wealthier and more tolerant nation, they also created a hyper-individualistic culture and an increasing sense of social exclusion among young, working-class men. Lammy also argues that the liberal attitude towards single parenting has de-emphasized the importance of family structure and, in particular, the need for positive male role models. In turn, young men turn towards alternative role models that provide them with twisted notions of masculinity:

The boys have usually grown up without positive role models, adopting the warped versions of masculinity projected by popular culture. They don't want to wear a suit or carry the toolbox of an artisan; they want the baggy jeans, the bling and the women from the grime videos. Theirs is a world of the alpha male, where 'respect' is everything. Look at someone the wrong way, or stray into the wrong postcode, and you could lose your life. Carry a knife or a gun and you are a real man. Become a 'baby father', have children with a string of different women, and people will look up to you. No one ever taught these boys that the inability to delay gratification, the obsession with status symbols and a worldview centred on the self are markers not of manhood, but of immaturity.

Lammy, 2011: 97

As Bauman (2012: 19–23) has argued, the absence of patterns, routines, and norms in the 'society of fluid modernity' does not necessarily bring about the sort of freedom or happiness eulogized by 'dedicated libertarians', but often results in doubt and fear. In our current form of modernity, problems need to be coped with individually and identities need to be learned and acquired through self-determination (Bauman, 2012). But those who are marginalized will often acquire identities associated with oppression and characterized by violence (Freire, 1972). In his analysis of the street violence of young men in the ghetto communities of Philadelphia, Anderson (1999) documents how the lack of realistic employment opportunities combined with the absence of 'old heads' and 'decent daddies' as positive role models fuels a sense of hopelessness and oppression. These young men subsequently become engaged in violence to uphold the oppressive identities they inherit and the oppositional culture they embrace (Freire, 1972).

Issues of status frustration bound up with today's lack of order, stability, and certainty thus breed a crisis of masculinity that may explain some aspects of youth violence. Messerschmidt (1993) also argues that, where issues of class and race combine to reduce conventional opportunities to achieve hegemonic masculinity, youth violence and crime are even more likely to occur (Muncie, 2009). Further, Hagedorn (2008: 100) argues that the de-industrialization process has devastated young men in ethnic minority communities and that, as a result, a new 'ghettocentric identity' has emerged. Wacquant (2008: 69) contends that the 'deliberate stacking of public housing in the poorest black areas of large cities' has led to a 'system of *de facto* urban apartheid'. 'White flight' followed by the exodus of upwardly mobile black families 'further pushes ghetto residents away from the regular economy and society' and accelerates the growth of the criminal economy among young African American men (Wacquant, 2008: 68). Authors such as Hagedorn (2008) and Pitts (2008) also suggest that the same combination of issues related to class and race that affect the black American ghettos also impact on deprived neighbourhoods in the UK. They argue that transatlantic patterns of street violence and gang culture do exist and may be linked to the vertiginous social and cultural inequality that characterizes deprived communities (Wacquant, 2008, 2009b).

Just as there are competing theories about the causes, nature, and consequences of youth violence and gang culture, over the years there have also been many competing views about the most effective way to police these issues. Central to the historical debates has been the tension between pre-emptive intervention and suppression strategies. In the next chapter, I explore these issues in more depth.

Chapter 2

Policing the violence: Challenges and opportunities

In democratic societies around the world, the police are often searching for the best means of reducing youth violence, and over the last several decades many different strategies have been implemented, with varying results. This chapter begins with a review of policing research as it evolved as a field of study. I describe what we have learned about police decision-making and what is known about policing young people in particular. I then set out the policing strategies that have been applied in the USA and UK to address crime and violence. Using the framework established by the National Research Council (2004) in the USA, I describe four general types of policing strategies – traditional, community, problem-solving, and focused – and point to the most promising options for violence-reduction. I discuss the impact these strategies have had on reducing violence, along with citizens' perceptions of police legitimacy. The chapter concludes with a thorough description of the recent policy initiatives to reduce violence that combine problem-oriented policing, multi-agency collaborations, and focused deterrence. I introduce the reader to the Cincinnati Initiative to Reduce Violence (CIRV, pronounced 'serve'), implemented in 2007, and the Community Initiative to Reduce Violence (CIRV – again, pronounced 'serve') implemented in 2008 in Glasgow. I also include a brief analysis of the statistics on crime-reduction achieved as a direct result of the strategies underpinning the CIRV projects in both cities.

History of community-oriented policing and police research

In the 1950–60s, a series of rich ethnographic studies describing police behaviour and organizations illustrated that an understanding of the law alone gave little insight into how police behaved in practice (Goldstein, 1960; LaFave, 1962; Goldstein, 1963; Skolnick, 1966; Wilson, 1968; Westley, 1970; Reiss, 1971; Muir, 1977; Black, 1980). It was discovered that police discretion was often indiscriminate and created a wide gap between the law-as-written and the law-in-action (Bernard and Engel, 2001). Further, Goldstein (1960) recognized that discretion was inherent in the police profession and necessary for the proper processing of offenders throughout the criminal justice system. However, uncontrolled discretion was a primary problem and needed to be addressed through a series of police reforms.

These studies set the stage for further inquiries over the next several decades. The findings were profound, bringing to light issues surrounding racial bias, abuse of force, corruption, and poor police–community relations (Skolnick, 1966; Bayley and Mendelsohn, 1969; Reiss, 1971; Muir, 1977). This body of research led to a significant rethinking of policies, strategies, and tactics (Goldstein, 1977; Walker, 1977; Skolnick and Bayley, 1986). Much of this work was informed by an implicit assumption that police decision-making was inherently biased and that exposure of these practices was necessary for reform. Given the tenor of the times, this assumption is unsurprising. For example, in the USA, the National Advisory Commission on Civil Disorders (more commonly known as the Kerner Commission) was created to examine the causes of the widespread rioting during the 1960s. It reported that a national crisis in race relations existed: 'Our nation is moving toward two societies, one white, one black – separate and unequal' (National Advisory Commission on Civil Disorders, 1968: 1).

The Commission's report illustrated the deeply rooted racial tensions and hostility between black citizens and the police. The Commission's recommendations emphasized the hiring of police personnel that reflected the demographics of the neighbourhoods they served, to improve police–citizen relations, which in turn led to an increase in hiring minorities within police agencies (National Research Council, 2004). The report also endorsed proactive policing and crime prevention that laid the foundations for community policing. Further, it stressed the need to increase the level of professionalism within policing, resulting in minimum standards for law enforcement personnel (ibid.).

Meanwhile in the UK, over the next decade there was a series of corruption scandals involving the Drugs Squad and the Obscene Publications Squad in the Metropolitan Police that tarnished the public image of policing (Newburn, 2013). These were followed by a number of urban disorders in the early 1980s, as a result of which the Scarman Report was 'scathing of the Metropolitan Police's communication failures' in communities such as Brixton (ibid. 629). Significant changes were subsequently made, initiated by Sir Kenneth Newman (then Commissioner of the Metropolitan Police) and involving a transition from confrontational, authoritarian models of policing to a focus on community-oriented practice. Influenced by models being developed in the USA at the time, English community policing emphasized the need to involve local community members in defining police priorities and local problems. Local citizens were encouraged to work alongside the police, to inform and supplement the operational work of officers (Tilley, 2008; Newburn, 2013).

In Scotland, the focus on community policing had begun much earlier. Donnelly (2010) draws attention to one particular initiative in Greenock that ran from the mid-1950s. Local constables were appointed to each area with the specific remit of working with local authority services and community groups. The initiative placed a particular focus on youth crime, and was underpinned by the belief that 'joint partnerships with all interested agencies would improve the quality of life and ... eventually reduce crime' (ibid. 203). Local authorities in the west of Scotland had hitherto invested in community involvement work and local participation more than anywhere else in the UK, and the Scottish police service had traditionally worked in close cooperation with its communities and public and private agencies. By the early 1980s, community policing had become embedded across Scotland (ibid.).

During the past three decades, in both the USA and the UK there has been an increased focus on problem-oriented policing (POP), which shares a number of characteristics with community policing. Originally coined by Herman Goldstein, the American professor of law who worked as an adviser to the Chicago Police Department, the term 'POP' places an emphasis on grouping incidents as problems, the need for systematic enquiry, analysis of the multiple interests in problems, and the uninhibited search for tailor-made responses (Bullock and Tilley, 2003). It also endeavours to shift the police away from a reactive model that focuses on individual events, towards a proactive approach that looks for 'patterns and commonalities' (Newburn, 2013: 626). Such patterns often include identifying hotspot areas for crime, violence, and prolific offenders – on the assumption that a minority of offenders are responsible for the majority of criminal incidents.

Against the backdrop of these new policing strategies that were being implemented on both sides of the Atlantic, numerous research studies set out to explain the coercive outcomes of police–citizen interactions. In the USA, the studies sought to determine whether the police used their considerable discretion in a morally defensible manner (Riksheim and Chermak, 1993; National Research Council, 2004). With a handful of exceptions, this work focused on police decisions to use specific coercive sanctions, including citations, arrests, and use of force. Only relatively recently has the research focus expanded to consider stop-and-search practices (Fagan and Davies, 2000; Gould and Mastrofski, 2004; Alpert *et al.*, 2005; Warren and Tomaskovic-Devey, 2009). Other types of police decision-making and behaviour (such as community policing, problem-solving, and service activities) or citizen behaviour towards officers have largely gone unstudied, with a few important exceptions (Mastrofski *et al.*, 1996; Parks *et al.*, 1999; Mastrofski *et al.*, 2000; DeJong *et al.*, 2001; Skogan, 2006). In short, despite the increase in studies over the decades, our collective body of knowledge about the use of police discretion remains limited. Our understanding of policing youth, in particular, is even more limited.

Policing strategies and effectiveness

While researchers grappled with understanding police decision-making during police–citizen encounters – and particularly encounters with minorities and youth – crime increased significantly across the USA in the 1970s–80s. Specifically, violent crime increased more than four-fold, rising from a rate of 161 offences per 100,000 people in 1960, to a peak of 758 per 100,000 in 1991 (US Department of Justice Federal Bureau of Investigation, 2013). In the same time frame, property crime also tripled. This trend was not limited to the USA – similar patterns were reported in the UK, where both violent and property crime rose in the 1980s, followed by a peak in the mid-1990s (UK Office for National Statistics, 2013).

A separate body of research examining the effectiveness of policing strategies at reducing crime and violence was undertaken. Studies from the 1970s and early 1980s demonstrated that the common policing strategies of the time (including random motorized patrol, rapid response to calls for service, foot patrols, police staffing levels, and investigative work) did not significantly reduce crime (Kelling *et al.*, 1974; Greenberg *et al.*, 1975; Greenwood *et al.*, 1975; Kelling *et al.*, 1981; Loftin and McDowell, 1982; Spelman and Brown, 1984). From the 1980s onwards, this led to an initial crisis in policing in the USA, followed by a period of tremendous change and innovation (Bayley and Nixon, 2010).

The combination of economic recession and the crack cocaine epidemic in the 1980s led New York City to experience an all-time high level of violent crime. As a result, zero-tolerance policing was introduced in 1993 at the hands of Bill Bratton, Chief of New York Police Department (NYPD) (Newburn, 2013). The strategy was informed by the 'broken windows' thesis, which asserts that an unrepaired broken window sends out the message that nobody cares and therefore leads to more damage (Wilson and Kelling, 1982). In the same way, if minor incivilities such as begging, drunkenness, vandalism, and graffiti go unchecked, 'more serious crime will flourish' (Burke, 2004: 2).

The strategies put in place in New York City and the variations of them that were implemented in other locations were therefore based on the assumption that a police presence that targets petty offenders on the streets can produce 'substantial reductions in the level of crime' (ibid. 3). Opponents of zero-tolerance policing argue that it largely focuses on failed military-style 'hard' policing measures introduced in England in the 1970s and early 1980s, which were blamed for the ensuing public disorders in Brixton, London (ibid.).

The strategies adopted in New York were responsible for a huge drop in crime in the 1990s. During a time when dramatic declines in crime and violence were being witnessed in both the USA and the UK, the rate of decline was greater in New York than anywhere else (Newburn, 2013). Yet, despite these innovations in policing strategies and the reduction in crime rates, concerns regarding racial or ethnic and age disparities in the criminal justice system in the USA were raised. These disparities focused on issues surrounding drug use, apprehension, and sentencing. The War on Drugs from the 1980–90s led to dramatic changes in criminal justice strategies used across the US, including the aggressive targeting of drug offenders at street level and increased sentence length and rates of incarceration (Scalia, 2001; Tonry, 2011; Engel and Swartz, 2013). Targeted enforcement strategies were especially felt by juvenile minority males, who were disproportionately subject to police surveillance and imprisonment for drug offences (R. Kennedy, 1997; Walker, 2001; Tonry, 2011; Engel and Swartz, 2013). A research summary by the American Sociological Association underlines this disproportionate impact by noting that, in 1980, the rates of drug arrests for young black and white males were similar, but by 1993 they were more than four times higher for black youth compared to whites (Rosich, 2007).

Police chiefs and politicians across the country suggested that the reduction in crime was due to their particular crime reduction strategies (such as zero-tolerance policing, Computer Statistics [COMPSTAT], and community policing), while researchers struggled to better document and understand the forces and factors behind the dramatic declines (Eck and Maguire, 2000). Many theories were advanced, with the reported drop in crime attributed to phenomena as diverse as shifts in the drug market, mass incarceration, and legalization of abortion (Weisburd and Green, 1995; Donohue and Levitt, 2001; Levitt, 2004; Corsaro *et al.,* 2012). The only thing that was clear was that success had many authors.

The National Research Council (2004) documented the predominant policing strategies from 1980 to 2000 using a four-fold typology classification scheme based on two dimensions: the diversity of approaches used by police agencies and the level of focus given to specific problems. The first dimension (diversity of approaches) refers to the content of the police strategies and tactics used, ranging from traditional to more innovative approaches. The second dimension represents the level of focus or targeting activities of the police, ranging from focused on specific places or individuals, to more generalized approaches. Using these two dimensions, they classified policing strategies as belonging to one of four models: 1) Standard Model (mostly law enforcement approaches with a low level of focus); 2) Community Policing (wide array of approaches with a low level of focus; 3) POP (wide array of approaches with a high level of focus); and 4) Focused Policing (mainly law enforcement approaches, with a high level of focus).

The Council used these groupings to summarize the effectiveness (in terms of crime-reduction) of the various types of strategies and tactics in each of these models, and to provide recommendations. In summary, it concluded that traditional policing strategies under the Standard Model provided little or no evidence of effectiveness. Likewise, it reported that strategies under the Community Policing Model generated only weak-to-moderate evidence of effectiveness. In contrast, strategies involving POP produced moderate-to-strong evidence of effectiveness. Finally, strategies characterized as Focused Policing ranged in levels of effectiveness from weak to strong based on the specific tactics used.

In the case of POP, at the height of the crack-fuelled violence epidemic in predominantly poor, minority, urban neighbourhoods in the USA in the 1980s and 90s, research had revealed several effective policing methods (Eck and Maguire, 2000). Goldstein's (1979) formulation of a problem-oriented approach to policing shifted the emphasis from the processing of calls, crimes, and citizen encounters, to addressing the proximate conditions that gave rise to the calls. This approach showed great promise at reducing highly localized crime and disorder problems (Eck and Spelman, 1987). Evidence of POP's effectiveness continued to mount throughout the 1990s and into the next decade (Weisburd and Eck, 2004). At the same time, the importance of place-based policing efforts started to be articulated and was confirmed over the next decade (Sherman *et al.,* 1989; Braga *et al.,* 1999; Braga, 2001). Statistical analysis of crime problems and mapping of crime hotspots also became relatively common in policing (Sherman *et al.,* 1989; Weisburd and Lum, 2005).

Applying a problem-oriented approach, Kennedy and Braga (1998) showed that focusing police efforts on the most violent offender networks could drive down gang homicides, and further research confirmed this (see, for instance, Braga *et al.*, 2001; Braga, 2008; Braga and Weisburd, 2012a). Later, Kennedy analysed how these strategies impacted on illegal drug operations, and identified positive results (Kennedy, 2009). He also found that this approach improved public perceptions of police equity and legitimacy, since it ensured that the community was directly involved in supporting and implementing the strategy. When properly implemented, these types of focused policing efforts can address racial and cultural tensions as well as conflicts between young people and the police. And while promoting positive police–community relations, over the long term they can also save lives.

Using focused deterrence approaches to reduce violence

In Chapter 1 I acknowledged the need to avoid becoming a 'gang talker', to widen my sociological lens beyond the 'gang gaze', and to consider the wider ecology of individualized street violence (Hallsworth and Young, 2008: 191). However, I also recognize that the available research on violence and street gangs demonstrates a convincing correlation between gang membership and criminal offending (see, for instance, Battin-Pearson *et al.*, 1998; Huff, 1998; Loeber *et al.*, 2001). Likewise, the relationship between gang membership and violent victimization has also received strong and consistent empirical support (Esbensen and Huizinga, 1993; Decker and Van Winkle, 1996; Rosenfeld *et al.*, 1999; Curry *et al.*, 2002; Thornberry *et al.*, 2003; Taylor *et al.*, 2007; Ozer and Engel, 2012). Therefore, police have often focused on interrupting gang networks in order to significantly reduce violence in communities.

The focused deterrence approach to violence-reduction was first used in the Boston Ceasefire during the mid-1990s (Braga *et al.*, 2001), when police put targeted enforcement pressure on gang members to discourage gun violence in the city. It has since been implemented in several other cities and states. As Robin Engel notes in the Foreword to this book, these multi-agency initiatives are based on the fundamental presumption that the majority of offences are committed by a small number of individuals who are often organized (to some degree) in groups or gangs. Although violence may be committed individually, violent incidents are often motivated by a group dynamic. Once the chronic offenders are identified, law enforcement agencies coordinate with one another to communicate consequences to these individuals. Young offenders are required to attend offender notification meetings or 'call-in' sessions where they are exposed to a series of powerful messages. They are told that, if a violent incident occurs, law enforcement agencies will employ all the legal resources necessary to punish those who commit violence as well as their associates or gangs. Meanwhile service and community partners also offer help in the form of social and job services for those who are willing to move away from violence (also touched on in the Foreword to this book).

Kennedy (2009) suggests that, by promoting a group-focused enforcement strategy, law enforcement agencies can ensure that gang members who participate in offender notification meetings take on board the warnings they are given and place peer pressure on their associates to move away from violent behaviour. But practitioners and community members need to consistently communicate the non-violence message to offenders. In this process it is expected that the group structure will play a role in both communicating the message regarding the changes in sanction risk, as well as establishing new behavioural standards in the offender social network based on these changes (ibid.). The resulting changes in offender decision-making are thus based on group-based informal social control and an altered risk–reward calculus. In addition, this approach narrows the focus of law enforcement to those at the highest risk of becoming a perpetrator or victim of violence, thereby adding legitimacy to the approach.

Cincinnati Initiative to Reduce Violence (CIRV), Cincinnati, Ohio

In response to escalating levels of violence, including a 300 per cent increase in homicide over an eight-year period, the City of Cincinnati implemented the Cincinnati Initiative to Reduce Violence (CIRV) in April 2007. Recognizing that violence impacts on a variety of groups in the city, CIRV brought together an assortment of stakeholders that included political leaders, law enforcement agents, academics, medical professionals, Street Advocates, social services providers, and community and business leaders, to develop and implement a comprehensive strategy to reduce violence. Through multi-agency collaboration, CIRV used a focused deterrence approach similar to that of the Boston Gun Project's Operation Ceasefire (Braga *et al.*, 2001). In Cincinnati, 0.3 per cent of the population was initially identified by police as being members of a violent group or gang. These gang members had lengthy prior criminal records (averaging 35 charges per person, with 91 per cent having a previous arrest for at least one violent offence). Further, analysis of the city's homicides in June 2006–May 2007 demonstrated that nearly 75 per cent of all homicides involved a group or gang member as the victim, suspect, or both (Engel *et al.*, 2013). The CIRV team targeted these individuals and the gangs they represented by promising swift and certain law enforcement and prosecutorial action against those who continued to commit violent acts. The team also offered social service support to those seeking to move away from crime.

The CIRV message was aimed at disrupting the group dynamics that promoted the use of violence to deal with conflict and gain respect. The primary method of message delivery was through offender notification meetings, known as 'call-in' sessions, in Hamilton County Court (Papachristos *et al.,* 2007). Individuals identified as members of violent gangs who were also under court-ordered supervision (probation or parole) were required to attend these sessions as a condition of supervision. The participants were mainly young black males, with an average age of 26 years. Call-ins followed a formalized process whereby CIRV partners presented the message from three different perspectives.

First, law enforcement officials pledged to increase pressure on gangs associated with violence. If an individual gang member was involved in an act of violence, law enforcement scrutiny was thrust upon the entire gang for any criminal activity in which they were engaged. The purpose was to encourage gang members to 'police themselves' by deterring their peers from getting involved in violent encounters, to avoid the full force of the law coming down on the entire gang (Engel *et al.,* 2013). Second, social service providers described the alternatives to a violent lifestyle and promised streamlined social service assistance to those willing to transition to a pro-social lifestyle (ibid.). Finally, offenders heard from community members and homicide victims' families, who illustrated the damage caused by violence and appealed to them to desist (D.M. Kennedy, 1997). These notification sessions were repeated as necessary to demonstrate the delivery on promises and reiterate the message of non-violence to the target population. As of 2010, 568 identified gang or group members representing 41 violent gangs had attended at least one notification meeting (Engel *et al.,* 2013)

A quantitative evaluation of CIRV found a statistically significant 42 per cent reduction in gang member-involved homicides in Cincinnati since its activities began (Engel *et al.,* 2013, and see also the Foreword to this book). A critical aspect of the continued evaluation and ultimate success of CIRV has been the on-going monitoring of its processes, which has allowed programme personnel to make data-driven decisions regarding potential changes in strategy.

Community Initiative to Reduce Violence (CIRV), Glasgow

Following the success of the Cincinnati strategy, Scotland's VRU implemented a similar initiative in Glasgow in 2008–11. The Community Initiative to Reduce Violence (CIRV) established a partnership between police, social services, education, housing, and community safety services, along with local communities, and delivered the clear message that 'the violence must stop' (VRU, 2011). The initiative was implemented in the east end and north of the city, targeting approximately 1,000 young people who were repeatedly on the police radar because of their involvement in violence. The majority of those targeted were young white men within an age range of 14–19 years, and many were known to be involved in gangs. For the purposes of the initiative, the VRU adopted a working definition of a gang in Glasgow, namely: 'a group of three or more people who associate together, or act as an organized body, for criminal or illegal purposes' (Centre for Social Justice, 2009: 41). In a similar way to the Cincinnati initiative, the Glasgow CIRV aimed to reduce youth violence through a mixture of enforcement and suppression strategies, support services and programmes, and the moral voice of the community (VRU, 2011).

While the 'stop the violence' message was communicated to individuals and groups, robust intelligence-gathering enabled police officers to focus enforcement on the gang structures that often stimulated the violence. Young offenders were warned that, if they continued to involve themselves in violence, then criminal justice repercussions would ensue. A Gangs Task Force had been in operation for several years, formed by Strathclyde Police as a tool to combat gang-related violence, and after CIRV's inception the Task Force became the enforcement arm of the initiative. Task Force officers ensured that prolific offenders were detected and that dawn arrests took place for those who continued to engage in violence. Alongside the message of enforcement was a softer message of hope, since CIRV made a range of services and programmes available to those young men who committed to change their lifestyles. The initiative thus drew on a range of existing services in Glasgow together with some new programmes that were tailor-made to meet the needs of the young clients and, in some cases, benefited from targeted Scottish Government funding (VRU, 2011; Donnelly, 2013). The implementation of CIRV also involved representatives from the communities affected by violence, who delivered the key messages that the violence needed to stop and that there were alternative choices available.

As in Cincinnati, the process of engaging with the violent young men was centred around call-in sessions. Young offenders were routinely brought into the Sheriff Court in Glasgow but, unlike in Cincinnati, they attended in a voluntary capacity (for further details on this, see Chapter 8). The young men were encouraged to attend these sessions by youth workers on the street, by police officers visiting homes, and through self-nomination as a result of young men hearing about the initiative from other attendees. The sessions themselves were amended from the Cincinnati model to take account of both the different socio-cultural context of Glasgow and the younger age group of targeted clients. Across the period of implementation, just under 500 clients participated in ten call-in sessions.

Following the Cincinnati approach, senior police officers made it known at the beginning of the sessions that law enforcement strategies had been put in place to punish those who continued to offend, as well as their associates. But then there were contributions from other essential partners, such as reformed offenders, young mothers, and members of local communities, who were able to express the impact of the violence on their lives and appeal to the young men to make alternative choices. The sessions always finished with the message of hope that 'there are better ways out' (VRU, 2011). Service providers presented the young men with opportunities to be fast-tracked to a range of programmes and opportunities – but their involvement in these initiatives was contingent on their commitment to stay away from violence.

The initiative led to an impressive level of violence-reduction being reported in Glasgow. Provisional results have illustrated that, on average, CIRV clients demonstrated a 46 per cent reduction in violent offending. In particular, significant decreases were recorded in the type of behaviours targeted by the programme, such as weapon-carrying and gang fighting (Donnelly, 2013). Although the initiative ended in 2011, the principles and approaches underpinning it live on, and have become subsumed within wider initiatives in Glasgow and across Scotland.

Chapter 3

Tales and confessions from an ethnography:
The communities, research methods, and ethical issues

Quantitative evaluations suggest that youth violence in Cincinnati and Glasgow is being managed more effectively as a result of CIRV (see Chapter 13). But my research set out to explore what lay beneath the positive statistics. Taking into account the sociological factors inherent in youth violence outlined in Chapter 1, I wanted to understand what caused the violence in both cities and how it impacted on people's lives. And, mindful of the issues surrounding the policing of youth violence outlined in Chapter 2, I aimed to analyse the principles that underpinned CIRV as it was implemented on both sides of the Atlantic. I also sought to comprehend the cultural shift that had taken place in the police departments in both cities to accommodate the interventions. And I wanted to hear the voices of young offenders from the two urban contexts, and better understand the role of Street Advocates, youth workers, and community service organizations in enabling marginalized and oppressed young men to desist from crime and become socially included. As a critical and radical criminologist, I wanted to get behind the positive statistics presented in evaluation reports and hear the personal accounts of those who were involved in implementing, supporting, or engaging with the initiatives.

In this chapter, I provide a more detailed picture of the two cities that were the focus for my research, which were characterized by contrasting cultures and demographics. I also present an overview of the research methods I adopted and the ethical issues I had to address during the study.

A tale of two cities

Industrial decline and violence in Cincinnati

Cincinnati is the third-largest city in Ohio, located on the north bank of the Ohio River at the Ohio–Kentucky border, near Indiana. Settled in 1788, and well known for its steep hills and river-front location, it was dubbed by Winston Churchill 'America's most beautiful inland city' (Staley, 2001).

With a peak population of 503,998 in 1950, the city steadily lost residents over a sixty-year period and, by 2010, the population had dropped to 296,943 (Mecklenborg, 2012). Once known as a great commercial port and pork-packing centre, the process of industrial development increased the gap between the wealthiest and poorest city residents. From the 1960s onwards, suburban growth led to racial polarization as white families fled city neighbourhoods and retreated to the suburbs, while African Americans moved into the inner-city area. As de-industrialization took effect, the African Americans found themselves in declining neighbourhoods as businesses closed and job opportunities diminished. Crime began to plague these communities as young black men found themselves disproportionately unemployed (Stradling, 2003). For instance, by the end of the twentieth century, the neighbourhood known as Over-the-Rhine (immediately north of the central business district) had become notorious for its poverty and had earned the label 'ground zero for inner-city decline' (Staley, 2001).

In April 2001, police officers shot an unarmed black man, Timothy Thomas, in Over-the-Rhine. Hundreds of Cincinnati residents took to the streets to protest over entrenched racism and economic inequities. Thus did the first major race riots of the twenty-first century in the USA begin (Staley, 2001; Seabrook, 2009, and see the Foreword to this book). Despite a national decline in gun violence during the mid-1990s across the USA, Cincinnati experienced a significant increase in homicides involving firearms during the first decade of the twenty-first century. Between 2001 and 2006, the annual average was 73.3, compared to just 41.3 during the 1990s, and with a modern-day high of 88 homicides in 2006 (Engel *et al.*, 2013).

Almost three-quarters of homicides during a one-year period in Cincinnati (June 2006–June 2007) involved a known violent group member as victim or suspect (Engel *et al.*, 2013). These authors observe that 'violence tends to stem from loosely-knit social networks of individuals who hang out together on the street and promote violence as a way to handle conflict' in the city's most deprived communities (ibid. 405). These groups do not rise to the status of 'gang' as typically defined by academics and practitioners. They do not have hierarchical structures, initiation ceremonies, common tattoos, or symbolic colours, and many do not even have a name but are identified only by the territory where they hang out. However, they do contribute significantly to serious violence linked to turf wars around drug territories (ibid.). Through a rigorous intelligence-gathering process in 2007–10, multiple law enforcement teams identified a total of 2,431 individual members of violent groups or gangs in the city at some point during that period. In 2010, a total of 46 active gangs were identified. Among the 1,761 known active members within them, the average age was 26.2 years (Engel *et al.*, 2013).

Urban deprivation and violence in Glasgow

Glasgow is the largest city in Scotland and is situated on the River Clyde in the country's West Central Lowlands. In the eighteenth century, the city was one of the UK's main hubs of transatlantic trade. Following the Industrial Revolution, the population and economy of Glasgow expanded exponentially and the city became one of the world's most distinguished centres of heavy engineering. With a peak population of 1,128,473 in 1939, subsequent urban renewal projects resulted in the large-scale relocation of people to new towns and peripheral suburbs, and reduced the inner-city population considerably, to a current figure of 598,830 (General Register Office for Scotland, 2011). The east end of Glasgow, which extends from Glasgow Cross in the city centre to the boundary with North and South Lanarkshire, now includes some of the most deprived areas in the UK. For example, suburbs such as Easterhouse have suffered a long history of social problems arising from the failure to provide basic amenities when the housing schemes there were first built, combined with sixty years of significant unemployment (Deuchar, 2009a). In the north of the city, some of the suburban residential areas such as Springburn and Maryhill are reported to contain the highest levels of unemployment and drug abuse in Scotland. Although many of the run-down tenement buildings have been refurbished or replaced, levels of poverty remain high in these communities. Inevitably, these social problems have brought with them significant levels of crime.

Of the 874,000 crimes in Scotland during 2010–11, 25 per cent were recorded as 'violent crimes', with assault accounting for 24 per cent of all crimes and a knife being used in 11 per cent of violent incidents (Scottish Government, 2011d). This represents a 30 per cent drop in incidents of assault in Scotland since 2008–9. However, it has been found that men under 65 living in the most deprived quintile of areas in Scotland have a death rate due to assault that is 31.9 times that of those living in the least deprived quintile (Leyland and Dundas, 2010). Further, 16–24 year-old males have been found to be at the highest risk of being a victim of violent crime compared with all other combined age and gender groups, and particularly those living in the 15 per cent most deprived areas of Scotland (Fraser *et al.*, 2010; Scottish Government, 2011d). In Glasgow, statistics immediately prior to the implementation of the CIRV initiative suggested that the homicide rates in the city were approximately three times those in Scotland as a whole (Leyland, 2006). Specifically, 32 of the total number of 94 recorded homicides across

Scotland took place in Glasgow city during 2005–6 (Scottish Government, 2007). By 2011, the number of homicides had dropped to 26 but Glasgow still had the second-highest homicide rate in Europe, after Amsterdam (Scottish Government, 2011b; Lindsay, 2012). Data recorded by the United Nations Office on Drugs and Crime (UNODC, 2012) indicate that, in 2007–8, the homicide rate in Glasgow was 4.1 per 100,000 of the population compared to 2.1 in London and 1.5 in Belfast; by 2009–10, these figures had dropped to 3.3 in Glasgow, compared to 1.6 in London (although they had risen in the case of Belfast, to 2.6) (UNODC, 2012).

Since 2000–1, Scottish Government statistics on homicide have included a category for 'rival gang member' in the 'relationship of the victim to the accused', and this figure has fluctuated between one and six homicides per year in Scotland between 2001–10 (Bannister *et al.*, 2010: 5). However, in general terms it has always been difficult to locate statistics of violence or homicides related specifically to 'gang-related' crime in Scotland since the data gathered by crime analysts from the VRU and the newly-formed Police Scotland tend not to be classified in this particular way. Specific geographical area statistics on the more generic category of 'youth disorder' in Glasgow are compiled by the Information and Intelligence Unit within the GCSS. Their figures suggest that the number of incidents of youth disorder has dropped from around 489 in 2008–9 to 112 in 2011–12 in the east end of Glasgow (GCSS, 2012). However, one senior officer I interviewed described the ambiguous nature of youth disorder statistics of this kind, explaining that they could encompass anything from 'drinking alcohol on the street' or 'having a noisy party' to 'throwing a petrol bomb at someone'.

In spite of the difficulties associated with finding clear definitions of, and statistics related to, youth disorder and gang-related offending, it has been found that young people living in housing schemes in the most socially deprived communities in Scotland are more likely to report having a fear of violence related to gang disorder (Fraser *et al.*, 2010). A rigorous intelligence-gathering process during 2007–8 enabled crime analysts from the VRU to identify the existence of 170 gangs in Glasgow (GCSS, 2008). The figure of 170 gangs compares with 169 identified by the Metropolitan Police Service in London, a city six times the size of Glasgow (Centre for Social Justice, 2009). Around 55 known and established street gangs were identified across the east end of Glasgow, comprising around 600–700 members, while a further 21 gangs totalling 400 members were later identified in the north of the city

(VRU, 2011). The average age of gang members was 16 years, and the knife was the most common weapon of choice.

Adopting an ethnographic approach to the research

In conducting my research for this book, I set out to create a qualitative analysis of the nature, causes, and impact of youth violence in Cincinnati and Glasgow. I also sought to examine the policy focus and cultural shift that took place in both cities to accommodate the focused deterrence approach to policing, managing, and reducing youth violence that was at the heart of CIRV. Although I was able to access statistics on violent disorder and the reduction in street violence and homicides that occurred at the time of CIRV's implementation, there was a lack of evidence illustrating the views of the people involved in the violence or influenced by the initiatives during their implementation. I was therefore dissatisfied with the existing accounts of the focused deterrence approach in the CIRV context.

I wanted to talk to the young people involved in the violence and to those responsible for designing and launching the CIRV initiatives. I wanted to hear from those who offered their services as police officers, youth and street workers, social workers, and mentors, and from those young offenders who accessed and supported the programmes. In short, I wanted to study the social phenomenon of youth violence and the policing and managing of it from the viewpoint of a naturalistic researcher.

I therefore set out to analyse the social and cultural worlds of offenders, reformed offenders, and social service partners in CIRV. I also aimed to observe, shadow, and participate in frontline police work and in youth and community work. My approach was a part-time sociological micro-ethnography (Hammersley, 2006), as summarized thus:

> Ethnographic field research involves the study of groups and people as they go about their everyday lives. Carrying out such research involves two distinct activities. First, the ethnographer enters into a social setting and gets to know the people involved in it; usually, the setting is not previously known in an intimate way. The ethnographer participates in the daily routines of this setting, develops on-going relations with the people in it, and observes all the while what is going on. Indeed, the term 'participant observation' is often used to characterize this basic research approach. But, second, the ethnographer writes down in regular,

systematic ways what she observes and learns while participating
in the daily rounds of life of others.

Emerson *et al.*, 1995: 1

In the following sections I explore the strategies I used to enter the social
settings under study, participate in the routines in those settings, and observe
what was going on.

Entering the field: Becoming a 'marginal native'

The majority of the data were gathered between spring 2011 and winter
2012–13. Table 3.1 summarizes the primary research participants from
whom insights are reported in the book. For ethical reasons, I have assigned
pseudonyms to the participants and also describe their roles and profiles
in loose terms, lest they be identifiable by readers. There is one exception,
namely American criminologist Professor David Kennedy who was
interviewed, and later consented to his real name being used during data-
reporting. In Cincinnati, access to police officers, offenders, members of
social service teams, and Street Advocates was facilitated via gatekeepers
from the University of Cincinnati Institute of Crime Sciences (UCICS),
of which the author of the Foreword is Director. The CPD entered into a
close partnership with researchers from UCICS during the first decade of
the twenty-first century to create opportunities for 'data-driven approaches
necessary to facilitate crime reduction' (Engel and Whalen, 2010: 113).
This pre-established relationship meant the process of accessing research
participants was relatively straightforward.

As a Scottish academic visiting Cincinnati for the first time, and
with much less experience of American policing than colleagues at UCICS,
I regarded myself as a stranger to the culture I was there to study in the
spring months of 2011. However, because of the closeness of the existing
relationship between researchers at UCICS and police officers at the CPD, the
police readily welcomed me as a visiting researcher linked to UCICS (Engel
and Whalen, 2010). With UCICS's support as gatekeepers, I quickly became
accepted and gradually assumed the role of 'marginal native' during the
fieldwork research, in a fine balance between being a stranger and a colleague
(Hammersley and Atkinson, 2007: 89).

Table 3.1: The primary research participants

Location	Number & gender	Names	Role or profile
Cincinnati	6 males	Ben, Brad, Dave, Joe, John, Tony	Senior police officers
	1 male	Josh	Senior police staff
	1 male	Charles	City council member
	5 males	Jason, Matt, Mike, Mitchell, Rick	Specialized unit cops
	1 female	Diane	Special surveillance officer
	1 male	Mark	Crime analyst
	11 males; 1 female	Aaron, Darius, Keenan, Lemar, Lester, Marcus, Mickey, Patrice, Rashan, Romeo, Sandra, Steven	Street Advocates and reformed offenders
	1 male; 1 female	Beverly, Samuel	Social service managers
	3 males	Barry, Jeremy, Kirk	Probation officers
	5 males	Arcus, Delroy, Jermaine, Rufus, Wesley	Current offenders
	1 male	David Kennedy	American criminologist
	1 male; 1 female	Alan, Laura	Criminal justice staff, UCICS
Glasgow	6 males	Ally, Brian, Iain, Kenny, Richard, Scott	Senior police officers
	1 female	Kate	Senior police staff

Table 3.1 continued

Location	Number & gender	Names	Role or profile
Glasgow	4 males	Stewart; Benny, Gary, Johnny	Gangs Task Force senior officer; Gangs Task Force officers
	1 male	Andrew	Crime analyst
	5 males	Billy, Colin, Lewis, Peter, Tom	Community agency managers
	1 male	Alex	Career adviser
	1 female	Karen	Housing officer
	1 male	Jamie	Senior education manager
	1 female	Alison	Senior social work manager
	1 female	Hannah	Case manager
	1 female	Alana	Intensive support worker
	1 female	Janice	Parent
	6 males	Cammy, Dean, Jordan, Ross, Sean, Shuggie	Current offenders
	8 males	Del, Donny, Graham, Grant, Jack, Jim, Kieran, Robbie	Reformed offenders, clients and volunteers
	1 male	Paul	Scottish academic

I was therefore able to negotiate access to six senior police officers who had played a key role in designing, managing, and implementing CIRV, plus one senior member of police staff and one city council member who was also a member of the CIRV Steering Committee. I also gained access to five operational police officers in Safe Streets, the specialized enforcement unit in the CPD, to conduct interviews and observe practice, and talked to one special surveillance officer and one crime analyst. The existing relationship between UCICS and the CPD also enabled me to reach the multi-agency partners that cooperated with the police on CIRV – namely 12 Street Advocates, two social service managers, and three probation officers. Additionally, I interviewed five current offenders, and I was able to talk to a number of Street Advocates who could authentically describe themselves as 'reformed offenders'. Finally, I also interviewed David Kennedy, an internationally renowned academic whose work had underpinned the Boston Ceasefire and influenced the CIRV initiative, and two criminal justice staff at UCICS.

In the case of Glasgow, access to participants was achieved thanks to a mixture of gatekeepers from the Scottish VRU, the then-Strathclyde Police (now subsumed within Police Scotland) and existing contacts in the field that I had established through my previous research (see, for instance, Deuchar, 2009a, 2010b, 2011, 2012). First, I gained access to five senior police officers and one senior member of police staff who were involved in designing, managing, or implementing the Glasgow CIRV, and one additional senior officer involved in implementing the wider anti-violence directive in Strathclyde Police and subsequently Police Scotland. I then worked with one senior officer and three operational officers who were members of the Gangs Task Force unit within Strathclyde Police, and liaised with a crime analyst within the VRU. Through existing contacts with local community youth work and voluntary organizations in Glasgow I reached five managers in community-based agencies that were key partners in CIRV. I also spoke to a careers adviser, a housing officer, a senior education manager, a senior social work manager, a case manager, an intensive support worker, the parent of a victim of gang violence, and a Scottish academic who had been involved in analysing the quantitative impact of CIRV.

To explore the causes, nature, and impact of youth violence and go beyond my earlier work in Glasgow, I also conducted life history interviews with both current and reformed offenders. These particular young men belonged to some of the communities in the east and north of Glasgow that were the focus for CIRV, and were accessed through various gatekeepers. I interviewed six young men who were serving prison sentences in Scotland's largest Young Offender Institution (YOI) for offences related to violence. I then interviewed a further eight young men who resided in the same communities but who had become engaged with the CIRV initiative as clients or volunteers. Further details about the access and data-collection methods used for this part of the research can be found at the beginning of Chapter 5.

As in Cincinnati, conducting the fieldwork in Glasgow required that I adopt the role of 'marginal native' (Hammersley and Atkinson, 2007: 89). I often moved among comparative strangers, while accident and happenstance shaped my approach as much as planning and foresight (Van Maanen, 1988: 2). By taking this approach I strove to build trust and form positive relationships with the young people and the members of organizations that helped to implement CIRV. In both cities, building these relationships enabled me to gather detailed and meaningful data through participant observation.

Participant observation and interviews

Ethnographic approaches to research usually involve fieldworkers 'participating', either overtly or covertly, in people's daily lives for an extended period of time. They involve researchers watching what happens, listening to what is said, and asking questions through informal and formal interviews (Hammersley and Atkinson, 2007). Gold (1958) provides a continuum of participant observation (adapted in Figure 3.1). At one end, researchers become full members of a social setting and refrain from revealing their researcher identities, conducting covert observation. At the other, they become overt observers but refrain from interacting with participants except during formal interviews. For a variety of ethical and moral reasons, I rejected both of these approaches and opted to fluctuate between the two middle roles. I thus aimed to spend time with participants and gain their trust, while also observing and analysing their practice or discussing their insights and views about their personal or professional lives.

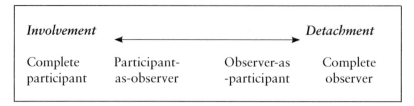

Figure 3.1: Participant observation

Source: Adapted from Gold, 1958.

I conducted semi-structured interviews with police officers, youth and street workers, and members of social service teams, as well as with the offenders and reformed offenders described above and listed in Table 3.1. I also engaged in part-time observation of specialized enforcement units in both cities, shadowing operational teams during patrols of neighbourhoods deemed to be hotspots for offending behaviour. Further, I observed the work of police surveillance teams in both cities and also made additional observations in Cincinnati communities, while working alongside police officers and Criminal Justice staff from UCICS. Finally, I participated in street and community work, observing Street Advocates in Cincinnati and intensive support workers in Glasgow as they made contact with young people within their own social and urban contexts.

The interviews and venues

I was committed to finding out more about the nature and causes of youth violence and gang culture in the two diverse settings. In addition, I wanted to:

- establish what the main goals of the CIRV initiative were in both cities, how social partners worked together to implement it, and the perceived impact it had had on violence
- examine how the initiative had been amended or adapted as it travelled from Cincinnati to Glasgow
- find out more about the prevention, intervention, and enforcement strategies in both cities
- understand the transition that police officers had gone through to embrace the principles associated with CIRV
- explore how – and to what extent – CIRV's strategic ideology had impacted on police culture, and had stimulated criminal desistance

I used these themes to form the basis of my interview questions. They needed to be focused but flexible enough to enable participants to elaborate on their responses and for me to follow up on issues raised with additional, supplementary enquiries when appropriate.

Although mostly conducted individually, where issues of availability or accessibility arose interviews were occasionally conducted with two or three participants at once. I interviewed the professional participants in police stations, community centres, universities, and public sector offices, and also gathered additional data on police culture and practice and the work of Street Advocates and intensive support workers through direct observation of police patrols and community work.

Interviews with current offenders in Cincinnati were conducted in probation offices and were arranged by the local probation team members who were monitoring offenders' behaviour. In such cases I met with a larger group of offenders, outlined the nature of the research to them, and sought volunteers to participate in interviews. For those who volunteered to participate, I met with them individually or sometimes in pairs to put them at ease. During the course of the interviews, probation officers were on hand but not present in the assigned interview rooms. Additional interviews were carried out with Street Advocates who were also reformed offenders, and these were conducted both at the University of Cincinnati and in the Street Advocates' own offices.

In Glasgow, some interviews were conducted with offenders in the largest YOI in Scotland. In such cases, access was negotiated through the Scottish Prison Service (SPS). Senior prison officers were able to identify those young offenders who belonged to the focused communities where CIRV was implemented but who had been sentenced for violent offences. I initially visited the YOI to meet these young men and seek their voluntary participation. Subsequent interviews were conducted in interview rooms, with prison staff on hand. Other interviews were conducted with those who had become clients of CIRV and had moved away from violence to some extent but who were still occasionally involved in offending. In some cases, these young men were awaiting court proceedings or were assigned to intensive support in the community. I visited local youth, community, or intensive support agencies to meet the men, build rapport, and, again, seek their voluntary participation. Subsequent interviews took place when keyworkers brought volunteers to the university or when I met informally with the young men along with youth and community workers in local cafés in Glasgow. Some reformed offenders who had become volunteers in the CIRV initiative were also accessed through the police and the various partner agencies. In such cases, I met with them informally and then conducted interviews with them in local cafés and bars.

Since violent offending is predominantly a male pursuit in both Cincinnati and Glasgow, all the offenders I interviewed were young men, and most were aged between 16 and 25 (with a tendency towards the higher end of this age continuum in Cincinnati). However, ethnic backgrounds differed across the two locations. While in the case of Cincinnati all of the youth participants were of African American descent, Glaswegian youth participants were all white. Reformed offenders were mostly between the ages of 25 and 37 in Glasgow but, in Cincinnati, there was a much wider age-span, with some of the reformed offenders (who were also Street Advocates) in the 60–70 years age range. I recognize that the majority of the professional participants were also male, and the limitations this places on my analysis. However, it was not possible to widen the gender sample as most senior police officers, members of social service teams, and professional associates who were involved in CIRV were male. That said, I did find more female involvement in the initiative in Glasgow than in Cincinnati.

Once transcribed, interviews provided a rich data set that I could then analyse to detect salient patterns and themes (Strauss and Corbin, 1990). I also assimilated the main themes with the existing analyses of social disorganization, strain, and advanced marginality as a stimulus for violent offending. This assimilation included the work of contemporary urban sociologists and criminologists such as Anderson (1999), Agnew (2006) and Wacquant (2008, 2009a, 2009b), as well as that of researchers associated with the classical studies outlined in the opening chapter. I also referred to previous policing research to theorize some of the insights I acquired from interviews about police culture and practice.

Observing police practice and street and community work

Two of my main research aims were to explore the transition that police officers had undergone to embrace the principles of CIRV, and to understand how – and to what extent – the initiative's strategic ideology had impacted on police culture. Despite the renewed emphasis on violence-prevention, I recognized that enforcement was still an essential element of CIRV. In both the CPD and Strathclyde Police, specialized enforcement or Task Force units were established to patrol high-crime communities and detect, disrupt, and deter those involved in youth disorder and gang violence. Decker (2007: 730) describes the formation of specialized units as a 'modal suppression strategy', and observes that the behaviour of the officers within them is often viewed as the antithesis of the principles underpinning problem-oriented, community policing strategies (see also Katz and Webb, 2006). In addition to conducting interviews, I therefore sought to observe first-hand the work of officers in the specialized gang enforcement units in each city. The aim here was to explore how, and to what degree, the renewed strategic ideology influenced the everyday practices of specialized frontline officers during their interactions with local young people. This approach would also enable me to consider to what extent the officers held on to the traditional hegemonic masculine identities associated with the tough, aggressive, street cop, and how this impacted on their interactions with youth (Chare, 2011).

Observing and participating in the work of specialized frontline police officers in both cities enabled me to understand their routine practices and explore the challenges that remain in terms of the everyday relationship on the streets between officers and local citizens. During the police patrols, I fluctuated between the roles of accepted incompetent, 'capable of shortening the long hours on patrol through talk but incapable of doing anything remotely connected to the job itself', and friendly helper, who could interact with perceived offenders and support officers with routine observations but who required 'continual supervision' (Van Maanen, 1988: 89). I also observed some of the office-based work conducted by police surveillance staff in both cities.

In addition to observing police practice, I accompanied Street Advocates in Cincinnati and Intensive Support Workers in Glasgow as they engaged with young people on the streets and in the low-income, high-crime communities. It was important to understand the challenges faced by the communities that were the focal point for CIRV, and the role that street and support workers played in re-engaging young men through pre-emptive strategies. I therefore shadowed street workers in Cincinnati while they walked around deprived communities that were characterized by violence. I also toured around the city's high-crime neighbourhoods by car and on foot with research staff from UCICS and senior and operational police officers. In Glasgow, I accompanied intensive support workers during keyworker meetings with young men out in the community and also observed the self-referral sessions that took place in Glasgow Sheriff Court.

Throughout my experiences of police ride-alongs and streetwork in both Cincinnati and Glasgow, and my informal tours of Cincinnati's neighbourhoods, I kept an ethnographic diary. I recorded jottings of 'fragments of action and talk' (Emerson *et al.*, 1995: 31–2) that would later serve as focal points for more detailed written accounts and fieldnotes describing key events. I also recorded my own personal impressions and feelings. Through applying analytic asides, commentaries, and in-process memos as a further means of analysis (Emerson *et al.*, 1995), I created impressionist tales characterized by dramatic recall, novelistic characterization, and textual identity (Van Maanen, 1988). Extracts from these impressionist tales appear in some chapters in Parts 2–4 to complement the interview data.

The ethical issues

The ethical and moral dilemmas I faced in collecting the data for this book were, at times, quite challenging. As with the research in Glasgow that preceded this work (Deuchar, 2009a), recruitment from youth groups raised particular ethical issues, meaning that informed consent from all primary youth participants would be required. To this end, I produced an information sheet providing full details of the nature, aim, and duration of the study in a form that was easily understood. Given that the interview questions could lead some young offenders to disclose criminal activities (as in Deuchar, 2009a), to avoid any legal obligation to report such disclosures, a statement was included in the information sheet for the young men. The statement was designed to reassure them that the only time that I would ever have to pass on information to the authorities was if a young person said something that showed that he or another young person was in immediate danger of serious harm, or where some very serious crime was identifiable but had either not been solved, or was about to be committed. Once the young men were aware of these issues, they were asked to indicate their consent verbally and this was audio-taped. Participant information sheets were also issued to all primary adult participants, who were asked to indicate their consent by providing their signatures.

In planning the participant observation of police patrols and community work, I was conscious that I would be collecting data in settings over which I would have very little control. To minimize the risks to myself, I adopted a reporting arrangement whereby I contacted assigned gatekeepers or family members via mobile telephone before and after the observations had taken place. In addition to observing the behaviour of primary research participants (police officers, Street Advocates, and intensive support workers) in the heat of a police operation or the midst of street work or community-based interactions, I was likely to come into contact with a secondary group of participants (local community residents, including young people) who in some cases might be unaware of my researcher identity. Fine (1993) sets out the compromises ethnographers frequently have to make with 'idealized ethical standards' and remarks that the goal of informed consent is often complicated by the fact that 'good ethnographers do not know what they are looking for until they have found it' (ibid. 274). Thus, I had to accept that the process of creating authentic portraits of street and community scenarios and police practice and culture would involve some subtle forms of deception (ibid.).

I therefore declared my intentions to police officers, street workers, and support workers in both cities, while recognizing the unpredictable nature of my encounters with citizens on the streets and in communities. In some cases I was able to make these secondary participants aware of the nature and scope of the research and to seek informed consent, but in other cases this was not feasible. I therefore sought advice from primary gatekeepers and reflected on how best to maintain an approach to data collection, analysis, and dissemination that was situationally ethical (Fine 1993; Hammersley and Atkinson, 2007). I finally decided to report on the data that arose from observations of local citizens and young people who were clearly aged 18 or older, but to ensure that the real names of neighbourhoods, streets, and secondary participants were never mentioned in my fieldnotes, so as to ensure complete anonymity and avoid any possible harm to all concerned.

In Parts 2–5 I describe the main themes that emerged from the study through sharing the interview data and fieldnotes from the ethnographic research.

Part Two

2

Violence in Cincinnati and
Glasgow: Insights from a
transatlantic ethnographer

Gangs, guns, and (dis)respect: The causes and nature of youth violence in Cincinnati

> *As we walk down to the bus stop, I notice a young black man who is wearing a t-shirt with a photograph of one of his deceased 'homies' on it. As the young man steps onto the bus, I notice the caption on the back of his t-shirt which reads, 'rest in peace'.*
>
> Author's fieldnotes, Cincinnati

This observation captures something of the impact of youth violence in Cincinnati. The t-shirt tells a sad story, and demonstrates how young lives are lost as a result of the gun violence that accompanies the drug trade and blights some of the deprived communities in the city. I sought to uncover the root causes of the behaviour that leads to such tragic circumstances and to explore the nature of the violence and offending itself.

Many authors have shown how poverty, unemployment, social disorganization, and oppression can stimulate violence among groups of young men (Shaw and McKay, 1942; Whyte, 1943; Cohen, 1955; Cloward and Ohlin, 1960; Anderson, 1999) (see Chapter 1). For those who are repeatedly rejected from the labour market or recoil at the idea of taking dead-end 'slave jobs' in the deregulated service sector, 'underground activities offer a bounty of full-time employment opportunities' (Wacquant, 2008: 66). Because drug dealing can offer the certainty of earning large sums of money very quickly, it provides the most marginalized with a sense of status and identity on the streets (Anderson, 1999; Wacquant, 2008).

Some young men may suffer from a lack of mainstream economic opportunities, combined with the absence of traditional male role models or 'decent daddies' in the family home (Anderson, 1999: 157). Hence, unconventional role models may influence them to participate in drug dealing, which is often organized around a code of violence and predatory activity that motivates them to possess guns for protection (Anderson, 1999). Drug dealing can also lead to gang culture, in which young offenders seek out 'running buddies' or 'homies' who can be relied on to back them up and defend their honour where disrespect from others is perceived (Anderson, 1999: 73).

As I also discussed in Chapter 1, some academics argue that young black males are the most profound casualties of advanced marginality in American towns and cities (Anderson, 1999; Hagedorn, 2008; Wacquant, 2008, 2009a). As white families have increasingly been supported by the government to flee from the central city areas to the suburbs, an 'urban colour line' has been drawn around a 'class fracture' (Wacquant, 2008: 58). Hagedorn (2008: 558) argues that 'racism shapes the identities of alienated, impoverished youth' in deprived American communities. Anderson (1999: 323) asserts that the profound social exclusion of African Americans has arisen against the backdrop of historical prejudice, discrimination, and the psychological scars of the experience of slavery (Du Bois, 1953).

In this chapter I explore the key themes from my interviews with young male offenders in Cincinnati and with those who had left offending behind and were now working as Street Advocates. I also provide additional data gleaned from police and probation officers (for details of participants, see Table 3.1), and interrogate some of the results of the participant observations conducted during my real and virtual tours of Cincinnati neighbourhoods. I explore the social and cultural disadvantage that young black men in deprived neighbourhoods in the city may become exposed to. And I examine how – and the extent to which – they deal with these social pressures through participating in the lucrative underground economy and in violence.

Family, role models, and street life

During my initial discussions with senior and operational police and probation officers, several participants told me they believed that young men became involved in violence and crime due to a lack of positive role models and support in the family home:

> The main issues are societal issues that the police can't do very much about – weak family structure, not a strong male presence in their lives too often ... so, you end up with young men ... they end up in the vulnerable position of livin' on the streets, usually what we call the 'street life' – usually involved in drug sales.
>
> Joe, senior police officer

> I would call it weakened family structure ... that's what I blame.
>
> Ben, senior police officer

> I think it's … lack of parenting … their parents don't discipline or watch them … and then when they're 18 or 19, they're starting to have kids of their own, and they're not in their kids' lives.
>
> Jeremy, probation officer

During subsequent interviews with current and reformed offenders, many of these views were affirmed. Most participants talked about how they had grown up without any positive male role models in their lives, and the impact they felt this had had on them:

> I started hittin' the street [as a teenager] when I lost my dad, when my father died that's when I went out on the streets.
>
> Keenan, Street Advocate and reformed offender

> I grew up in a single-parent home … I had a step-dad that was kind of on and off and my dad was pretty much absent.
>
> Lemar, Street Advocate and reformed offender

> We didn't have no good, no positive role model or especially not no male. Now, the women – I mean like my mother wasn't a bad role model but she's a woman … I love women but I want to be a man … he's powerful, he's a boss, I want to be like that.
>
> Darius, Street Advocate and reformed offender

> Like, you need a mentor … someone over your back like, 'do this, do that … make sure you do that.' It wasn't really like that when I was growing up … there weren't really no father figure.
>
> Delroy, current offender

Some young men grew up with the knowledge that their fathers were incarcerated. And some reformed offenders also talked about how the adult males they had in their lives were often abusive, while the females were victims. Where young men lacked positive mentors in the home, they turned towards alternative role models on the street who embraced them and encouraged them to sell drugs for material gain:

> The street will embrace them … encourage them and accept them.
>
> Rashan, Street Advocate and reformed offender

All them years from age seven, the neighbourhood raised me ... you are looking up to males and the males in my neighbourhood was selling drugs.

> Darius, Street Advocate and reformed offender

Them older guys, they got like two cars, got that money, a house, they got money 'cause they put it up, they smart and you wouldn't even know they're doin' nothin' ... 'cause they low-key with it.

> Wesley and Jermaine, current offenders

It seems, then, that the current and reformed offenders in Cincinnati identified the social pressures associated with family upbringing as a major factor in stimulating their involvement in the street life. The young men I interviewed felt they had missed out on having access to a strong male mentor in their lives and conceptualized the image of a father figure in hegemonic terms, characterized by strength, power, and dominance (Connell, 1987). Alternative, street-oriented role models encouraged them to become involved in the underground economy, and they embraced exaggerated, defensive images of masculinity associated with drug dealing and crime (Anderson, 1999; Hagedorn, 2008).

Status frustration, anomie, and drug dealing

In addition to family pressures, some of the participants became motivated to sell drugs because of the lack of employment opportunities. Both current offenders and those who had now moved away from offending reflected on the impact of these pressures:

It's a Catch 22 situation because, you know, [young men] can't get work, they can't get welfare support so obviously they're gonna choose the street life, I suppose.

> Rashan, Street Advocate and reformed offender

I couldn't get a job and then I got fired from my job ... [I sold] just a little marijuana, some here and there.

> Delroy, current offender

You had to learn how to get another trade – the street life trade.

> Aaron, Street Advocate and reformed offender

Those who were caught up in the criminal justice system due to recent offences referred to the lack of opportunity to make money through conventional means. For instance, Jermaine expressed his frustration at how he was demonized because of his previous convictions:

> It's hard to get us a job, you see ... it's my record, what they look at first and try and judge me ... they check our background before they try to know us, you feel me? So that's when you ain't got no choice but to turn around and go straight to the streets. What more can we do?
>
> Jermaine, current offender

Other offenders and reformed offenders described the difficulties they came across when looking for employment that would provide them with an adequate level of pay that matched the 'fast cash' they gained on the streets:

> I got a job at Wilma's [restaurant] ... it was 7 dollars, 30 cents ... most guys go to the streets.
>
> Delroy, current offender

> If you're around people ... you see the fast money they get, compared to the money that you've gotta wait for ... quicker money ... making double my pay cheques in a couple of days.
>
> Lester, Street Advocate and reformed offender

> I didn't want to grow up struggling so I was more enticed to making money in an illegal way because I knew I was making a lot more money.
>
> Lemar, Street Advocate and reformed offender

Some reformed offenders reflected on the social and cultural pressures to achieve material gains. They described how some young men tried to live up to media-induced role models, achieve particular standards of success, and aspire to live the 'American dream'. Combined with the lack of opportunities to access legitimate means of achieving these goals, this led to increased participation in the informal economy:

> You have no one to look towards, and the person you do look towards is maybe a rapper ... an artist, a basketball player ... you're trying to pursue this dream [to be like them] ... So within doing so you're doing things like selling drugs, robbing, to try to have that lifestyle that America tells you that you should have.
>
> Lester, Street Advocate and reformed offender

Drugs play a big part in it because … it's a medium by which every young guy believes he can be a millionaire overnight, you know? That impacts on him to the point where he doesn't feel like he has to prepare himself, 'I don't have to go to school … I can be a rapper, I can be a sports star'.

Rashan, Street Advocate and reformed offender

In some cases, the status frustration that led young men to seek social support on the streets and economic security from the drug trade was associated with cultural, as well as social, pressures.

'Fitting the description': Marginality, racial prejudice, and policing

Some interviewees felt that there was a lack of recognition and celebration of African American heritage both in Cincinnati and in America as a whole. Lester felt that this led to an identity crisis among many young black males:

Here we have no heritage. The black African American in the United States … we are so confused and trying to figure it out … what you belong to, where you came from. If you go and ask a lot of African Americans in the inner-city about common knowledge of … our history, they don't know because in our schools they teach us nothing about ourselves … so you have this identity crisis your whole life … of not knowing who you are.

Lester, Street Advocate and reformed offender

Others also talked about how social deprivation and disadvantage affected black communities the most. And perceptions about police prejudice caused frustration and anger:

It's just – they stereotype us. Like, us three here, I swear – we go right outside right now and stand on a corner and we would just be stopped … they goin' to try and ask us what we doin' or just … they goin' to be lookin' at us and stuff … and it could be us three again dressed different or doin' right on another corner and they'd pay us no attention. Sometimes there's a dress code.

Jermaine, current offender

It could be the clothes, it could be the guys you're with … this happened like three weeks ago … like I come out my house, my boys is rollin' up a joint … the police ridin' by and just keepin'

> lookin' at the car, we pull out and like five police cars blitz us, like
> they just hit the car ... they thought I was makin' a drug deal ...
> they just tore the car apart, lookin' for guns, dope, whatever ...
> that's all we had, a little joint.
>
> Arcus, current offender

Observation of frontline police practice among specialized officers in the
city suggested that suspicion was indeed sometimes unevenly aimed at black
citizens in deprived communities. My fieldnotes illustrate that the cues of
criminality that were given most attention were not always racially neutral:

> A young black male is walking along the side of the road in front
> of us. Matt, the police officer I am with in the car, is unhappy
> about this. He slows down and begins rolling down the window
> but the young man is on his mobile phone and continues with
> his conversation without making eye contact. Matt addresses
> him: 'Hey, excuse me, could you put the phone down please?' The
> young man puts the phone away and Matt asks him for his social
> security number. Having put away his phone, his hands are still in
> his pockets. 'Take your hands out of your pockets please,' he asks,
> 'and back-up ... hey, if you could not walk on the street when
> there is a sidewalk available, sir'. The young man obliges and
> now begins to pay more attention to the officer as he continues to
> question him.
>
> Author's fieldnotes, Cincinnati

Engel and Johnson (2006) find that, when compared with Caucasians, black
males generally display significantly higher levels of gaze avoidance, speech
disruptions, and hand gestures during normal interpersonal interactions.
Officers who are trained to interpret these non-verbal cues as indicators of
deception may 'unnecessarily view interactions with blacks as suspicious'
(Engel and Johnson, 2006: 611). During police ride-alongs, I found that some
specialized enforcement officers were apt to react with suspicion to non-
verbal cues among young people, such as gaze avoidance, selective attention
deriving from mobile phone use, and casual body language. In Matt's case (in
the previous excerpt from my fieldnotes), the police officer also adopted an
authoritarian stance during his interceptions, attributable to the combined
impact of his sense of mission, attention to perceived danger, and suspicion
(Reiner, 2010).

My interview and observational data illustrated the strained
relationships between police officers and young black men in Cincinnati.

Wesley, Jermaine, and Arcus all felt that there were 'good cops' and 'bad cops', and that 'bad' cops tended to frame young black men for crimes they hadn't committed:

> They put two dirty cops together it's goin' to be murder ... somethin' gonna happen bad, man. They'll pull us over, the car ripped, drugs on the scene, guns found ... everythin', man.
>
> Jermaine, current offender

And, 'we fit the description'.

> Arcus, current offender

Every time I get locked up I 'fit the description', every time!
> Wesley, current offender

However, some also conceded that the same issues affected other neighbourhoods that were predominantly white:

> You go to [name of district] and it's the same deal ... it's all a lot of white people, so it don't make a difference ... they carry guns too, they got bigger guns ... they're crazy!
>
> Jermaine, current offender

Jermaine (among others) recognized that violent offending linked to social marginalization could take place in white neighbourhoods as well as black. However, the majority seemed to feel that African American communities had been the most profound casualties of advanced marginality (Wacquant, 2008). From the time of the Kerner Commission report onwards, research findings have indicated that minority citizens in the US have a greater distrust of, and more negative attitudes towards, police than do white citizens (Webb and Marshall, 1995; Weitzer, 2000; Engel, 2003). The young black offenders I interviewed confirmed their intense distrust of police officers, and felt disempowered and marginalized by their experiences of 'fitting the police description'. The process of 'othering' that they experienced strengthened their tendency towards an oppositional culture (Young, 2007).

Gangs, guns, girls, and violence

Although the links between gang membership and violence have been identified (as described in Chapter 2), Klein *et al.* (2006) argue that most American gangs do not conform to the commonly held inter-generational and highly organized stereotypes associated with the Bloods and the Crips (two primarily African American gangs founded in Los Angeles). In Cincinnati, some current offenders also felt that street violence was not necessarily related to what they would describe as 'gang' culture, as Jermaine described:

> There are no gangs here … the closest to gangs is shoot-outs … gettin' shot at, or shootin' at someone.
>
> Jermaine, current offender

During interviews and informal discussions with police and probation officers, participants confirmed that many young offenders failed to identify with gang culture, because they associated gangs with organized hierarchies. Nonetheless they did 'group up' to sell drugs and conduct violence:

> When they think of gangs they think of Crips and Bloods, and that's 1980s stuff. Now they just have 'people'. So, these are my 'people' … [but] there's no difference. They might not wear all the same colours, but ultimately they are together, they all sell drugs together, they do shootings together … they're on the same corner together.
>
> Barry, probation officer

> Different groups are associated with different corners and blocks … but it's not like other gangs that you would identify in the country that are organized, have a hierarchy and structure.
>
> Kirk, probation officer

> We're fortunate that we don't have the born-in gangs, like you would see if you go to Los Angeles. Like my grandfather was a Crip, my dad's a Crip, I was born a Crip. We don't have that here … we don't have a lot of formalized gangs … with the real established hierarchy and things like that.
>
> Dave, senior police officer

The young men I interviewed acknowledged having 'running buddies' or 'homies' who would back them up if they required it, and admitted that fear often led to a need to 'group up':

> I mean I've got homies, but it's family … or someone I've grown up with … or been around, someone I've known since my childhood.
>
> Rufus, current offender

We definitely have [guys] that are grouped up and the reason is because of the fear of another group that they know is there.

Steven, Street Advocate and reformed offender

Some current offenders explained that they felt it was essential for them to own and carry a gun to ensure they had a sense of protection out on the streets, since everyone else in the neighbourhood tended to be armed. They talked about how violence in the 'hood' was often centred around disputes arising from rivalries over girls or money (Yablonsky, 1967; Anderson, 1999). Where such issues erupted, group or gang-related violence often came into play as a response to perceived disrespect. This reality was also articulated by reformed offenders, and backed up by police officers:

Just the slightest thing can start the chaos and when I say the smallest thing, I mean it could have been a girl that he likes and this girl likes me ... once the tension builds up now I got 'beef' so my whole crew that I hang with doesn't like him ... and one of my boys could see one of his boys ... and that's when the guns come into play.

Lemar, Street Advocate and reformed offender

Most of it's based on respect-type issues – you know, you disrespected me ... you owe me 20 bucks from a crack game you didn't pay me, and when I asked for it back you punked me out in front of my boys, you disrespected me ... so we're gonna hunt you down and kill you.

Dave, senior police officer

For some young men, holding and using a gun provided a sense of status and power on the streets:

You feel like Superman – you are unstoppable, you feel like it don't matter who it is, you feel like, you just feel like 'that's power'.

Darius, Street Advocate and reformed offender

Yes, it definitely feels like ... it's like having a million dollars here, you feel powerful because money represents power, because a gun also represents power because you feel unstoppable. I mean you visualize all these gangster movies you've seen like Rambo or old gangster movies.

Lemar, Street Advocate and reformed offender

·Drawing these accounts together, we can see that the participants viewed youth violence in Cincinnati as being centred around the underground economy associated with drug dealing. The code of violence was based on upholding respect and retaliating against perceived disrespect. It could sometimes be attributed to a defiant culture, in which offenders acted as individuals to uphold a sense of personal honour (Jankowski, 1991). However, group-related violence was also in evidence. Other reports have suggested that violence in Cincinnati tends to stem from 'loosely knit social networks of individuals who hang out together on the street' (see Chapter 3). While these groups do not rise to the status of gang as typically defined by academics and practitioners, they do contribute significantly to serious violence linked to turf wars around drug territories (Engel *et al.*, 2013).

The data confirm this, but also suggest that the violence can arise as a result of more trivial issues, such as rivalry over girls and disrespect towards others' street reputations (Yablonsky, 1967). In the context of these volatile situations, the young men I interviewed embraced toxic forms of masculinity that fostered the need to dominate others and a readiness to resort to violence (Kupers, 2005). They carried guns for protection and used them to demonstrate a 'blunt display of power' (Anderson, 1999: 125).

Interviews with offenders and reformed offenders helped to illuminate the social and cultural disadvantage that characterizes Cincinnati's deprived communities, and the nature of the crime and violence that spring up as a result. First-hand observation of the real and virtual worlds of the offenders helped to deepen this analysis further. Box 4.1 summarizes the observations I made during ride-alongs in the Cincinnati neighbourhoods and in the surveillance unit of the CPD.

BOX 4.1: REAL AND VIRTUAL TOURS OF CINCINNATI'S 'BADLANDS'

A marginal native on the streets of Cincinnati

I get into the car with Laura, a research associate, and Alan, a crime analyst, both from UCICS. As we motor around the streets of the city, I am struck by the intense socio-economic contrasts. One moment we are driving around affluent downtown, and the next we are surrounded by evidence of poverty and social deprivation. As we drive into one neighbourhood, the impact of the drug wars becomes more apparent to me as Alan and Laura point out a small playground beside a run-down apartment block. 'This is the territory of the Tot Lot, one of the most notorious groups or gangs in the city,' Alan explains. 'Offenders tend to congregate around that playground, and the shootings against rival gang members have affected children before, who have been caught in the crossfire.' The implications of this seem horrific to me, as I stare at the playground where innocent childhood meets the hard-edged impact of the 'code of the street'.

As we begin to head back along the main road to go back to the university, Laura spots something of interest. We stop at the kerbside, where a wooden post holds a small shrine to two murdered gang members. A t-shirt hangs from the post, with a photograph of two young black men wearing t-shirts belonging to their gang. Their dates of birth and dates of death are listed – both were in their twenties. On the ground lie some flowers. One of them was murdered on Christmas Day 2007. As Laura says, 'gang violence takes no vacations'.

Author's fieldnotes, Cincinnati

The virtual world of the violent gangster and 'gangsta rap'

During my visit to the CPD surveillance unit I am introduced to Diane, a specialist surveillance officer who helps lead the team in apprehending offenders through the use of advanced visual and audio technologies. Diane shares some insights with me about the virtual world of gangsters in Cincinnati. 'They tend to vocalize through song and videos that they have what they call "beef" with somebody ... and they will tell you their crimes through their songs – their shootings and their drug sales.' As Diane enters the name of an infamous young Cincinnati offender (whom I will refer to as Leroy) into the search engine, I am surprised to see a wide array of online videos that this particular individual has created on YouTube. As Diane clicks on one of the videos, I sit back and watch the images unfold ...

As the screen opens up, the outline of a police patrol car is quickly followed by the image of a young, African American male captured within the letters of his name ('Leroy') and accompanied by the intense, hard-core beats of hip hop and gangsta rap music. Within seconds, the full screen opens up to briefly reveal Leroy smoking and carrying an assault rifle. The screen then changes again to reveal some close-up shots of multiple packets of cocaine, followed by a close-up of the rifle before cutting again to Leroy as he sings along to the rap music. The screen is then filled with an image of a hand, carefully transferring measures of cocaine into plastic bags and containers, before cutting back to Leroy staring out of the window followed by another image of a passing police squad car. As the images keep on coming, one shows Leroy blatantly hold up the gun and point it at the screen.

A new image then appears, revealing an unmarked police car parked in a nearby street and accompanied by a lyric that translates into 'I know you are here'. Over the next three minutes, images of Leroy loading his rifle with bullets are interspersed with images of an undercover SWAT [Special Weapons and Tactics] vehicle, illustrations of Leroy observing police operations from his window, and the blatant singing of lyrics that celebrate the use of .223 Remington rifle cartridges and AK.45 assault rifles. Various other young men are depicted singing the same lyrics as the film-maker, and close-up shots of the street where they hang out are also depicted. Towards the end of the film, the music continues to blast out with the accompanying lyrics that suggest that Leroy is 'creating a recipe'. He places the ingredients into a pot and cooks them, while he ceremoniously creates a line of cocaine and heats up a jar of boiling water to cook it with. The final images depict close-up shots of the young man's street and house, and a shot of him walking along the street with a young child. Thus, gangster turns father and the prospects of another generation of violence begin to emerge ...

As the video comes to an end, Diane highlights that, within the first three seconds of the film, Leroy had demonstrated his involvement in drug offences, gun possession, and police offences that would give them enough evidence for arrest. Members of the surveillance unit systematically gather these sources of evidence to compile overall reports. As Diane says, young guys like this know the police can see these films but do not seem to care about the potential consequences.

Author's fieldnotes, Cincinnati

The observations recorded in Box 4.1 illustrate the socio-economic contrasts that define Cincinnati's neighbourhoods, and the presence of 'concentrated ghetto poverty' (Anderson, 1999: 26). In such circumstances, young men become attracted to the street life, where they jeopardize their own and others' lives inside the 'isolated perimeter of the collapsing inner city' (Wacquant, 2009b: 210). As Anderson (1999: 32) notes, the inclination to violence 'springs from the circumstances of life among the ghetto poor – the lack of jobs that pay a living wage, limited basic public services ... the stigma of race, the fallout from rampant drug use'. Young men develop an internalized identity and sense of self-respect and honour by defending their drug turfs through violence (Anderson, 1999). My visits to the city's deprived neighbourhoods and conversations with UCICS staff portrayed first-hand the nature of this territorial behaviour in Cincinnati. Control was exerted by groups and gangs over particular corners, and defended against others (Holligan and Deuchar, 2009). In some areas, the impact went further than the intimidation of other violent individuals, groups, or gangs. From a young age, children learned the first lesson of the streets from notorious local gangs such as the Tot Lot: that they 'cannot take survival itself, let along respect, for granted' (Anderson, 1999: 49).

There were also tragic consequences for the young men who engaged in the violence. In his book *The Comfort of Things*, Miller (2008) describes how material objects are often viewed as integral and inseparable parts of all relationships and help to maintain human ties. At the roadside shrine referred-to in the first section of Box 4.1, the wooden post and the t-shirt provided a physical reminder of lives stifled by violence as a result of the code of the street and the class and cultural disparity that stimulates it. The dates of birth and death conjured up the image of lives unfulfilled against the backdrop of subterranean capitalism and failed criminal enterprise. The shrine was a poignant reminder of how those excluded from the mainstream eventually surfaced as citizens in a parallel world and adopted an oppositional culture (Anderson, 1999; Alvarez, 2009). But engaging in this parallel world sometimes meant being extinguished by the very danger that characterized it.

Glimpsing the virtual world inhabited by some of the violent young men was also enlightening. For Leroy, the hip hop gangsta rap performance channelled via YouTube illustrated an extreme form of defiance. Hagedorn (2008) argued that hip hop was created as an oppositional form of identity, providing marginalized young people with opportunities to become empowered against the backdrop of bleak surroundings. It thus enables youth to join 'pleasure and rage while turning the details of their difficult lives into craft and capital' (Dyson, 1996: 177). In particular, gangsta rap enables gang members to express 'black rage' and articulate their 'defiance of the white man's system' (Hagedorn, 2008: 97). It glamorizes violence and romanticizes the culture of guns to draw attention to complex dimensions of ghetto life ignored by many Americans (Dyson, 1996). A 'ghettocentric' identity is evident in many of the lyrics, where the image of the gangster is celebrated and the 'white supremacy' associated with dominant institutions is rejected and defied (Hagedorn, 2008).

In Leroy's case, his creative cultivation of gangsta rap enabled him to blatantly showcase the alternative economy he had engaged with, in spite of the risks of becoming exposed to criminal justice sanctions. The oppositional culture he promoted via his music will inevitably influence other members of marginalized communities like him on the Internet, hence life may continue to imitate art imitating life (Hagedorn, 2008). And the violence will continue.

The next chapter focuses on Glasgow and some of the marginalized young men who inhabit its deprived neighbourhoods.

Chapter 5

Strains, critical moments, and street violence:
Tales of Glasgow's lost boys

Watchin' my mum and dad usin' drugs gave me a lot of anger ... I was in surroundings where you were taught if somebody's bigger than you, you pick up a brick.

Kieren, reformed offender

In *Gangs, Marginalized Youth and Social Capital* (Deuchar, 2009a: 144), I observed that some young people in Glasgow 'drift into gangs for a while; they vie for territory and engage in moderate violence for recreation and to help cope with social exclusion'. I also noted that, for those with particular social and emotional difficulties, gang membership occasionally leads to more extreme forms of violence and recruitment to serious crime (see also Kintrea *et al.*, 2008, 2011). It is not my intention to replicate my earlier work here, but rather to deepen the reader's insights into the issues relating to youth violence and crime that can arise both alongside, and independently of, territorial gang culture in Glasgow.

Some young men's violence may have little to do with gangs but everything to do with issues of social exclusion and oppression. This chapter therefore focuses on the lives of those who have engaged in urban violence both within and beyond the context of the street organization that we might associate with gang culture (Hallsworth and Young, 2008).

As part of my research, I wanted to explore the ways in which street violence among young men in Glasgow might be encouraged or shaped by the types of socio-cultural issues I uncovered in Cincinnati. I was also interested in the sanctions these young men became exposed to. Agnew (2006) argues that, used in isolation, punishment does not deter individuals from engaging in further offending since the punishment itself often functions as a social strain *conducive* to crime. Against the backdrop of CIRV's implementation and the mainstream adoption of a public health approach to violence-reduction in Glasgow, I was therefore keen to explore current and reformed offenders' experiences of the criminal justice system.

As explained in Chapter 3, all the participants who were interviewed for this part of the research were young white males from those communities that were the focus for the CIRV initiative. They resided in communities with the highest levels of social deprivation in the east end and the north of Glasgow. I wanted to talk to young men who had benefited from CIRV but also to those who had continued to offend and had become exposed to criminal justice sanctions.

In total, I worked with 14 young men. First, I gathered intelligence from gatekeepers such as youth workers and social workers about those who belonged to the communities in question but who were serving prison sentences. Through subsequent liaison with the SPS, I made contact with six youths aged 16–18 who matched the criteria and were willing to participate in interviews in prison. This enabled me to capture the views of a small group of young men from the target communities who had progressed to the more extreme end of violent offending. Although some had attended CIRV self-referral sessions in Glasgow Sheriff Court, they had continued to engage in violence until they were incarcerated.

I was interested to know what stimulated these young men's continued offending. Conducting life history interviews, I explored their original motivations for, and attraction to, participating in street violence. The aim was to uncover the salient events and turning points in their lives and how these might have accelerated or limited their involvement in violence and criminal activity (Laub and Sampson, 2003). It was also important to explore their experience of being incarcerated and the impact this may have had on their self-confessed commitment to desist from violence.

Second, thanks to help from the former Strathclyde Police, the Scottish VRU, and a range of statutory and voluntary agencies, I was able to make contact with a small group of young men who resided in the same communities but who had become engaged with the CIRV initiative as clients or volunteers. I interviewed eight men who were between the ages of 16 and 37. Those who were clients had been referred to CIRV because of their violent offending and had engaged in the self-referral sessions and the workshops, courses, and interventions implemented by the partner agencies. While some had moved away from violence, others were still offending in other ways. The volunteers I met had already begun to desist from crime by the time they became involved with CIRV, although some were originally referred to the initiative as clients and later became recruited to work with other young men to encourage them to leave violence behind. Again, I used life history interviews, encouraging participants to explore the significant turning points in their lives (including their involvement in CIRV) and how these events may have heightened or curtailed their involvement in violence and crime. Although mostly interviewed individually, on one occasion three of the men who came from the same local community opted to be interviewed together due to their established relationship with each other and their desire to save time. Further details on data collection methods, ethical issues, and interviewee profiles can be found in Chapter 3.

In later chapters I will outline the journeys towards desistance that some of the young men embarked on, and the role that CIRV played in enabling this process. However, in this chapter I focus on what led them into the violence to begin with, the nature of the violence itself, and the impact of the criminal justice sanctions they experienced. The data from their stories are presented in the form of short biographies; in Boxes 5.1–5.4 I have summarized the salient events that four of the most vulnerable young men I met referred to in the interviews. Each biographical description is followed by a short discussion in the light of relevant themes and issues raised in the literature. While all of the personal accounts communicated during interviews were unique, it could be said that many of the issues in the biographies featured here are fairly typical of those expressed in the interviews with the other ten participants. Hence, I occasionally draw on illustrations from other interviewees to provide some cross-case observations.

BOX 5.1: BIOGRAPHY 1 – DONNY

Donny began gang fighting when he was 13, and felt that boredom was the root cause of this. He noted that most of his friends became involved in gang violence from a young age because there were few facilities and opportunities within their local community in the east end of Glasgow: 'You either dae absolutely nothin' and you're bored, or you go oot and fight.' The violence was centred around territorial behaviour and a strong urge among the young men to defend their housing scheme from external threat (as in Deuchar, 2009a). Donny had started smoking cigarettes after his grandmother died, and later progressed to smoking cannabis. Although he felt that cannabis often made him feel relaxed, on some occasions it could stimulate aggression, particularly if mixed with alcohol: 'If you're smokin' and somebody pissed you off then obviously … that buzz is gone. It's just turned into rage n' that … and mixed with booze it isnae really a good combination.' Donny developed a difficult relationship with local police officers. He resented them because they regularly stopped and searched him on the street. He was eventually given a short-term prison sentence for gang violence, which made him more committeed

> towards moving away from crime on his release: 'It was really bad … I was like, "sack that … I'm no' gang fightin' again".' However, Donny left prison and immediately returned to his local community, with no after-care support. Some of the other members of the local gang tried to bully him into participating in violence again. However, by the time I met him at age 16, his interests had moved on. He had begun selling drugs within his local housing scheme as a means of earning fast cash: 'You can make a whole lot of money … like a quarter of it goes to the person that gave me the weed and so I get the rest of it.'

Barry (2006) observes that some young people begin offending because they view it as fun, exciting, and a means of relieving boredom. The adrenalin rush that some gain from gang fighting has also been documented elsewhere (Deuchar, 2009a). For Donny, a sense of boredom and lack of opportunity led to regular engagement in street violence, which was centred around the drifting-together of young men who shared status problems and who became focused on 'hyper place attachment' (Cohen, 1955; Kintrea *et al.*, 2011: 68). Donny used alcohol and drugs as a form of relief from the social strains he experienced, which further increased his propensity towards violence (Agnew, 2006). He developed an uneasy relationship with local police officers because of his street-oriented behaviour. Previous research has demonstrated the fragility that often characterizes the relationship between young people and police officers in socially deprived communities in the UK (Crawford, 2009), and the resentment that arises because of police stop-and-search procedures in Scotland (McAra and McVie, 2005; Gormally and Deuchar, 2012). As in Cincinnati, several of the interviewees in Glasgow had similarly negative views of the police due to their perceptions that officers were 'out to get them':

> They're searching you for no reason at all because maybe you're standin' on a corner at the end of the day … people need to live, especially young people. Young people that stand on corners – it's up to young people. It's no' against the law.
>
> Grant, reformed offender and CIRV volunteer

> I've got that opinion that the polis are always oot to get you, that's the way it is … it's a true saying, 'good cop, bad cop' … but I seem to think there's more bad oot there to get you.
>
> Jim, reformed offender and CIRV client and volunteer

Some of them are arseholes … but if they're arseholes to you, you're arseholes to them.

Dean, current offender

The interviews with Donny, Grant, Jim, and Dean illustrate that, in spite of the principles underpinning CIRV, police were often viewed as being prejudiced against young people in socially deprived communities. As with the young black males in Cincinnati's ghetto communities, police presence among the young white men I interviewed in Glasgow was regarded as an unwanted invasion by an external force (reflecting earlier findings by Campbell, 1993; Anderson *et al.*, 1994; Carr *et al.*, 2007). In terms of the criminal justice system, the punitive aspects of Donny's prison experience had had a short-term deterrent effect. However, his short custodial sentence was devoid of opportunities for rehabilitation or aftercare. Barry (2011) notes that 76 per cent of all custodial sentences issued in Scotland are for less than six months, leaving little scope for meaningful intervention. As with some of the young men in Cincinnati, peer pressure, combined with the attraction of monetary success from the lucrative drug trade, led Donny to spiral back into offending on his release.

Box 5.2: Biography 2 – Jack

Jack grew up in a deprived community in the north of Glasgow in a home where violence was an everyday occurrence. His father was often violent towards his mother and she dealt with the pressure through heavy drinking, and was therefore unavailable to Jack in an emotional sense. When Jack was five, his father battered him violently and he never forgot this traumatic experience. He would often arrive home from school and his mother would tell Jack and his brother that they were leaving the house and going to live in a women's refuge. After a few days there, they would return home and the cycle would repeat itself again. At primary school, Jack was always getting into trouble for fighting and was labelled the 'bad boy' by his teachers. He was referred to a psychologist but he was always too afraid to tell her what was going on at home. His childhood was dominated by fear, and much later a trauma counsellor told him that he had evidently been 'programmed for violence' by the time he went to primary school.

Once he had made the transition to secondary school, Jack became involved in gang violence on the street. He picked up a two-year prison sentence for knife crime when he was 15 for slashing a rival gang member's face. When he was released, he found that his mother's drinking had worsened and his father was rarely at home. Jack continued to build a reputation for himself through participating in gang violence, driven by a sense of fear: 'See when I was a young boy, I was full of fear and everything I displayed was about showin' you how I wasn't fear't. So I was the wee guy that would be at the front of the gang fight throwin' bricks … one of my pals says to me, "see when you were younger, you were game as f*** – you know, you were always up front in gang fights." I says to him, "no, I wasnae, I was the most frightened".'

Following several other charges and criminal justice sanctions, Jack got involved in a fight one night with his friend at a bus stop. During the scuffle, Jack hit his friend who then fell onto the road and went under a bus and lost his life. The incident devastated Jack as well as the families of both young men: 'Everybody knew about it – my ma' and da' knew his ma' and da' and he stayed round the corner. I didnae realize then it would leave an imprint on me – it affected my mental health to a level that even the day [today] it can still affect me.'

Jack began his prison sentence at 20, having been convicted of culpable homicide. He was released three years later without any of his issues of trauma having been addressed, much less resolved. He returned briefly to his own community where he met a girl and became a father but still found it difficult to function in relationships and in the environment where his friend had lost his life. For the next few years, he sold and took drugs and became isolated in his mother's home as he seemed to always become involved in fights whenever he tried to go out and socialize. In the end, after being stabbed and not being able to get free from his past or address his issues, he ended up in a homeless unit in the city centre. One of the homeless support workers put Jack in touch with an alcohol and drug counsellor. Now in his early thirties, he had finally begun to find the courage to challenge many of his deeply ingrained attitudes: 'There were times when I just thought, "what's the point in it – you've failed in your life". There's a part of you that wants to fight on, but you think, "what's the point … you've failed your life, you're never goin' to amount to nothing". All the stuff I was told when I was growin' up I was replayin' – all lies. Hardwired into me. I'd been in the bad square from Primary One all the way through – you know what I mean? And the messages off my ma' and da'.

Sprinkle (2006) argued that children from homes in which violence occurs have a 'myriad of developmental, physical, and psychological difficulties'. For Jack, domestic violence was a recurring strain associated with his childhood. Combined with the emotional detachment that his mother's alcoholism created, this led Jack to experience persistent feelings of emotional isolation and fear (Agnew, 2006). Meltzer *et al.* (2009) note that children who witness domestic violence often become fearful and inhibited and can react by presenting trauma symptoms, and that these symptoms can often persist into adulthood. While girls may react by experiencing internalized problems, boys will often display externalized behavioural issues. Drawing on social learning theory, we can posit that Jack learned about violence through a process of observation, behavioural rehearsal, and reinforcement. He observed violence from a young age at home, then rehearsed the use of violence in gangs, and was rewarded by achieving peer respect and a criminal reputation that he then needed to continue to uphold (Sprinkle, 2006). Some of the other young men I interviewed also talked about having negative role models in the home that may have stimulated their involvement in similar types of violence and crime:

My da' … used to live with us until I was about 13 or somethin' … you used to get a laugh wi' him, sitting aboot wi' my pals … he's the co-accused for the crime I'm in [prison] for now.

Sean, current offender

My mother went through a lot of things wi' my da' … he used to do drugs and that and done a lot of time … he was involved in gangs when he was younger … and he ran a lot of drugs and stuff like that.

Ross, current offender

Negative school experiences also played a part in perpetuating Jack's violence; teachers labelled him as 'bad', and so he felt compelled to live up to this identity. Like other young men in both Cincinnati and Glasgow, Jack's continuing participation in violence was driven by the need to sustain and enhance the criminal and violent reputation he had established among his peer group, and by a fear of losing that reputation and the sense of identity that went with it (Barry, 2006). The death of his friend and the culpable homicide charge he picked up had a huge impact on his mental health and self-esteem. And his experiences of prison were limited to containment and punishment, with no corresponding focus on rehabilitation or aftercare. Barry (2011: 165) argues that most prisoners are 'traumatized because of addictions, mental health problems, and former abuse'. Jack left prison without having any of these issues resolved.

> ## BOX 5.3: BIOGRAPHY 3 – JIM, ROBBIE, AND DEL
>
> Jim, Robbie, and Del grew up in one of the most deprived housing schemes in the east end of Glasgow, where territorial issues were very much to the fore. They carried knives and became involved in violence from a young age, as a means of defending their housing scheme from opposing gangs. They now identified the lack of opportunities for employment and poverty, combined with peer pressure in their local community, as the main causes: 'We're still recoverin' from the 1970s Thatcherism ... [name of scheme] is the worst poverty place ever ... what they've done is make the place look cleaner but the poverty's still there ... it's just what you dae ... as young boys, we grew up and we saw this happenin' in the street'. The young lads referred to the pressure they were under to establish and uphold a street reputation. This was essential to ensure they avoided becoming targets for violence themselves: 'You've got a rep to protect ... if you're stood-on, you'll be stood-on again' [Del]. Indeed, carrying a knife was seen to be an expression of masculinity within their community: 'When you've got a knife in your pocket, you were ... it's as if you're no' a wee boy – I'm a man.' [Jim]. The boys cited poverty as the reason they each progressed from gang violence to selling drugs within the community, and they regarded the opportunity to make 'fast cash' to be worth running the risk of going to prison. Moreover, Robbie indicated that the threat of imprisonment was not a deterrent: 'The kinda sentences they've been dishin' oot nowadays for drugs is nothin'.

Previous research in Glasgow has found that territoriality is a cultural norm in some deprived communities and that an acute sense of place attachment and group solidarity can often be felt (Kintrea *et al.*, 2008; Deuchar, 2009a, 2010b; Deuchar and Holligan, 2010; Deuchar, 2011). As with Donny (Biography 1), territoriality in Jim, Robbie, and Del's housing scheme was shaped by the oppressive world outside their neighbourhood that had left them socially excluded, stigmatized, and with few opportunities or resources at their disposal (Kintrea *et al.,* 2011). Other young men in the wider sample also identified that territorial rivalry was ingrained in their communities and could create considerable tension for them:

> It's just backin' up your scheme … it's always been there for years and years.
>
> Shuggie, current offender

> My area's not even a quarter of a mile end-to-end … it's postcode wars … just constant tension.
>
> Kieren, reformed offender and CIRV volunteer

For Jim, Robbie, and Del, participating in violence was also stimulated by relational factors – the need to follow the crowd and gain a sense of identity among friends (Barry, 2006). Kupers (2005: 714) identifies toxic masculinity as the 'constellation of socially regressive male traits' that foster a need for domination of others and a readiness to resort to violence. As with many of the young men I met in Cincinnati, for Jim, Robbie, and Del weapon-carrying became a means of both protecting themselves and also engaging in 'toxic' masculinity, where no other forms of self-expression as men were available (McDowell, 2003; Kupers, 2005). Whereas guns were prominent in Cincinnati, the knife was more often the weapon of choice in Glasgow for many of the young men I interviewed. The oppressive influence of poverty and the desire for financial 'success' led Jim, Robbie, and Del to progress from gang violence to offending associated with selling drugs (echoing Barry, 2006). This was also a stimulus for other young men in the Glasgow sample, whose subsequent involvement in weapon-carrying and violence worsened with their increasing involvement in drug dealing:

> I was 15 and I was sellin' smack right up until I was 17 … gettin' more involved wi' the polis, hundreds of stabbings.
>
> Jordan, current offender

> You picture yoursel' havin' to go and sign on … so you're sellin' drugs, sneakin' into my hoose wi' a gun in my jacket.
>
> Kieren, reformed offender and CIRV volunteer

The threat of prison was not great enough to act as a deterrent for Jim, Robbie, and Del, since their desire to make money was so intense. Cammy also talked about how his experiences of multiple prison sentences had desensitized him to the threat of incarceration:

> After my third time [in prison], I was like, I didn't care any mair
> to be honest wi' you because it's just a holiday camp ... the time
> flies in there because you are doin' about six different things a day.
>
> Cammy, current offender

Grant also made the point that having a prison record made him look tough
in front of his peers and he had begun to view it as a badge of honour. He
also felt that the lack of aftercare following his release meant he soon became
re-acquainted with drugs:

> Automatically you think you're a big man cause you've been in
> the jail. So I went and got a drink, I went up the toon and just
> started takin' drugs from the day I got oot ... so [prison] didn't
> really help me.
>
> Grant, reformed offender and CIRV volunteer

In Scotland, a high proportion of young people sentenced to YOIs are re-
convicted within two years of release. And the challenges for those young
people returning to their communities after prison are reflected in the high
levels of reoffending (Scottish Government, 2011c). It has been reported that
87 per cent of the population of Scotland's largest YOI have been there prior to
their present sentence, and that issues related to alcohol and drug use, difficult
relationships, and mental health problems hinder their successful transition
back into the community (Scottish Government, 2011c). Although current
public policy signals the need to develop community integration plans and
identify agreed priorities and supportive contact points for young offenders
on release, Grant's experiences (like Jack's; see Biography 2) illustrate that
this does not always happen (Scottish Government, 2008a, 2011c).

BOX 5.4: BIOGRAPHY 5 – KIEREN

For Kieren, watching his parents become drug abusers when he was
young created an intense need to develop a sense of status through
knife-carrying on the streets, and to engage in gang violence. In turn,
this led to drug dealing and firearms possession: 'Watchin' my mum
and dad usin' drugs gave me a lot of anger ... I was in surroundings
where you were taught if somebody's bigger than you, you pick up
a brick ... it's a time bomb isn't it? ... So there's a lot of fear, a lot of
tension ... if you're a young boy and you're 15 ... and you're involved
in drugs and you can get your hands on a gun ... that pressure leads
you to more and more types of weapons, to try and protect yourself

---

really.' When he became homeless, Kieren began experimenting with cocaine to combat his sense of paranoia about being attacked by others, which led him to become even more paranoid: 'When I was sleepin' in a close, I'd be takin' more cocaine because I was fallin' asleep and was hearin' noises and I'd be paranoid ... so I'd have another line of coke.' Kieren was in his late twenties when I met him. Reflecting back on his experiences, he felt that violence had become a survival instinct against the backdrop of the highly volatile family life and violent community in which he lived: 'I'm no innocent – I've been involved in knife fights, I've been involved in gun battles ... that's the way it was. If I didnae I wouldnae be here, I would be dead.'

As in the case of Jack and several of the other young men I met, Kieren grew up in an aversive family environment and a poor and socially excluded neighbourhood. Parental rejection, combined with lack of opportunity, led to anger, which increased Kieren's propensity towards offending. Agnew (2006) argues that negative emotions such as anger and frustration create a pressure to correct a perceived injustice or to satisfy desires. Further, angry individuals are 'less likely to consider the long-term consequences of their behaviour' (Agnew, 2006: 33). As was the case with Jack, Kieren's involvement with violence, drugs, and weapon-carrying created a pressure to uphold a reputation in his community, driven by fear.

Subsequently, Kieren's increasing drug dependency, combined with his desperate experiences of living life on the margins, led him into a hyper-volatile world. Hallsworth (2011: 188) argues that the streets of deprived and stigmatized communities are often populated by 'unpredictable young men from chaotic backgrounds whose psychological instability is often compounded by long histories of violent victimization'. In such circumstances, violence is a competence that has to be learned and mastered where 'street survival is literally the name of the game' (ibid. 189). Although some young men gravitate towards gang violence to gain status and identity, others may become involved in norm-less and unregulated violence. This type of violence lacks a social orientation or territorial motivation, but can nevertheless result in tragic circumstances. An older interviewee provided a clear example of this. Graham described picking up a murder charge as a teenager, following a meaningless and unorganized street chase:

> I was told that three grown men – three brothers – were chasing
> a boy. He wasnae even a pal of mine … I remember chasing after
> the guy and I'd taken the knife oot my pocket. And I don't know
> why I did this but I lunged oot wi' the knife. I mean I didnae know
> the guy, it was nothin' to do wi' me. And as I done that he turned
> around and it caught him in the neck. And I knew, I knew straight
> away that I'd killed him. I found out at court I'd severed a major
> artery … I have to live with that, even about 18 years later.
>
> Graham, reformed offender and CIRV volunteer

In line with Hallsworth's (2011) observations and my own experiences in Cincinnati, territorial issues in Glasgow were only one part of a more complex urban landscape for men like Kieren and Graham. Their lives were led on the disorganized periphery of the hostile and volatile communities they inhabited. And their violence was often centred around the upholding of an internalized identity that resonated with Anderson's (1999) code of the street.

Discussion

Social support theories of offending and crime are premised on the principle that involvement in such activity is inversely related to the presence of protective factors that challenge oppression and exclusion (Cullen *et al.,* 1999; Agnew, 2006). In all of the biographies outlined in this chapter, the young men had experienced a complex blend of social strains and status frustration. For instance, all of the young men lived in economically deprived communities with scant opportunities for accessing youth facilities or meaningful employment. The oppressive impact of poverty thus brought about economic marginality (MacDonald *et al.,* 2011). Added to this, all of them identified what MacDonald *et al.* (2011: 148) describe as 'critical moments' – events or experiences that the individuals remembered as 'highly consequential'. In some cases it was exposure to peer pressure that encouraged them to participate in recreational and territorial violence. Others suffered the traumatic experience of witnessing domestic violence or parental rejection due to alcohol or drug abuse.

The combination of the oppressive conditions arising from the economic wreckage that de-industrialization had brought about, and the highly consequential 'critical moments', stimulated negative emotionality. It also brought about a tendency towards criminal coping mechanisms among the young men (Agnew, 2006; MacDonald *et al.,* 2011). For instance, Kieren's experience of anger energized him, lowered his inhibitions, and created a desire in him to seek revenge for perceived injustice (Agnew, 1992). Jim,

Robbie, and Del adopted toxic forms of masculinity by which they sought to achieve status through weapon-carrying and use. And Jack lived his life in fear, responding to unresolved trauma with aggression and the building of a local reputation. In all cases, violence was used to reduce and escape from the social strains and marginality they experienced.

Some of the young men I interviewed gravitated towards what Hallsworth (2001) describes as the 'organized core' of the street worlds they inhabited, participating in territorial gang culture as a stimulus for violence. However, others inhabited the socially disorganized periphery of the street – selling drugs individually or engaging in unregulated violence. They embraced violent identities that created a pressure on them to enhance and maintain their local reputations. These young men's violent activity became removed from the sub-cultural social structure implied by criminological theories on gangs (Cohen, 1955; Cloward and Ohlin, 1960). In some cases, gang culture was an *initial* stimulus but violence later became unregulated and norm-less, within the context of hyper-volatile street worlds (Hallsworth, 2011).

A number of researchers have argued that efforts to control violence with an exclusive focus on enforcement, punishment, and 'law and order' principles may actually increase the likelihood of further crime by producing additional anger and frustration (Cullen and Gendreau, 2000; Agnew, 2006; Deuchar, 2011). Several of the young men I interviewed had served prison sentences that provided little or no opportunity for rehabilitation or aftercare. Bereswill (2011: 206) argues that the integration of former prisoners into society often becomes an 'obstacle course of overcoming social discrimination and marginalization'. Further, she asserts that young prisoners are often 'multiply distressed' following their release, due to unresolved family conflict, problems of addiction, lack of employment opportunities, or homelessness. The biographical accounts of Jack and Grant, in particular, illustrate the barriers to integration they faced when leaving prison. In addition, despite claims about the 'pains of imprisonment' (Sykes, 1958: 286), the words of Robbie, Cammy, and Grant illustrate how criminal justice sanctions used in isolation failed to deter these young men from engaging in further crime. So although incarceration should both punish and rehabilitate, the young men in my sample indicated that it often achieved neither.

The nature of the violence in Cincinnati and Glasgow differed, as did the cultural backgrounds of the young men involved. But the root causes were often the same. To reduce youth violence in these contexts, young people need to be exposed to interventions that deter while also providing purposeful activity and valued support (MacDonald *et al.*, 2011). Thus, a crucial part of my research was to examine the role the police can play in implementing such interventions and stimulating social support, and to explore the remaining challenges in terms of changing frontline police culture. In Part 3 I explore this in the context of the focused deterrence principles underpinning the CIRV initiative on both sides of the Atlantic.

Part Three

Policing the violence
through focused deterrence:
Opportunities, transitions,
and challenges

3

From zero tolerance to 'PhD cops': Police journeys and the CIRV model in Cincinnati

It's been really effective and you can see out of it a real increase in trust and relations between the police department and virtually every neighbourhood in the city.

Tony, Senior police officer, CPD

In Chapter 4 I discussed how the young African Americans in Cincinnati were marginalized as a result of status frustration, oppression, and family upbringing. Defensive and toxic masculine identities had come to the fore as they strove to adapt to a new de-industrialized world, unemployment, the inadequacy of welfare support, and their continuing lack of faith in the police and judicial systems (Anderson, 1999; Hagedorn, 2008; Wacquant, 2008). Some became attracted to the drug trade because of its extravagant financial rewards that so often serve as a 'subterranean welfare system' (Wacquant, 2008: 67). For these young males and others like them, participation in the alternative economy had altered the rules of masculine confrontation on the streets and led to groups of 'armed young men ... who exercise power over areas' (Hagedorn, 2008: xxv).

Five years after the race riots in Cincinnati had engulfed the city in three days of violence, arson, and looting in 2001, several brutal street killings in the Over-the-Rhine area of the city convinced the public that violence was again out of control. Young black men were shooting each other over drug deals and, by the end of 2006, the total of 88 homicides in the city was the highest number since record-keeping had begun (Seabrook, 2009). Nearly three-quarters of these homicides involved a 'known violent group member as either a victim or suspect' (Engel *et al.*, 2013: 404). Until this point, police responses to these issues had been characterized by a conservative focus on suppression and enforcement. An elite 60-man crime-fighting squad named Vortex (now renamed the Safe Streets specialized enforcement unit) was assembled and became the 'jump-out squad' that aimed to tackle this increase in violence (Kennedy, 2011: 238). However, as I reported in Chapter 2, by

2007 Cincinnati's political leadership had partnered with law enforcement officials, academics, medical professionals, Street Advocates, and community and business leaders to form CIRV, driven by a focused deterrence strategy (Engel *et al.*, 2013).

Prior to CIRV's implementation, violence in Cincinnati was mainly tackled through aggressive policing tactics. The renewed focus on POP and focused deterrence thus required a fundamental reorientation of police culture in the city (Engel *et al.*, 2013). In this chapter I focus on the voices of senior police officers and staff from the CPD as well as members of the CIRV team. I examine their thoughts about previous policing strategies and the more recent focused deterrence approach to managing youth violence. Through data derived from semi-structured interviews, the chapter explores the CPD's journey and the reorientation that was required to adopt the problem-oriented, intelligence-led, and welfare-based policing strategies that underpinned CIRV.

Zero tolerance policing and alienated communities

Zero tolerance policing approaches prioritize strict enforcement as the 'antidote to the spread of urban decay' (Karmen, 2004: 26). These 'get tough' approaches to law enforcement in New York City during the 1990s were associated with a rapid plunge in the murder rate from an all-time high of 2,224 in 1990 to a 40-year low of 580 in 2002 (ibid.). These approaches were replicated in numerous towns and cities across the USA and around the world. But such aggressive tactics also reduced public confidence in the equity and legitimacy of police practice (see Chapter 2). Karmen (2004: 29) argues that zero tolerance crackdowns can be counterproductive if they drive 'already marginalized people even deeper into lives of desperation and deviance'.

Members of the CPD and community partners in Cincinnati identified the problems associated with using zero tolerance strategies in Cincinnati. They drew attention to the resentment that arose among the African American populations in the city's ghettos:

> I think the biggest issue has been there has always been one way of doing police work, and that is to flood an area with police officers and in our mind that was suppressing criminal activity, but from the other perspective, there was a very high degree of mistrust between the African American community – the black community – and the police department. And there was always a big give and take, or push and shove, whatever you want to call it – that, look, 'we've got all this crime, we're bringing in all these police officers'

but the African American community would holler back, 'we're all being treated the same, we're all being policed in a way we don't want to be' – over-policed, if you will, and we were referred to as an 'occupying army'.

Tony, senior police officer

... for 20 years there would be a spot where you would just send a bunch of officers in and everybody gets swept up and so when you sweep everybody up instead of doing this focused thing, you get individuals swept up that may have been involved in something – but they weren't really causing the problem that you're trying to stop.

Josh, senior police staff

As a senior officer in the CPD, Tony recognized the mistrust that had existed between minority citizens and the police force. This reflected earlier findings about the pain, anger, and frustration felt by African Americans in Cincinnati after the black citizen Timothy Thomas was shot and killed by a white police officer in 2001 (Gillen, 2009, and see also the Foreword to this book). During the early part of the twenty-first century, Cincinnati was described as being the 'ground zero' for racism (Kennedy, 2011: 2). More generally, a number of researchers also suggest that racial prejudice among American officers can be a by-product of police and societal culture. Some claim that suspiciousness, hostility, and prejudice are unevenly targeted at black citizens, against the backdrop of vertiginous social and cultural inequality (Wacquant, 2008; Westmarland, 2008; Reiner, 2010).

For many minority citizens, police officers have thus become the 'ultimate symbol of an unjust society dominated by white supremacy' (Engel, 2003: 478). Josh confirmed that this had been the case in Cincinnati when he referred to the 'sweeping up' of individuals in deprived, ethnic minority neighbourhoods who may not have been the main perpetrators of crime (Weitzer, 2000). Officers admitted that zero tolerance had indeed widened the gulf between the police and the communities it patrolled. The race riots in Cincinnati were seen as a major turning point that alienated the African American community in Cincinnati, as one senior officer described:

We had serious race riots in 2001 that were very racially based ... what really seemed to spark the riots was a white police officer killed a black citizen under circumstances where he shouldn't have. That's what started it but what really seemed to fuel it were another set of confrontations and critical incidents between the police and the community where black citizens ended up dead. Sometimes it was a white officer, sometimes not ... the community felt they were being victimized. And it all came to bear in 2001.

Joe, senior police officer

The killing of Timothy Thomas (see Chapter 2) led to protests that called for an end to racial profiling and systematic discrimination by the city's police force. The incident forced communities in the city to 'confront unpleasant truths about themselves' (Gillen, 2009: 112). The civil unrest of 2001 was therefore a major catalyst for re-thinking how policing should be carried out in Cincinnati. The resulting move towards a more focused and inter-agency approach was a potential means of re-engaging the target populations of young, African American citizens. Interviewees described how this strategic reorientation was guided by community-building and public health perspectives:

I was on the commission at the time we had civil unrest in the year 2001. One of the roles that I was charged with during that period of unrest was to try to be a buffer between the citizens and police as related to the concerns that the citizens had and how do I try to mediate that process?

Charles, City Council member, Cincinnati

And then growing out of that, the Collaborative Agreement – you may have heard of that, it's almost like a contract with the community to be more transparent and be more communicative. That has helped a lot – we switched to a problem-solving model of policing that involves the community as much as we can and when we started our CIRV initiative it had a strong community component and that's why it's been widely accepted within the community.

Joe, senior police officer

Hence, community partnership work and POP were both regarded as important means of responding to African Americans' sense of alienation. These two approaches offered a creative way to tackle youth violence that involved talking to the communities and earning trust. In other words, zero tolerance gradually became 'zero wastage policing ... zero stupidity policing ... zero offend-the-community policing' (Kennedy, 2011: 264). As part of the new approach, the focus on training officers changed to become more oriented towards building effective community relationships. Although older officers resisted this approach to begin with, Charles indicated that the focus on community service gradually increased and became embedded into initial training:

> … the old guard would still try to find ways to circumvent the process, but as time continues to move on a lot of those officers are beginning to retire and a new, re-defined police officer is hitting the streets on a regular basis in terms of new classes of officers. We require the officers to spend time in the community doing community service and that's part of their initial training. We want officers to be community-oriented officers now – that's the new, defined police officer now, not so much law enforcement.
>
> Charles, City Council member, Cincinnati

Charles' comments reflected the growing tendency in police departments in many large cities across the USA to adopt 'changes in their missions, strategies and tactics during a time generally recognized as the community era in policing' (Novak *et al.*, 2002: 71). Cincinnati officers began to work with local partners to address the underlying causes of violence, and to draw on alternative methods aside from the use of criminal sanction (Goldstein, 1979, 1990; Novak *et al.*, 2002; National Research Council, 2004).

Problem-oriented policing and focused deterrence

Re-conceptualizing policing in Cincinnati on the basis of a community-oriented, social support model was seen as crucial in enhancing trust in local neighbourhoods. I interviewed David Kennedy, an American criminologist, professor, and author who first introduced the principles of focused deterrence in the Boston Ceasefire to combat gang-related violence there. He described how the strategy developed by talking to frontline police officers, focusing on the most prolific violent offenders, and communicating with them directly both about the consequences of violence and also about alternative opportunities (Braga *et al.*, 2001; Kennedy, 2009):

> The gang guys in the Boston Police Department said 'here's what's going on, we know all these kids, everybody who gets killed, and we know them personally, we almost always know who killed them and we know who killed them personally. They are in gangs, most of what's getting people killed is various kinds of personal-based vendettas' … They were exactly right and 60 to 80 per cent of the youth homicide in Boston came out of a couple of score of drug

crews, maybe fifteen hundred, not even fifteen hundred people. Of the fifteen hundred people maybe 20 per cent were really active so it's not even fifteen hundred people ... it wasn't about selling drugs or crime as such, it was 'the shooting is going to stop' and it turned out that when they did this thing it was invariably effective at which point our outside research team looked at this and said 'this is miraculous' ... and systematized it into what became Operation Ceasefire and combined it – as the original home-grown Boston Police operations had been combined – with two other elements. So one was the offer of help to gang members with social service and job placement and job training, and the other was something that we didn't characterize very well at the time which later became absolutely central – which was direct engagement about right and wrong.

David Kennedy, American criminologist

Ten years later in Cincinnati, the CPD formed close working relationships with the University of Cincinnati. As in Boston, there was a focused approach to crime analysis and urban policing:

I think that number one, the greatest thing we were able to do is to form a working relationship with the University of Cincinnati ... [the academic lead] introduced us to graduate students and suggested that they be embedded in the agency and that helped us do a better job of analysing data, of mining our databases ... I think from the onset they showed us that our data would reveal that three tenths of 1 per cent of the population of Cincinnati were responsible for 75 per cent of the homicides. It allowed us to sit back for a minute and say, 'Oh my gosh', this practice of taking 200 officers and storming into a neighbourhood and arresting anyone for anything and zero tolerance and all the other practices we had been involved in for so many years – we realized that those were highly ineffective ... it's clearly a focused style of policing rather than just swarming an area, stopping everyone. It's been really effective and you can see out of it a real increase in trust and relations between the police department and virtually every neighbourhood in the city.

Tony, senior police officer

Tony's description of how the university began mining the CPD's databases represented a fundamental shift in traditional practice. For the first time, the police gave academics full access to databases and to senior officers. The academics extracted information from everywhere, including arrest records, case files, field interrogation reports, incident reports, citations, bond histories, court histories, surveillance photographs, tattoo photographs, and automated licence-plate readers (Kennedy, 2011). Research participants recognized the invaluable impact of this relationship, which Kennedy (2011: 264) describes as 'the only such relationship ... anywhere':

> Cops do law enforcement very well, and we're getting more involved in the academic side of things; however we're not there yet, and the services that academia provides – they're invaluable.
>
> John, senior police officer

> I think we've really become laser-focused on the issue we're trying to address. And then I think people see – 'yeah, they're getting the people that's affecting my quality of life' instead of swooping up somebody that may have had a beer outside, that the community perceives really didn't do anything wrong.
>
> Brad, senior police officer

The close working relationship between the CPD and the University of Cincinnati enabled the transition towards a finer-tuned, intelligence-led policing – or 'PhD policing':

> What the University of Cincinnati has brought to the Cincinnati Police Department as it transitions from being an authoritarian law enforcement-type agency to a more community-oriented agency, what they have brought is the ability for us to laser-focus our response to calls for services ... In other words what it has done is brought us into what I term 'PhD policing' ... PhD professors with the University of Cincinnati helping us analyse our crime and our statistics, and all of that factors into how we deploy our services and it has made a phenomenal impact ... it just causes the police to work much smarter.
>
> Charles, City Council member, Cincinnati

These officers recognized the huge benefits of working with the university to bring in fresh ideas and different ways of looking at policing strategies. As Kennedy explained, it was no longer the case that officers routinely used 'patrol or rapid-response or detective investigation'. Officers used an intensely focused, problem-oriented approach to identify the specific individual offenders responsible for the majority of the violence, and as the first stage in implementing CIRV. Senior officers described how focusing on the real offenders and adopting multi-agency approaches to intervene earlier enabled police–community relationships to improve and develop:

> Overall, I think the very best thing that comes out of this are the wonderful working relationships that blossom in the community between the police and the community ... the mutual respect that grows out of this, the true relationships, the resolution of years of conflict and mistrust and almost hate for each other ... it creates an opportunity to tell your police officers, 'don't think of yourself just as an officer, but think of yourself as an ambassador', not just the city but this entire region of the city or this entire region of the world. That is what a community sees in its governmental agencies and the most high profile governmental agency, a police department, in that relationship with the community – one of tolerance, one of acceptance, willingness to learn – a willingness to say, 'hey, we weren't doing it the best way we can'.
>
> Tony, senior police officer

> The community intervention strategies that we've employed ... it's generated acceptance around the whole methodology in the community, and so that's a good thing.
>
> Joe, senior police officer

CIRV: Enforcement, community engagement, and social services

As I referred to in Chapter 2, the CIRV initiative adopted a three-pronged approach, focusing on law enforcement, service provision, and community partnership (Engel *et al.*, 2013). Law enforcement was based on a 'pulling levers' strategy, which enabled police officers and partner agencies to coordinate efforts to raise awareness of the consequences of violence during offender notification meetings or call-ins. This strategy also ensured that all and any resources were channelled into targeting the most prolific offenders in the city. For instance, police crime analysts and probation officers supported the police in focusing their efforts on high-tariff drug dealers and their violent associates, to maximize detection and apprehension rates (D.M. Kennedy, 1997; Braga *et al.,* 2001):

> If there's a guy we know is a drug dealer and we know he's been selling dope all day and he jay walks, we're gonna stop him and ride him a ticket, 'cause then it gives us an opportunity to pat him down which then might lead to a gun or something else.
>
> Barry, probation officer

> We had a gentleman go to court on gun charges in the morning and he was out afterwards on bail. On the way, he decided it was a good idea with an iPhone or one of them smart phones to make a video right out after he got outta jail. Well, he was on this video where he lives, with a gun. Se we reached out to parole and said 'he's been outta jail for an hour and this is what he posted' ... so we were able to send people out there and make an arrest.
>
> Diane, special surveillance officer

> During my visit to police HQ I sit and have a chat with Mark, a young cop who has recently moved into crime analysis. On the computer screen in front of us, he brings up a map of Cincinnati with red dots scattered around some of the most deprived communities in the city. 'You see this here, these dots illustrate that there have been 20 shootings in [this community] so far this year. Most of the shootings are in this street here ... so these areas are on our radar and a lot of our efforts are focused there.'
>
> Author's fieldnotes, Cincinnati

Chapter 7 provides further evidence of how frontline officers focused their efforts on detection and enforcement. However, the moral voice of the community also was a particularly influential component of CIRV. As Kennedy argued, it was important to engage with offenders and focus on moral reasoning, rather than purely on enforcement:

> Everybody has an easy time thinking about sanctions and punishment. Everybody has an easy time thinking about 'I'll get you a job' and nobody's imagination goes to 'we need to tell these gun slingers that shooting people is wrong and their community needs it to stop'.
>
> David Kennedy, American criminologist

Community engagement involved exposing offenders to the voices of influential groups in society that they might be prepared to listen to, such as young mothers who had lost their sons to gang violence. Dave (a senior officer) confirmed that, during call-in sessions, 'you can hear a pin drop when the mum talks about what it's like', and that gun shootings would tend to reduce for the first six weeks following a call-in session. At the same time, Street Advocates were seen to play an essential role as motivators and mediators (see also Chapter 10 for further details):

> The Street Advocates come in spending time with them and motivating and encouraging and 'you can do this, I did it and it's going to take work but you can do it and these will be the fruits of your labour'.
>
> Beverly, services manager, CIRV, Cincinnati

> One of the things they did, and it was very helpful to us – they started showing up at crime scenes, at non-fatal shooting scenes. They would mill around in the little crowd that would gather, they would talk to people, calm emotions ... they never got involved in 'snitching' per se, but some of them weren't shy about picking up the phone the next day and sayin', 'hey while I was walkin' around the crowd, everyone was sayin' that "so and so" did this, or "the car looked like that"' or whatever, so we never put them in a position of being a witness for the information that they passed on to us but they were able to pass on helpful information at times.
>
> Joe, senior police officer

A range of tailored social-development and job-readiness programmes coordinated by social service agencies were offered to those offenders who were prepared to leave the violence behind. Beverly managed the case-management process that matched offenders with the most appropriate types of service in the city. She described the assessment process that was conducted in collaboration with Street Advocates, to ensure the team made the right type of referrals:

> We would do that in conjunction with the Street Advocates – we would sit down and conduct an interview that probably was two hours in general to collect that information to determine what the needs were and then make referrals and continue to follow them.
>
> Beverly, services manager, CIRV, Cincinnati

Follow-up referrals could involve offenders participating in cognitive behavioural therapy programmes to help them make changes in the way they thought about, and reacted to, social strains in their environment, and to make transitions to pro-social lifestyles (Agnew, 2006):

> We used a curriculum called *True Thought* or *How I think: Thinking for Change*, and helped them identify what their thinking errors might be, how they view the world, how they view themselves ... to help them to see that there may be some distortion in terms of their thinking and [that] that distortion then can impact the limitations they would put on themselves ... they would typically say things like 'you know, I can't get a job or I can't do this, I don't do that'. So it takes a lot of intense work, it takes collaboration with mental health agencies, social agencies, and certainly agencies that deal with the employment piece.
>
> Beverly, services manager, CIRV, Cincinnati

Offenders were referred to organizations such as Cincinnati Works, a non-profit job placement and retention agency that is funded privately and without government subsidies (May, 2009). The organization provided job-readiness programmes and workshops for young men that included opportunities to build confidence and learn about the best way to fill in job applications and gain interview skills. Elsewhere, the Urban League of Cincinnati was a private corporation with board representation from business, education, service professions, and the media, specializing in providing job training, youth development, and empowerment programmes to strengthen communities. Its manager, Samuel, was himself a reformed offender, and he endeavoured to provide the young men with the motivation to move on to employment:

> My most direct involvement in CIRV was to try and be a change motivator ... because of my own personal past of being an ex-offender myself and being able to transition from my past life into what I do now, so I think they kind of used me as an individual to motivate some of the participants and to try to inspire them and let them know that you can transition successfully from a life of anti-social behaviour to become positive members of society ... we have a three-week programme addressing personal issues, professional development such as resumé- [Curriculum Vitae] writing, and making sure you are participating actively and thoroughly, as well as computer exploration, matching up your personality with the

type of opportunities that would be fitting for your own personal interests.

Samuel, workforce manager, Urban League of Cincinnati

Working alongside other partners such as Street Advocates, members of social service teams such as Beverly and Samuel liaised with potential employers with the aim of getting young men placed in jobs after they had completed their training. They were committed to early intervention and to a holistic, multi-agency approach to make the interventions successful.

However, in spite of the focus on early intervention, social integration, and service provision, some senior police officers focused their attention mainly on the 'pulling levers' element of the CIRV strategy. They welcomed the practice of using any of the legal resources available – including the use of federal prosecution – to punish those who committed violent acts:

> The best thing we've actually done is federal prosecution. The state system does not scare our gangs. As you hear all the time, 'I can do 18 months, four years standin' on my head' – they come out of state prison and wear it like a badge of honour. You can rock their world by puttin' them in the federal justice system because that's a world that they just don't understand … they have no earthly idea how this works and it scares the hell out [of] them.
>
> Dave, senior police officer

> With the state system if I'm a bad guy and I go to court, I'm pretty much looking at the minimum sentence unless I have aggravating circumstances. With the federal system, you basically start at the higher level and the only way to get lower … is to cooperate with the police, so through that we've been able to close several homicides.
>
> Ben, senior police officer

> The home visits take place in between the call-ins … we show up at the offenders' homes and spread the message further. One officer showing up at the door does not have any effect. Four officers showing up with a fed agent and probation officer will have a greater effect.
>
> Dave, senior police officer

This focus on the 'get tough' strategies associated with federal prosecution suggested to me that some police officers still favoured authoritarian enforcement and carceral affirmative action. Some of the participants described the challenges of confronting traditional police culture. They struggled to convince some officers to see alternatives to the patriarchal ideology associated with the 'hard charger' image of the street cop, whose only desire is to handle the streets through enforcement (Chare, 2011: 24):

> Cracking the police culture was one of the early challenges ... I think it's still a work in progress. I think we have buy-in at the command level and it's filtering that down to the line level. When you're a cop you're used to doing things the same way. You go out and make an arrest and you just say you've recovered a gun and you recover a gun again and again in the same place and you say 'it's working' but then you've really got to look at the outcome of it – have the shootings been reduced? And often times, they weren't, and so what we've become is just gun collectors. And that's the mind-set that we're working on, but it takes time.
>
> Brad, senior police officer

> [It's] showing the beat cops, the guys that are on the ground, the benefit of doing this work and how it will really change ... you go through the Academy and the first three years you learn ways that police have made available to do that – and that is 'make arrests, take the gun off the street, get the bad guy off the street' and so you fall into that rhythm that that's what you do.
>
> Josh, senior police staff

Most senior officers thus rejected an exclusive focus on enforcement and were committed to working towards re-engaging 'urban outcasts' (Wacquant, 2008). In CIRV, a collaborative, intelligence-led approach was used to integrate suppression, social intervention, and community organization (Spergel, 1995; Braga, 2008; Wacquant, 2008; Kennedy, 2009, 2011). But some officers continued to emphasize the threat of sanction, so although the strategic vision of the CPD had changed, it was evident that re-aligning the culture associated with frontline policing was indeed a work in progress. Josh revealed that 'cracking the community culture' and getting them to trust the police department also continued to be a huge challenge.

The tensions between command-level strategy, police culture, and frontline practice that were raised in the interviews piqued my interest, and I wanted to seek the views of specialized frontline officers about the main principles and values that underpinned their work in Cincinnati, while also observing frontline practice. Decker (2007: 730) describes the formation of specialized enforcement and gang units as a 'modal suppression strategy', and notes that the behaviour of officers within them is often viewed as the 'antithesis of the principles of effective community policing' (Decker, 2007: 731). The Safe Street unit of the CPD therefore became the focal point for my follow-up interviews and participant observation. In Chapter 7 I present the results.

Guns, tasers, and 'hard chargers':
Police culture on the streets of Cincinnati

> *I like the adventuresome side of it ... I guess you would call it the risk-taking activity. The adrenalin ... the fun, the chases ... the game side.*
>
> Jason, specialized unit cop

Police culture is by no means monolithic. Reiner (2010) argues that individual officers and groups of officers can create sub-cultures based on particular values, attitudes, and professional preferences. Chan (1997: 65) describes how academic analyses of police culture often fail to take account of 'internal differentiation and jurisdictional differences'. The culture found at command level in some police departments may well differ from that found at street level. Drawing on both Bourdieu (1990) and Wacquant (1992), Chan argues that the policing *field* represents the structural conditions of police work, which develop against the backdrop of specific social and political contexts (Chan, 1997: 71), while the police *habitus* refers to the cultural knowledge and system of dispositions that characterize policing (ibid.). But Chan emphasizes the role of police actors in influencing cultural knowledge and institutional practice:

> ... structural conditions do not completely determine cultural knowledge, and cultural knowledge does not totally dictate practice. Working within the structural conditions of policing, members have an active role to play in developing, reinforcing, resisting, or transforming cultural knowledge. They are not passive carriers of police culture ... any structural conditions are taken into account by officers in their practice. Whether a structural change results in any change in cultural knowledge or institutional practice depends on the nature of the change and the capacity of officers to adapt to the change.
>
> Ibid. 73–4

Individual officers must thus be viewed as active decision-makers and not passive entities, and some will adopt the structural orientation and cultural knowledge established at command level, while others will not (ibid. 75). In this chapter I examine the extent to which the strategic police reorientation that took place in Cincinnati through CIRV (the new policing *field*) influenced the culture (police *habitus*) of those who were on the streets and the practices they engaged in.

Safe Streets (formerly known as Vortex) is a specialized unit that was established as a 'jump-out' squad to deal with violence on Cincinnati's streets through zero tolerance strategies (Kennedy, 2011). When CIRV began, the unit refocused its purpose to work specifically with chronic offenders and specially targeted groups or gangs, and take responsibility for the enforcement aspects of the initiative. In the sections that follow, I report on insights from semi-structured interviews conducted with specialized unit officers from Safe Streets. I also provide illustrations of police practice gleaned from participant observation, in which I shadowed unit teams during specialized operations in Cincinnati's deprived neighbourhoods. In reading these insights, it is important that the reader be aware that the officers in the Safe Streets unit are not representative of typical patrol officers in Cincinnati. The specialized unit officers are hand-picked for a very specific but limited function; they are not assigned to routine patrol and neither do they respond to calls for service. They focus on specific locations in the city where recorded crime is the highest, and are expected to target those offenders who continue to engage in violence and crime despite warnings and opportunities to leave that lifestyle behind. I therefore cannot make any claims that these officers' views, attitudes, or practice are representative of those of other officers or of policing in general in Cincinnati.

Focused deterrence and 'hard chargers'

During interviews with the specialized cops in the Safe Streets unit, I found strong support for an intelligence-led, focused deterrence approach to policing:

> I think at first people were like, 'oh great, here's just another initiative that won't work' … but I think it's been the best thing that this department has done as far as focusing on the main bad guys, for lack of a better word.
>
> Mitchell, specialized unit cop

You have to be goal-specific. You know, we used to ... address problems by sweeps. We'd go out, saturate the community, go and arrest everybody and take 'em to jail ... well, you know, the jail would let 'em back out. And two days later they're standin' just where they were ... you can't just go in and just arrest your way out of a problem.

Rick, specialized unit cop

One frontline officer, Danny, talked about how his daily work on the streets went hand-in-hand with problem-solving and deterrence. Another officer, Matt, described how the higher level of sophistication in crime analysis that had been achieved thanks to the CPD's relationship with academics meant that he now tended to 'focus on those individuals that are targeted' as prolific offenders. Danny also talked about the benefits of working with non-traditional partners; for example, he described how Street Advocates provided an important and credible means of appealing to offenders to change their lifestyles (as illustrated more fully in Chapter 10):

[The Street Advocates] are more familiar with these guys. They're familiar with the culture. They're familiar with the lifestyle that these guys live ... and it's easier for them to get out and walk the streets and go up to them and talk with them about changing the things they're doing in their lives, as opposed to me, a police officer, coming up and telling somebody, 'you know you need to do this'. 'Cause frankly, I haven't lived the life that they live – I haven't been to jail, so I don't really know what it's like.

Danny, specialized unit cop

However, despite vocalizing a strong commitment to the reoriented strategic approach underpinning CIRV, several of the officers held on to traditional police values. In his analysis of the frontline police culture portrayed in early episodes of *The Wire* – a US television police drama that ran from 2002 to 2008 – Chare (2011) identifies how the increasing importance of surveillance technologies in Baltimore Police Department's practice caused a crisis of masculinity among some male officers. This was driven by an anxiety that the surveillance team had become labelled as 'station queens' rather than 'hard chargers'. 'Station queens' were stereotyped as those whose roles enjoyed the 'sanctuary of the inside' – the archetypal feminine space associated with the office and the dullness of using technology and completing paperwork. Conversely, 'hard chargers' were 'aggressive and courageous street cops' who were seen to be physically capable, authoritative, and confrontational, and occupied the archetypal masculine space of the street (ibid. 24; see also Herbert, 2001). It was evident that some of the specialized frontline Cincinnati officers identified most with the patriarchal ideology of the 'hard charger' street cop (Chare, 2011: 24), favouring traditionally masculine activity characterized by spontaneity, physical superiority, personal confrontation, and enforcement:

> I love it, I love it – drug work, guns … our goal here is to really address the violent activity … pretty much our responsibility is to target those individuals, and take 'em off the street … if you can put the right leverage on some of these guys … they're gonna spend some serious time in prison.
>
> Rick, specialized unit cop

> It's a matter of being out there and paying close attention to what we see, you know … so I get a kick outta that.
>
> Mike, specialized unit cop

In his 1978 paper 'The asshole', John Van Maanen noted that, when American police officers got the opportunity to engage in what they viewed as 'real police work' – searching, chasing, and capturing offenders – their self-image was 'affirmed' and their morale 'enhanced' (Van Maanen, 1978: 312). Several of the officers in Safe Streets had internalized the nature of the 'cop on the beat using the tough approach to policing' (Schulhofer *et al.*, 2011: 343) and their morale was enhanced by making what they viewed as masculine, authoritative interventions. When asked about the strategies they might use if they encountered volatile situations while out on patrol, some officers focused on enforcement and suppression through the use of guns and tasers (a non-lethal electroshock weapon):

> You would obviously want your firearm pointed at them … now if somebody already has theirs out, you're behind the ball … it takes less than a second to pull the trigger … if you've already got a gun out and you've got your finger on the trigger, that's four shots – if he's slow on the trigger.
>
> Jason, specialized unit cop

> If there's evasive action … it leads me to believe that they have a firearm, then I'm going to draw a firearm and let them know that I'm watching them and the potential for me to protect myself and others exists … if it's a deadly threat then … there's no question, a firearm comes out. If it's a threat of fleeing from me during an

investigation in which case I could be hurt, the person that I'm trying to apprehend could be hurt, I'm gonna give a warning and I'm gonna try to let them know that I have a taser that's ready to be used.

Matt, specialized unit cop

While shadowing narcotics investigations with these officers and becoming immersed in participant observation of confrontational police work, I often found the adrenalin surge contagious:

I notice that Matt has his taser on the left side of his belt, his gun on the right, and his shiny CPD badge in the middle. Suddenly the radio crackles to life. 'Uniform, are you poised? When Matt gets behind the vehicle can you get there quick?' 'Sounds good to me,' Matt responds. As my heart begins to race with adrenalin, I look ahead and see the undercover SWAT vehicle turn round the corner. Matt pounds his foot on the accelerator and we turn the corner, just in time to see the SWAT team storm into the house with assault rifles.

Author's fieldnotes, Cincinnati

Beyond Safe Streets, I found that those officers who had made the transition to crime analysis and surveillance work reluctantly accepted alternative police strategies. But they still admitted a preference for high-adrenalin activity:

We're bringing in more of a focus on analysis of crime statistics – a problem-solving focus. It's been very good for me ... [but] I enjoyed being really active. If I could do the transition, anyone could. I'm willing to open my mind up, it's always a challenge – steering clear of excitement gets frustrating.

Mark, crime analyst

I wanted to gain further, first-hand analysis of the extent to which the strategic reorientation in the CPD had reached those who might view themselves as the 'aggressive and courageous street cops' in a specialized unit such as Safe Streets (Chare, 2011: 24). While observing the work of police officers in the unit, I found motorized surveillance of high-crime neighbourhoods to be the most revealing. Box 7.1 captures one of the observations I made during participant observation of one particular police–citizen encounter when I rode along with Matt.

BOX 7.1: IMPRESSIONS OF AN ETHNOGRAPHER ON THE BEAT IN CINCINNATI

As we turn into Red Street, Matt notices something unusual in his wing mirror. 'Hold on, look at this guy!' he says. I look out of the window and see a reasonably young man of colour walking along the sidewalk with a leash in his hand. Several metres in front of him is a large dog, running along the sidewalk. Matt stops and pulls down his window. 'Hold up a minute', he shouts, 'why do you have a leash and no dog on it?!' The officer's initial approach appears fairly authoritarian in nature, although his remarks could almost be interpreted as containing an edge of sarcastic humour. A response with a similar amount of humour could have defused the situation, but I am quite unprepared for what comes next. With a huge amount of aggression, the man approaches the police car and shouts in the window, 'you want to say something to me? Hey, man, if you want to say something to me, say it to me!'

Matt tries to defuse the situation by re-iterating his question in a calm and rational manner, but the man's aggression worsens. 'What is your problem? You're aggravating me', he shouts. By this time, Matt is out the car and approaching the man and I can tell that his anger has been ignited. 'Hey, you're about an inch away from going to jail – you're getting disorderly', he declares. I am amazed at how quickly this situation has escalated and it occurs to me that this man's reactions probably represent the common response to the police in this neighbourhood – reasonable interaction with them is to be avoided at all costs. At the same time, I am surprised at Matt's reactions and find it astonishing to think that the guy with the dog has just been threatened with a potential arrest.

Matt asks the man for his social security number, and he gives it but also continues to shout, 'no one in this neighbourhood has a problem with this dog but you – there ain't no-one on this whole block that's got a problem with this dog!' Matt attempts to ignore the man, gets back in the car and begins to fill in a citation. He enters the man's details into the Computer-aided Dispatch (CAD) unit system and alerts his patrol colleagues to the incident. 'Hey, hurry up – I've got to go to work', the man continues to shout, 'I got a job – I am a productive member of society, you know … you saw me calling that dog back – but this is what you wanted – you wanted to issue me with a citation.' Matt begins to speak, but the man ignores him and begins to recite Islamic prayers. 'Is that because you don't want me to understand what you're saying?', Matt asks. 'I'm praying', the man replies aggressively. I realize that the resentment the man feels is not only a social one but a cultural one as well – the dominant white are viewed as the enemy in this neighbourhood. Matt issues the man with his citation, and he walks away – still grumbling. 'Hey, what's your name, CLOWN?', the man yells as he continues to walk along the sidewalk away from the car.

Matt closes the car door and drives off. I comment on the aggression the man just showed, and Matt explains that he talked himself into a ticket – he only asked him why his dog was off the leash and if he had replied in a civilized way, there would have been no further difficulty. I ask him how common it is to find this type of reaction, and he replies: 'It's very common – people in this neighbourhood hate the police. Islamic people are very resentful about us – they see us as white members of the establishment and it's ingrained in their minds from a young age – "don't talk to the police; they're racist" ... I mean I picked him out because his dog was off the leash, something very simple that I was trying to just correct through a verbal, "hey, just put the dog on the leash." And you saw what happened. It just was totally... it wasn't consistent, his response, with what I was asking. He accelerated it through ... a strong dislike for authority. Anybody that represents that ... anybody that tries to tell me what to do.'

I ask Matt what he would have done if the man had become violent. 'I was watching his hands the whole time', he replies, 'in case he pulled out a gun'. Until that moment, the possibility of this happening hadn't even occurred to me ... I ask Matt what he would have done in this situation. 'If he pulled a gun out and I felt threatened I would pull my own gun out ... I would aim for the centre mass – first the stomach and then the head area.' Finally, he adds, 'and I was watching that dog as well – if it had tried to attack me, I would have shot it.' Matt shows me the gun he was carrying: an MP 9 mm. 'Some guys on the street would have one of these', he adds. He reaches up above his head and pulls down his backup: a shot gun. 'This one contains smaller bullets', Matt explains, 'it's used for close-range shots to do more damage to someone'.

As our shift comes to an end, I feel relieved to be going back to the day job and the simple life of an academic.

As I have observed, research findings from the past forty years have illustrated that minority citizens in the USA have a greater distrust of, and more negative attitudes towards, police than white citizens (National Advisory Commission on Civic Disorders, 1968; Bayley and Mendelsohn, 1969; Webb and Marshall, 1995; Weitzer, 2000; Engel, 2003; National Research Council, 2004). Non-white juvenile suspects are much more likely to resist white police officers' authority based on their perceptions of discrimination (Engel, 2003: 476). In turn, officers tend to respond to perceived disrespect, not necessarily because of illegal behaviour but mostly because forms of resistance are viewed as 'affronts to their authority' (ibid. 476). Evidence of this could be seen during several of my ride-alongs with specialized unit police officers, one instance of which is captured in Box 7.1 (see also Chapter 4). A complex intersection of class, race, and gender underpinned the interactions between Matt, the frontline officer, and the young Muslim citizen on Red Street. Matt embraced a working culture focused on upholding police authority at all times, while carrying out the specialized work of targeting potential offenders in high-crime neighbourhoods (Westmarland, 2008; Reiner, 2010). His initial intervention with the man, although laced to some degree with humorous sarcasm, projected an authoritarian approach that was fairly inflexible and provoked resentment from the young Muslim citizen. His desire to force the individual to put the dog on its lead could be read as a metaphor to control and dominate the dog walker himself.

The young man had no expectation of having an exchange with a police officer that would convey feelings of dignity and justice. Furthermore, the officer's opening lines reinforced his deeply ingrained and (perhaps) socially conditioned perceptions of the police force as an authoritarian, discriminatory, and racist organization (Hodgson, 2001). Thus, his immediate reaction was to reject the officer's approach towards him and respond through confrontation. Matt's instinctive position was to adopt the 'tough approach to policing', as one might expect in a specialized unit focused on enforcement (Schulhofer *et al.*, 2011: 343). His immediate response to the young man's aggression was thus to issue a threat of arrest and incarceration. However, Matt issued the threat because the young man's resistance was perceived as being an affront to his authority, and not as a result of any illegal activity (Engel, 2003). Elsewhere, Dave, a senior member of the CPD who coordinated Safe Streets, was aware of the macho, competitive culture that some officers continued to uphold. He spoke about the 'contempt of cop' where arrests were made simply because local citizens disrespected officers:

> It's what I call the 'contempt of cop' … cops that go from zero to
> sixty, attitude-wise, very quickly, and with whom every citizen can
> talk their way into jail very easily … the true underlying cause of
> the arrest is that they pissed off the cop and caused him to look
> that much harder for a charge so as to 'win' the encounter.
>
> Dave, senior police officer

In the words of Patrick (2013: xiv), Matt reacted 'just like a gang whose masculinity has been publicly challenged'. Gutierrez Riviera (2010) has found that authoritarian operational police responses like these can create a tension within those police agencies that are attempting to implement problem-oriented strategies. Further, they can increase the social gulf between police officers and citizens. The exchanges between Matt and the young Muslim male illustrate the complexities resulting from the 'imploding dark ghetto' meeting the agents of the 'exploding carceral apparatus' (Wacquant, 2009b). The young man fought back against his feelings of marginalization and alienation through the chanting of Islamic prayers while he was subjected to the issuing of a citation by what he viewed as the dominant white class. Matt's resentment of the perceived ingrained animosity towards the police and other authority figures led to a desire to regulate the de-skilled fractions of the working, and subordinate cultural, class (Wacquant, 2009b). At the end of our shift, Matt's reference to his defensive weaponry – his highly valued guns – demonstrated the need felt by specialized officers to hold on to the traditional image of adventurous and risk-taking masculinity. Matt projected the image of being willing and able to 'charge the tower at the sight of crime' – or, even, police *perceptions* of crime (Garcia, 2005: 68).

Box 7.1 provides one illustration of the resentful, distrustful, and even explosive confrontations that may still take place in Cincinnati between the black urban outcasts of the fallow ghettos and the predominantly white, masculine officers who patrol them (Wacquant, 2008). In spite of the reoriented *field* in the CPD, focused on problem-oriented, preventive policing and building positive relationships with communities, there were frontline sub-cultures in the specialized unit that created tension. The cyclical distrust and antagonism that characterized the incident described in Box 7.1 were a result of the continuing dominance of an authoritarian frontline *habitus* among some officers (Bourdieu, 1990). At the same time, deep-seated perceptions of discrimination led the young ethnic minority citizen to view the police as intruders in his community and to regard their intervention as synonymous with invasion by an external force. If these types of confrontations continue to flare up on the streets, it may mean that the impact of the CPD's attempts to re-strategize through initiatives like CIRV are limited, in terms of the extent to which officers and their collaborators can lure young men away from the 'code of the street' and challenge the class and cultural disparity that stimulate it (Anderson, 1999).

Game-playing and war zones

As well as focusing on 'hard chargers' and the frustrations that male officers experienced as a result of the 'institutional roadblocks to good policing', early episodes of the television series *The Wire* also underlined frontline officers' focus on game-playing (Bandes, 2011: 7). The 'game' was characterized by continuing attempts to curb the drug trade and outwit the dealers on the street. Similarly, in describing their work, Cincinnati-based specialized frontline officers and their associates often focused on the 'game-playing' elements:

> I like the adventuresome side of it ... I guess what you would call the risk-taking activity. The adrenalin ... the fun, the chases ... the game side.
>
> Jason, specialized unit cop

> I mean, it's just part of the game sometimes – it's the 'cat and mouse' game.
>
> Jeremy, probation officer

Jason talked about how he even found being shot-at exhilarating – as long as he outwitted his opponents in the end:

> There's a lot of adrenalin and excitement in this part of the work. It's an exhilarating experience being shot-at ... I was shot-at once by someone who robbed and stole a van. He ran from the car and got stuck up a fence. He was trying to reach the ground to get his gun – he hung upside down shouting 'I'm not going back to prison!' I didn't oblige by shooting him, but I did send him back to prison.
>
> Jason, specialized unit cop

During specialized police investigations, I saw the way officers sometimes won small battles and felt they had got the upper hand over their opponents, particularly when drug raids were carried out, houses were searched, or dealers were arrested:

On the kitchen table in front of me I see a large rock of heroin, a pan, and two mobile phones. I am amazed at the size of the rock, and it's strange to think that this is the motivation for most of the violence that occurs out there on the streets. In the living room next door, one officer counts the bundles of dollar notes that are scattered across the sofa, while the other cops rip the sofa apart and search the cupboards for other drugs or firearms. Expensive designer clothes are strewn around the floor in front of me. And in the middle of the living room, cuffed to a chair, is the young drug dealer. 'A pretty successful warrant,' comments one of the frontline officers as he un-cuts the flex cuffs attached to the young man while leaving the metal ones on.

Author's fieldnotes, Cincinnati

However, in spite of these small victories there was a realization that the game-playing needed to continue. In the first series of *The Wire*, police officers recognized that the war against drugs and violence never ended (Mittell, 2009, and see season one, episode one, *The Wire*). In a similar way, I found that frontline officers continued to battle and try to out-manoeuvre their opponents through subtle game-playing. When I rode along with Jason he taught me how to play the 'burned/not burned' game. He used strategies to demonstrate how our undercover status could be maintained or exposed:

As we move along Main Street, I notice a young black guy walking along the sidewalk. 'Let me show you a little game I like to play', says Jason, the frontline cop driving the car. 'Everyone here is gonna look at us, because we don't fit in', he continues, 'but I want you to deliberately not look at this guy as we pass him'. I keep my eyes on the road in front of us, but as we pass the young man by I can see out of the wing mirror that he is staring at the car. 'You see, he's looking at us, checking out the licence plate and hangin' around but we're not burned. If we had looked at him, he would have reacted and gone inside'. We turn another corner into Fifth Street. 'See this guy up ahead, I want you to look right at him', Jason tells me. As we pass another young black man hanging around on the corner, we both look out of the passenger window right at him, and the young man looks up nervously. 'You see – now we're burned – he knows we're not customers and we've unnerved him!'

Author's fieldnotes, Cincinnati

Although the strategic direction of the CPD had changed to become more focused on intelligence-led, proactive prevention at command level, frontline officers in Safe Streets still largely viewed 'real' police work as being about detection, subtle game-playing, and acting out the 'symbolic rites of search, chase and capture' (Van Maanen, 1978: 7; Reiner, 2010). These officers were very aware that their main remit was to focus on persistent violent offenders and to take responsibility for enforcement, and so they tended to gravitate towards traditional police values. However, my discussions and observations suggested that arrests could sometimes be made because officers resented local people disrespecting them, and there was evidence of authoritarian approaches to maintaining order. Some officers focused their efforts on battling to take control of the streets and viewed local citizens in deprived communities as opponents that needed to be outwitted and defeated at all costs.

The CPD's policing *field* had become oriented towards problem-solving and violence-prevention as a result of the social and political context in Cincinnati. In turn, the dominant *habitus* had become centred on social intervention and building positive community relationships. But frontline officers in Safe Streets played an active part in constructing their own sub-culture, and this led to practices that created tensions with the strategic ideology. Although the approach of the specialized officers I referred to in this chapter cannot be regarded as representing wider police practice in Cincinnati, it is clear they adopted the roles of 'hard chargers' and 'game players' as portrayed in fictional television series such as *The Wire* – which is perhaps not so fictitious after all.

In 2008, Glasgow adopted its own version of CIRV to intervene in the lives of young men such as those described in Chapter 5. In the next chapter, I examine how the model was adapted as it travelled across the Atlantic, and the personal journeys made by police officers in Glasgow to embrace the focused deterrence principles underpinning it.

Chapter 8

Transatlantic connections, transitions, and lessons: Designing and delivering CIRV in Glasgow

> *We described ourselves as 'critical friends' speaking 'uncomfortable truths'.*
>
> Kenny, senior police officer

Biographical analysis of young men's lives in Glasgow (see Chapter 5) shows how poverty, lack of opportunity, and particularly salient critical moments led to emotional vulnerability and crime. The violence that occurred was often territorial and recreational but could also be individualistic and unregulated, related to the need to build a sense of status and identity and uphold a reputation. Those who became incarcerated often left prison without having addressed the underlying issues that had provoked their violent responses. The tendency of these young men to re-offend following their release from prison was not untypical; it has been reported that almost 75 per cent of young offenders serving short-term custodial sentences in Scotland go on to commit a further offence within two years (Reid, 2011).

Prison is the most costly and least effective method of reducing both offending and re-offending. And violence as an issue needs to be addressed not only by justice services but also by health and education services (Scottish Executive, 2002; Scottish Government, 2008a). Over the last decade the Scottish Government has increasingly taken a public health perspective on tackling crime, reflecting the World Health Organization's (WHO) approach to violence-prevention (Krug *et al.,* 2002). Thus, primary prevention in Scotland is aimed at preventing violence from occurring in the first place; secondary prevention focuses on preventing violence from escalating to serious criminality; and tertiary prevention aims to prevent violent offenders reoffending (Scottish Government, 2008a).

The Scottish Government policy document *Preventing Offending by Young People: A framework for action* emphasized the need to intervene early with young people at risk, to offer 'positive choices and chances', and to 'build their capacity to capitalize on opportunity' (Scottish Government,

2008b: 2). The Government produced Single Outcome Agreements between themselves and Community Planning Partnerships, setting out how each would work towards improving outcomes for local people in a way that reflected local circumstances and priorities (Scottish Government, 2008c). One desired outcome was for communities to live their lives 'safe from crime, disorder and danger', and the Scottish Government emphasized the need for timely and effective intervention. Agencies were to plan and work together in partnership with children, families, and others to do 'everything possible to provide early and effective responses to problematic behaviour' (ibid. 10). The Government's *Equally Well* strategy document endorsed a public health approach to violence-prevention that had inter-agency work at its centre (Scottish Government, 2008a). These strategies were underpinned by the principles of *Getting it Right for Every Child* (GIRFEC), based on streamlined planning, information-sharing, and high standards of cooperation to ensure young people's social inclusion (Scottish Executive, 2006).

It was against this policy backdrop that Glasgow's version of CIRV was first implemented in 2008. Learning from the innovative practice initiated in Cincinnati and developed from earlier interventions in Boston, Massachusetts, the Scottish VRU drew upon focused deterrence principles, POP, and a public health approach towards violence-prevention to underpin CIRV. The initiative was aimed expressly at reducing violence, not at dismantling gang structures in Glasgow (D.M. Kennedy, 1997), and those involved recognized the need for a coordinated effort among agencies (Engel *et al.*, 2013). This chapter explores interview data with police officers and members of the wider partners within CIRV. It also examines how the Cincinnati model was adapted as it travelled across the Atlantic, and the personal journeys that police officers in Glasgow had to undertake to embrace the principles.

Targeting and preventing violence through a shared agenda

When senior police officers reflected on the causes of youth violence in Glasgow, they often cited poverty, deprivation, lack of opportunity, and the high degree of anger, frustration, and trauma that witnessing domestic violence can cause. This confirms the perspectives described in Chapter 5. They also referred to the impact of parental rejection due to alcohol or drug abuse, the influence of peer pressure, and wider family involvement in crime. However, although many of the causes of violence were the same as those found in Cincinnati, officers noted that the nature of the violence itself was very different:

> In the States I always think that there's an element of criminality
> involved in it – they're protecting their drugs turf. Over here ... I
> mean we coined the term 'recreational violence' because it was
> about 'what are we doin' Friday night? Will we go for a beer? Och
> no, let's go and fight the other gang over there!'

> Kenny, senior police officer

Although territorial issues were seen as a strong stimulus for violence in
Glasgow, interviewees emphasized that CIRV was not preoccupied with
eradicating gang membership. On the contrary, it recognized that many
young men did not even identify with gang membership and that, where
they did exist, gangs could bring some good things to some young people.
These views were consistent with literary evidence that suggests that many
young violent offenders do not necessarily associate with gang culture and
that street violence is sometimes far removed from the sub-cultural social
structure implied by criminological theories on gangs (Hallsworth and
Young, 2008; Hallsworth, 2011). Therefore, solutions had to be focused
on violence-reduction, whatever its context – but with a particular focus on
territorial rivalry since the majority of the youth violence in Glasgow was
known to arise in this context. In seeking to prevent this violence, there was
a recognized need to offer social support and empathy:

> I mean, Barlinnie [prison] has got eighteen hundred people in it
> today ... 94 per cent of them are re-offenders. Now that means ...
> probably 1,750 of them have gone and re-victimized or victimized
> someone else. I'm not sure that it's working! ... What we were
> saying is that these [young men] are alienated ... what we were
> saying was 'actually, don't be alienated, because we care for you' ...
> that old Adam Smith thing, empathy's the glue that keeps society
> together.

> Kate, senior police staff

Some senior officers talked about their frustrations with traditional police
work. Stewart, for instance, had come to realize that the police cannot simply
'arrest their way out' of the problems associated with violence, and Richard
talked about the frustrations he had often experienced at seeing the same
young people locked up over and over again, with no positive outcomes.
Hence, these officers had begun to see the weaknesses in traditional police
enforcement that emphasizes containing and managing individuals involved
in violence (Nicholson, 2010). Those senior police officers who coordinated
the CIRV project realized they needed to approach violence-reduction as an

issue that could only be resolved through a holistic, multi-agency approach based on prevention (thus reflecting the principles underpinning Scottish Government policy, outlined earlier). Echoing some of the views I uncovered in Cincinnati, they emphasized the need to target only those who were engaging in the most prolific violence, through an intelligence-led model:

> The big issue that I had right from the start was making sure that we were targeting the right individuals – you know, the real problematic individuals. At the top end of that, I wanted what we called our Cat A's – the ones that were causing us the most problems … there's no point in putting a young boy that's actually come out of school wi' three 'O' grades into an employment programme for six weeks –'cause to me, that's no' value for money 'cause that wee boy's only done three vandalisms and a breach o' the peace.
>
> Ally, senior police officer

> We were looking at people who were hard to engage with, violent individuals … we were trying to target the right people, the hard-to-reach ones.
>
> Iain, senior police officer

Reiner (2010) stresses that the development of 'intelligence-led' policing has been accompanied by a proliferation of proactive tactics, including a growth in inter-agency partnership work. But, unlike in Cincinnati, close partnerships with academics were not a feature of the intelligence-gathering approach in Glasgow. Rather, it was driven by the high level of police analysis that already existed in the Scottish Intelligence Database (Halpin, 2010). Police complemented and enhanced this existing data through consulting with other service agencies and also with young people. They were able to build a comprehensive picture of local territories and relationships, as a first step towards identifying the sources of violence:

> The police would provide the reports from their intelligence managers – that would then get submitted onto the Scottish Intelligence Database … This allowed us to develop a profile of the gang members as we knew it – in terms of who they were, their ages, their family relationships, where they lived … but a lot of that information was derived through actually going out and speaking to people – going out and getting the information first-hand. So you'd start wi' the police and the community cops who worked in those areas to draw out what they thought the gang

> territories were. And then we'd get the ... voluntary agencies to do
> the same ... and then we'd actually get gang members to do that
> themselves.

Andrew, crime analyst

Andrew's emphasis was on gangs, and senior police officers recognized that the only way to tackle youth violence was to gather intelligence about one of the biggest motivations for that violence – namely territorial rivalries. Following this intelligence-gathering phase, senior officers engaged in proactive networking, identifying agencies that could come on board and work with the police. They also identified a 'positive architect' in each agency who would be amenable to supporting a new initiative focused on early intervention and violence-prevention. They believed that violence-reduction could only be achieved through a collective approach that spanned across sectoral boundaries, since the causes of crime lay beyond the police and justice systems (Scottish Government, 2008a).

The public health model, which emphasizes preventing violence from occurring rather than treating its consequences, therefore articulated with these officers' professional values. A focus on intelligence-led, problem-oriented approaches to violence-reduction was centred around a shared agenda (Carnochan and McCluskey, 2010: 419). Through embracing the need to work alongside key partners in the public service landscape, prevention was seen as the 'cornerstone of violence reduction', with an emphasis on focused deterrence (ibid. 419).

Focused deterrence and CIRV: Transitions, emulation, and realism

The Cincinnati version of CIRV was designed around a focused deterrence and problem-oriented strategy that offered offenders alternatives to violence through referring them to a range of appropriate social support agencies (see Chapter 6). But also inherent within it was the threat of sanction and the deployment of federal enforcement powers on those who continued to offend (D.M. Kennedy, 1997, 2009). One Scottish academic who was involved in analysing the quantitative impact of CIRV in Glasgow described it as a 'carrot and stick' approach, in which incentives and enforcement complemented each other well:

> It was quite a revolution in terms of ... it was the beginnings of
> looking at violence from a public health perspective, rather than
> purely as focusing on it from a criminological perspective ... it

has a carrot as well as a stick. The stick is still there ... I mean enforcement is still an integral part of CIRV. What CIRV adds is more in the way of incentive ... an enhanced opportunity for young guys to do something different.

Paul, Scottish academic

However, as Scotland's legal framework and criminal justice principles differed greatly from those in Cincinnati, a focus on draconian enforcement was not a feasible option for the Glasgow version of CIRV:

The concept of treating a gang as one group and so huckling them all in and arresting them all – we can't do that within our current legal framework ... we do not have the same legal positioning in this country as they do in the States. We're a very different country – we don't have the same reliance on, or the same belief in, heavy judicial enforcement – whereas in America it's the 'three strikes and you're out'. It's very much a punitive society – we're not a punitive society.

Andrew, crime analyst

So although the principles underpinning the focused deterrence model were adopted in Glasgow, the offender notification meetings needed to be quite radically changed from the American model. While those who were brought in to the Hamilton County Court in Cincinnati were under probation or parole and were therefore 'called in' to the court as a condition of their court supervision, in Glasgow young men were invited to attend the sessions voluntarily:

In Cincinnati, they compelled people to attend the call-in. They used their powers through parole and probation ... but it quickly became apparent in my initial discussions with the judiciary and the prosecution and defence that we didn't have those powers to compel people to attend court ... so on reflection I decided that obviously we couldn't call it a call-in session any more ... and to reflect that we called it a 'self-referral' session because we were asking people to refer themselves and come along voluntarily.

Iain, senior police officer

Invitations were issued through the police liaising with social work services, youth services, and education. Some interviewees had attended the Cincinnati call-ins and identified several elements that needed to be changed for the Glasgow context of adopting a self-referral session that was voluntary and less coercive (Graham, 2012):

I obviously had to 'tartanize' the call-in. I sat through the call-in (in Cincinnati) and I thought, you know, 'that would work, that wouldn't work'.

Ally, senior police officer

In the States ... it was almost like, 'oh my goodness, this was theatre' almost. They had a number of prisoners there who were handcuffed and who'd come straight from, you know, prison to be there, along with people who'd been brought in who were on probation or parole.

Alison, senior social work manager

I think we were kind of a bit gob-smacked that young people were still brought in shackles and chains into the call-ins [in Cincinnati]. And, you know, when you see them being managed by a sheriff with a double-barrel shotgun – you begin to think, 'well actually I would choose the alternative [the opportunity to be referred to social services] without much of a hope'.

Jamie, senior education manager

Interviewees also identified that the religious elements of the call-ins in Cincinnati needed to be withdrawn, due to the secular nature of Scottish society, the historical issues associated with sectarianism, and the cultural tendency for Scots to favour realism over evangelism:

So many of the young people we're talking about just wouldn't have been anywhere near one [a church] ... church equals older people to them, you know?

Alison, senior social work manager

It was definitely the whole 'let's go and pray' and that's not gonna work in the west of Scotland because there's too many Catholic–Protestant issues and these sort of things.

Hannah, case manager

It couldn't be done the same way in our culture ... it had to be based on realism in Scotland, not evangelism. Because I think as a nation we respond very well to that – we respond very well to reality.

Jamie, senior education manager

'Realism' in the self-referral sessions was nevertheless based on the key messages from Cincinnati. Senior police officers made it clear that there would be repercussions if the young men continued to be violent. But the 'moral voice of the community' appealed to them to leave the violence behind, while the 'services and opportunities' message offered them the hope of gaining access to programmes and courses if they did. Box 8.1 is an outline of my observations during one of the self-referral sessions I attended. It illustrates the range of inputs that young men were exposed to, to convince them to distance themselves from violence (see also Donnelly and Tombs, 2008; Deuchar, 2009b, 2010a).

BOX 8.1: SILENCE IN COURT

'This is a sad place. A place where young people walk downstairs from the dock, and are driven away to custody. But it doesn't have to be that way for you – you have a choice.'

The words of the sheriff signalling that Court Room 8 in Glasgow Sheriff Court is in session certainly attracts the audience's attention. From where I sit, I can see that the court is packed with parents, friends, and invited guests, all of whom have a common interest: to support the young men in leaving the violence behind. The event now begins in earnest with an introduction by the coordinator of CIRV, a Detective Chief Inspector from Strathclyde Police. He stresses to the young men that something has to be done to reverse Glasgow's reputation as the leaders in gang violence in Western Europe, and that today's event provides them with an opportunity to make a choice. In short, they can choose to continue with violence, and be faced with strong police enforcement, or become engaged in a range of alternative recreational pursuits, training, or employment opportunities offered to them by CIRV.

These choices are then illustrated to them more clearly through the appealing voice of Peter, Managing Director of a sport-oriented, personal development company that provides pioneering diversionary projects for young people across Glasgow. His words of reason encourage the youngsters to question the purpose of territorial violence and to consider the huge impact of violent crime on people's lives. I then hear several reformed offenders and gang members urging the young people to choose a different path, including one ex-murderer who describes himself as a 'coward' and pleads with the young men not to end up like him. And one ex-footballer cautions

---

> the young people against being drawn in as 'message boys' by older men on the streets, who vie for the energy and loyalties of younger recruits.
>
> But the most powerful voice during the session undoubtedly belongs to Jane, a young mum who lost her own son through gang violence when he was just 18. I can feel my eyes well up as Jane brings the court to a hushed silence and describes how she lived through a five-hour surgery to try to save her son's life following a knife injury, only to witness his death at the end of it. 'The next time you go the kitchen drawer to pick up a knife, think about my face', is her simple plea. As I look around the court room, I'm not surprised to see that many of the young men choose to look at the floor instead of looking at Jane's face at this particularly emotive moment.
>
> Author's fieldnotes, Glasgow

The inputs from the young mothers that contributed to the Sheriff Court sessions were often highlighted as being the most powerful, as they were in Cincinnati (see Kennedy, 2011):

> [When] Jane stood up … everybody became a bit emotional … I remember the first time sitting up beside the Sheriff and thinking, 'I'm ready to go here!'
>
> Richard, senior police officer

> When you have that mother speaking you definitely notice the difference in court. The boys put their heads down and it's totally different … well, everybody's got a mother.
>
> Hannah, case manager

> Everybody loves their mother. It doesn't matter what their mother did to help them or didn't help them growing up – they've got an association where they all love their mum … that worked well in the call-ins.
>
> Karen, housing officer

As an example of the full impact of one mother's involvement, Box 8.2 illustrates Janice's story – a young mother whose son was the victim of violence at the age of 13, and whose story was communicated to me during a lengthy interview. Janice regularly drew on her experiences to talk during the self-referral sessions about the sense of fear and helplessness that families can experience as a result of violence.

Box 8.2: Janice's story

Janice lived in a reasonably quiet neighbourhood within one of the most deprived communities in the east end of Glasgow. In 2004, she and her daughter graduated from a college course and were due to go out to celebrate their achievement one evening by having a meal together in a local restaurant. But when Janice phoned home, she discovered her 13-year-old son, Keith, had not yet returned from a trip to McDonald's with one of his friends. Janice and her daughter made their way back home, and Janice later received a phone call from the police to tell her that Keith had been stabbed. Arriving at the local police station, she found Keith lying on the floor covered in blood. He had severe head and bodily injuries and was rushed to the Accident and Emergency department of the hospital. After six hours of surgery to repair some of the damage, it transpired that Keith had lost some of his fingers and that his skull had been fractured as a result of a vicious attack by a local group of young men who had mistaken him for a rival gang member because he came from a different housing scheme from them. The young men had chased Keith and his friend. Keith had stumbled and fallen and was hit repeatedly with a scaffolding pole and a machete.

In the weeks and months following the brutal attack, Keith's independence was taken away because of his severe injuries and disfigurement. Watching him suffer in this way had a huge emotional impact on Janice as a mother: 'At that time, your child's going from a 12-year-old to a teenager … there's a lot of stuff they need to deal with wi' teenage years on its own. But for that to happen and then … to need somebody to feed you, to clothe you, to bath you – to do all the things you should be able to do independently … all of that independence is taken away. He was required to have his hands in stirrups for weeks – it was awful seeing your son crucified'. In time, Keith was able to have several operations that helped to repair his injuries but Janice remained extremely protective of him, which led to conflict between them. She subsequently faced the additional pressure of seeing Keith become involved with local gang members because he felt this might protect him from further violence. She struggled for several years to try to keep him away from the influence of peer pressure.

When CIRV began, Janice was approached by the Violence Reduction Unit and asked if she would be willing to talk to the young offenders during the self-referral sessions in court. Although she had mixed feelings about contributing, she agreed to participate. During the first session she spoke at, Janice was extremely anxious about talking to the groups of young men, but was driven by a need to share her own and Keith's experiences. Once Janice started speaking, she clearly noticed a change in the body language of some of the young men in the court: 'One particular guy was really quite, "so, tell me your story, I've heard it before" kind of thing. The body language was – "I'm no' interested" … to all of a sudden making eye contact with me – his face really changing, a look of sadness in his eyes, and really making that connection with me … a real look of empathy, and really reaching out to me to say, "my God, is this what this is doing to you?".' Over the next two years, Janice contributed regularly to the Sheriff Court sessions. Although she had been disappointed in the way the police had handled the incident with Keith, she felt that the support she received from the senior police officer who organized the court sessions enabled her to gain confidence and a strong level of renewed trust in the police.

Janice now believes that her inputs in the Sheriff Court and her involvement in CIRV took her on a long and worthwhile journey. She was able to reflect more deeply on her own experiences and also see the value in agencies working together to prevent violence from occurring: 'I think the reality of what's happened is somewhere blocked in your memory … so when you're talking about it, it really brings it to the fore – what you've been through as a family … but also it was a journey of really looking at a lot of these young guys and really seeing a lot of the issues … it's a whole approach, a collaborative approach from various agencies within the community – it's got to be everything in place, you've got to look at their housing situation, family situation, benefits, education, feeling positive about what they're taking part in.' Janice's enthusiasm for the project and the journey it had taken her on led her back into education, and at the time of writing she was entering the second year of a university degree in Community Learning and Participation. She was finally realizing an ambition she had held on to for eight years – since the night she had graduated from college and Keith was attacked.

The focused deterrence principles underpinning CIRV led police to prioritize violence-reduction, share information with other agencies, and develop comprehensive, coordinated responses (Engel *et al.*, 2013). The policy transfer process that enabled CIRV to make the transition across the Atlantic initially focused on copying the Cincinatti approach; however, it soon became apparent that a process of emulation was required. The agency partners' knowledge and insights regarding the ideas underpinning the Cincinnati model were used to develop responses in Glasgow, but with a focus on 'lesson-drawing' (Dolowitz and March, 2000: 13). The nature of the legal and social service frameworks in Scotland, combined with the renewed policy focus on crime prevention, led senior Scottish police officers to place less emphasis on punishment and more on addressing the causes and consequences of violence (Krug *et al.*, 2002).

The account of the Glasgow self-referral session in the Sheriff Court illustrates the wide range of inputs from social and community partners who appealed to young men to stop the violence. The messages delivered by the young mothers whose sons had become victims of violence were perhaps the most powerful. While Jane provided young men with a highly emotive illustration of the tragic and fatal circumstances that can derive from violence, Janice told of the emotional strain that violence can bring. Like many of the reformed offenders involved in projects in CIRV (see Chapter 12), Janice's own journey was characterized by the gains that can be achieved from generativity (Maruna, 2001). Some researchers have argued that, during the process of helping others, help-givers often benefit more than help-receivers (Maruna, 2001; Barry, 2006). By devoting her time to helping young offenders change their lives and persuading them to leave the violence behind, Janice was able to reflect more deeply on her own family's experiences, and she became more aware of the causes of violence and more committed to addressing these causes alongside other social partners. Her sense of trust in the police was deepened, her confidence in her own academic abilities restored, and her commitment to inter-disciplinary youth and community work enhanced.

Alongside the emotional appeals, participants in the self-referral sessions provided messages of hope through offering constructive alternatives to violence (VRU, 2011). Unlike in Cincinnati, where one or two charitable organizations normally took responsibility for case-managing service delivery, in Glasgow a wide range of statutory, voluntary, and third-sector agencies already existed. They offered opportunities for anger management, alcohol and drug addiction counselling, education, employment training, and work placements. Following each session, the multi-agency CIRV team members met to decide where to place those who had agreed to sign up to the initiative. Representatives from the police, social work, education, housing, and the careers service would engage in a painstaking case-management process:

> We would sit around the table and share information ... it would be a case of 'what do you know? What do you know? What do you know? ... OK, this is everything we know about the individual and what's the best route to go down – what can we sign them up to?'
>
> Hannah, case manager

Informal mentoring was provided by staff from organizations such as Skills Development Scotland and by volunteers trained by a team member from Glasgow Housing Association to work intensively with the young clients. The mentors ensured that a tailor-made approach was adopted to place the young men with the appropriate agencies at the right time:

> With the mentoring, it was about looking for triggers and identifying them and about giving them alternatives, identifying their goals, where they want to go, and finding the right agency that could do that.
>
> Alex, careers adviser

> [We identified] who would be a good match of mentor to work with a particular boy, depending on what his background was, what his needs were, [and] what he was going through at that particular moment in time.
>
> Karen, housing officer

Social service teams worked alongside the police and were committed to early intervention and the need for a holistic, multi-agency approach to make the interventions successful. Further information on the agencies themselves and the support they provided can be found in Chapter 11.

Police journeys and cultural tensions

The Scottish police service has traditionally worked in cooperation with its communities and with public and private agencies through its policy of 'policing by consent'. However, from the mid-1970s onwards Scottish Executives encouraged the police to prioritize enforcement strategies to tackle crime (Donnelly, 2010). More recently, Scottish Government policy has emphasized the need to address the root causes of offending behaviour, and CIRV was designed to take a proactive approach to reducing youth gang violence. Some participants I talked to believed Scottish police officers had had a shorter journey to travel than those in Cincinnati to embrace the principles underpinning the initiative. But there were some officers who felt that it had been an on-going struggle to convince some of their colleagues – or even themselves – of the need to adopt alternatives to traditional police work:

> Even although I thought of myself as a wee bit more liberal-minded, looking back on it now I went on a journey through CIRV.
>
> Richard, senior police officer

> Police culture's a whole myriad of cultures ... it's a very masculine culture, and they don't like difference.
>
> Kate, senior police staff

> We've still got some cops that don't see it. They'll say, 'no, it's no' our job to do that, our job's to do this' ... so we spent lots of our time trying to convince cops about the right thing to do. We described ourselves as 'critical friends' speaking 'uncomfortable truths'.
>
> Kenny, senior police officer

In spite of the commitment of senior officers to adopt a different approach to policing, Jamie (a senior education manager) said he felt the police force was still an authoritarian institution. As in Cincinnati, he felt that the wider police culture beyond CIRV still needed to change, to shift the emphasis away from the patriarchal ideology associated with tough enforcement (Chare, 2011):

> I still think there's a hard core of police that still need to change over the period. You know, but like any kind of organization like that, they are both structurally and organizationally set up to be in an authoritarian position. No matter how much training you give the police or whatever else, they still behave in a way which is unacceptable ... you know, that culture [of CIRV] hasn't really permeated itself all the way down the ranks – but it needs to.
>
> Jamie, senior education manager

Further, Ally (a senior officer) revealed that some police who worked in the communities targeted by CIRV continued to see their job as being only about enforcement, and viewed CIRV strategies as being a 'softer option'. And other participants alluded to the tensions that could surface between the 'management cop culture' in CIRV and the 'street cop culture' among those who patrolled the communities and dealt with the young people they were trying to engage with:

> You've got two relationships there. You've got almost like the 'CIRV police' and then you've got the other police who are doing the enforcement ... I mean, we had an example of a young boy who was in trouble – he'd done something stupid and there were some warrants out for him and he didn't know what to do ... at one point, there's these beat cops chasing him for something and the boy's panicking, so he phones the other police within CIRV to help him through it!
>
> Andrew, crime analyst

> There was a group of boys waiting at a pick-up point where we had arranged transport for them [to the self-referral session] ... the Gangs Task Force were passing and found half a dozen gang members standing around a street corner, and they gave them a bit of hassle and they moved off, so we didn't get them.
>
> Iain, senior police officer

One academic, Paul, reflected on the work of the Gangs Task Force – the frontline enforcement agency that was at that time situated within Strathclyde Police (now subsumed within Police Scotland). He felt that the Task Force had been established to 'detect and punish' young offenders, and that frontline Task Force officers did not tend to see their jobs as being about 'helping to develop these young people' who were involved in violence. Elsewhere, crime analyst Andrew described the tensions that could potentially exist between CIRV and the members of the Gangs Task Force:

> You had guys going out in the Task Force that were there to do their job – the kind of traditional policing model. You had ones sitting in CIRV doing an entirely different job looking for a different outcome from these young boys ... So there was probably a little bit of tension between the two of them ... they all wanted the same outcome – they wanted the violence to stop. But one wanted it by disruption and ... one wanted it through changing behaviour.
>
> Andrew, crime analyst

As noted in the previous chapter, many academic analyses of 'cop culture' fail to take account of internal differentiation and jurisdictional differences (Chan, 1997). During one of the interviews, Kate (see earlier quote) acknowledged the existence of a 'myriad of cultures' in Scottish policing, but also drew attention to the pervasive emphasis on patriarchal ideology and conservatism. The emphasis on focused deterrence and preventive approaches to violence that were at the heart of CIRV succeeded in changing many of the structural conditions of police work at command level (the *field*) in Glasgow, as it had in Cincinnati (Bourdieu, 1990). A liberal democratic model of soft policing began to develop as a result, but with a corresponding emphasis on radical perspectives associated with hard policing tactics such as the detection and disruption of violent offenders (Button, 2004).

However, as I argued in Chapter 7, structural conditions do not completely determine cultural knowledge (the *habitus*) or entirely influence frontline practice (Chan, 1997). Frontline police officers or individual police units have an active role to play in 'developing, reinforcing, resisting or transforming cultural knowledge' and are not 'passive carriers of police culture' (ibid. 73). Thus, although management culture may have changed in Glasgow to embrace CIRV, the culture and practice of individual frontline officers or units may still embrace a masculine, conservative ideology and the coercion and rigidity associated with 'authoritarian peacemakers' (Hodgson, 2001: 536).

Gormally and Deuchar (2012) find that police stop-and-search procedures in Glasgow often cement young people's opposition to the police and perceptions of procedural injustice. In spite of the insights Kenny offered in the interviews about 'critical friends' speaking 'uncomfortable truths', Andrew's accounts of the cultural tensions between the strategic ideology associated with CIRV and the frontline practice associated with the Gangs Task Force were telling. As in Cincinnati, the Gangs Task Force specialized unit in Glasgow became the focal point for frontline interviews and participant observation. I document the insights from these interviews and observations in the next chapter.

Chapter 9

Cops, lads, labels, and searches:
Insights from the Gangs Task Force in Glasgow

I've had this jacket for years, but I keep it and still wear it because it creates a point of connection with the young lads.

Johnny, Gangs Task Force officer

The cornerstone of modern policing in Scotland was, until recently, the Police (Scotland) Act 1967. Section 17 of the Act declared that the main duty of a frontline police officer was to 'guard, patrol and watch', to prevent crime, and preserve order (Donnelly and Scott, 2010: 8). However, contemporary strategic priorities emphasize early and effective intervention through engaging directly with young people in the social environment that 'effects, shapes and moulds them as Scotland's future' (Association of Chief Police Officers in Scotland [ACPOS] 2011: 11). The Police and Fire Reform (Scotland) Act 2012, which led to the formation of a new national police service for Scotland, highlights that the main purpose of policing is to 'improve the safety and wellbeing of persons, localities and communities in Scotland' (Scottish Parliament, 2012: section 32). The new policing principles emphasize the need for community engagement, and the overarching need to 'prevent crime, harm and disorder' (ibid.; see also chapter 13).

These principles were spearheaded by CIRV, with its focus on intelligence-gathering and analysis, youth engagement through self-referral, and individual case-management through interdisciplinary teamwork. CIRV also offered a range of personal development and employability services to meet young people's needs (VRU, 2011). But against this backdrop, enforcement was still seen as a priority. In its quest to support the creation of safer communities and contribute to violence-reduction, the Gangs Task Force (at that time under the auspices of Strathclyde Police) targeted those individuals who failed to take heed of the overarching message that 'the violence must stop' (VRU, 2011: 3).

In the ever-changing environment of preventive policing, operational officers need to be prepared to adopt alternative methodologies and to prioritize proactivity over reactivity (Clarke, 2006). They need to become 'humanitarian peace keepers' who believe that words are more effective than physical force during conflict-regulation (Hodgson, 2001: 536). They also need to view themselves as philosophers, guides, and friends in the communities they serve (ibid.). However, evidence suggests that police officers around the world value crime-fighting roles more highly than the provision of social service, and that individual officers may rely on conservative influences that undermine innovative new strategies arising from police reform (Garcia, 2005; Karp and Stenmark, 2011). Duran (2009: 153), for example, argues that many officers use criminal stereotypes in their decisions to stop and search young people on the streets; they often see urban clothing styles as a 'symbol of their criminal inclination' (see also Fine *et al.*, 2003). And Garcia (2005: 68) maintains that 'real police work' is often still associated with crime-fighting, and that 'good' officers are seen as those who are adventurous and brave, and who 'charge at the tower' at the first sight of crime.

Frontline officers in Cincinnati's specialized enforcement unit often expressed a preference for traditional, high-adrenalin, street-oriented patrol work (see Chapter 7). Given the nature of the unit's aims, this was perhaps unsurprising. However, on occasions their emphasis on authoritarian enforcement in response to seemingly innocuous street behaviour revealed a tension with the principles underpinning CIRV. So I was interested to see how the work of the Gangs Task Force in Glasgow supported or undermined the wider strategic focus of the Glasgow CIRV. In the sections that follow, I outline the insights gained from interviews with Task Force officers as well as from observation of police patrols and investigations. I intersperse my reflections on the data with observations from the relevant literature, so as to create authentic but interpretive cultural portraits (Van Maanen, 1988). As with the data from Cincinnati, it is important for the reader to be aware that the officers in the Gangs Task Force in Glasgow are not representative of typical patrol officers in the city. As in Cincinnati, these officers are not assigned to routine patrol, and neither do they respond to calls for service. They focus on specific locations with the highest recorded levels of crime, and are expected to target those offenders who continue to engage in violence and crime despite warnings and opportunities to leave this lifestyle behind. Therefore I cannot make any claims that these officers' views, attitudes, or behaviour represent those of other officers or of policing in general in Glasgow, or any other part of Scotland.

Insights into strategy and practice in Glasgow

During interviews, senior Task Force officers described the work of their police unit thus:

> The absolute main aim [of the Task Force] is to disrupt, deter, and detect those that are involved in youth disorder ... but primarily those that are involved in territorial fighting.
>
> Stewart, Gangs Task Force senior officer

> I think my main job as a supervisor at the Task Force is basically to deliver enforcement strategy at an operational level ... when I'm sending officers out on a daily basis, basically to give them the tools and the backing to go out and exercise their police powers.
>
> Benny, Gangs Task Force officer

The team's work focused on gang-related violence while also addressing unregulated violence and youth disorder. The senior officers saw the Task Force unit as a vehicle for delivering enforcement, and felt that the use of stop-and-search procedures was essential:

> If we look at the year-on-year figures ... stop-searches have steadily increased and I think that's, you know, we take a big part in that in the Gangs Task Force when we're out there. And, you know, it's powers that we're exercising all the time.
>
> Benny, Gangs Task Force officer

But although the focus was on detecting and disrupting violence through stop-and-search and police enforcement, Task Force officers also placed a strong emphasis on communicating effectively and building positive relationships with young people:

> When I came as Sergeant you obviously got to know your troops and see how they work and what goes on and ... I would regularly go out with them. They'd certainly identify themselves as police officers ... but it wasn't a case of 'come here, wait a minute' and very in-your-face – there's no point. All you are doing is getting off on the wrong foot. You're gonna end up gettin' folks' backs up ... I have always said, 'if you remember one thing, remember "do as you would be done by".'
>
> Stewart, Gangs Task Force senior officer

Your mouth's the best thing you can use, you know … it's being able to 'chew the fat' – just being able to talk to people.

Gary, Gangs Task Force officer

Despite the police rhetoric, I wanted to dig deeper to understand whether frontline officers still gravitated towards traditional police values, as in Cincinnati. Reiner (2010) argues that police cynicism and suspicion often arise as a result of the constant threat of danger experienced by officers. And some officers may adopt autocratic responses, to project authority and maintain power (Westmarland, 2008; Reiner, 2010). Benny, a sergeant with the Task Force in Glasgow, indicated that this may sometimes be the case:

The most important resource that they [officers] take out with them on patrol is their experience and their police powers … just knowing, being able to look at a situation and knowing that something isn't quite right.

Benny, Gangs Task Force officer

However, Benny's focus on police profiling and the use of statutory powers to intervene through stop-and-search procedures was complemented by building positive relationships among the young officers in the unit. Interviewees also talked about how important positive communication was when dealing with young people, whether they were searching a youngster on the street or conducting a dawn arrest:

You break down a wee barrier … if you talk away to them. And then the next time they see you they'll kinda, they'll give you the time of day, these are wee tiny things, I think, that make a difference – just talking to somebody rather than just saying, 'right, put your hands on your head, up against the wall.'

Gary, Gangs Task Force officer

You wouldn't usually [break down the door] unless you have a search warrant – if I was looking for drugs possession then I might do that, but usually there's no need to do that. It can sometimes provoke hostility and you sometimes get a better result if you just knock on the door and talk to the families.

Johnny, Gangs Task Force officer

When I shadowed frontline officers during a dawn arrest in Glasgow I found that they entered the house in an assertive but non-aggressive manner. Further, they created an opportunity to create a positive relationship with the young offender who was being charged, through informal conversation and friendly advice:

> As the time approaches 6.30 a.m., Johnny rattles the letterbox of the door several times but there is no reply. 'They'll come eventually', he says determinedly, and continues to rattle. Still no reply. He then knocks on the door, and several seconds later it is finally opened. In front of us stands a young man of medium height and with dark hair. He looks very groggy, and has clearly just woken up. Within seconds a woman in her thirties appears who is evidently his mother. 'It's police, can I speak to Craig please?', asks Johnny. 'Aye, this is Craig', answers the woman, pointing to the boy. The woman ushers the officers into the living room. Johnny and Benny sit down on the couch and provide the mother and son with some background information. 'Basically, on the 7th January Craig was involved in a gang fight with other boys – he was identified on CCTV camera footage and he was carrying a knife.'
>
> … A few minutes later, Benny and Johnny emerge from the flat with Craig in handcuffs. Benny is holding the cuffs in the middle to ensure the boy does not try to escape. We descend the stairs, out into the street, and get into the car. Craig sits in the back with Johnny while I take the passenger seat. 'There must have been a big squad of you kickin' aboot that night', enquires Johnny. 'Aye, about 30 of us', answers Craig. 'Aye, you need to rap that gang fightin', says Johnny, 'I've been dealing with the older boys fae your area for years – you're the new breed. And you don't want to end up where they are – most of the older ones are in jail now.' It is evident that Johnny is attempting to build a positive relationship with the young man, while still carrying out his enforcement role. I wonder if Craig might be prepared to listen to Johnny because of his young, trendy appearance – even although he might normally regard all police officers as the enemy.
>
> Once we arrive at the station, Johnny guides Craig out of the car. 'Come on let's go, mate.' As he grabs hold of the young man's arm, he asks 'do you do the weights, wee man?'. 'No,' replies Craig. 'You feel really solid, man', Johnny observes, and again I realize this is an attempt to build a relationship and find a point of connection.
>
> Author's fieldnotes, Glasgow

Task Force officers described how they preferred wearing plain clothes because it created a stronger link with young people. This was often because young men on the streets associated plainclothes officers with the CID, and thus tended to revere them:

> One day in uniform, you're walking about high vis [in high visibility clothing] and people just don't talk to you. And then it's almost as if … because they always make the mistake 'oh, you're CID and that'. And when you're wearing plain clothes, I dunno what it is. They seem to think that 'oh, aye, you're alright, I can talk to you'.
>
> Gary, Gangs Task Force officer

> I think – when we're out in plain clothes and we stop people, they say 'oh, it's the CID that have stopped me'. And some people think that they're a wee bit more important if they've been stopped by a plainclothes, it's a wee bit of kudos for them – 'oh, aye, it was the CID that stopped me' rather than just, 'aye, it was two beat men'.
>
> Benny, Gangs Task Force officer

The officers often deliberately wore fashion accessories on the street that would attract attention from young men during patrols. In particular, the Stone Island brand of accessories was seen as important due to its popularity among football fan casuals (a subsection of the football culture characterized by hooliganism and the wearing of designer clothing) (Thornton, 2003). Both Johnny and Benny wore this brand regularly when out on patrol, and had seen the benefits:

> You see this jacket I'm wearin' – it's Stone Island, a make that a lot of the young gang members like. It's associated with the football casuals, from films like *Green Street*.
>
> Johnny, Gangs Task Force officer

> It's a label that's been used in the past by football hooligans so they don't expect a police officer to be wearing it … but if something like that can get people talking then it's valuable.
>
> Benny, Gangs Task Force officer

So although the Task Force officers viewed their role as principally about enforcement, the way they conceptualized their duties juxtaposed the traits associated with 'hard' and 'soft' policing styles. Through interviews and observations of frontline operations, I identified that reactive policing styles complemented their focus on support, prevention, and consensus (Button, 2004). While Cincinnati officers favoured traditionally masculine policing styles characterized by spontaneity, aggressive confrontation, and enforcement, this was not as prominent in Glasgow (Chare, 2011). I felt that further first-hand observation of the work of Task Force officers would be helpful. I wanted to explore how – and the extent to which – the renewed strategic ideology behind preventive policing and the patriarchal ideology associated with authoritarian enforcement influenced the everyday practices of frontline officers on the streets.

Impressions of an ethnographer on the beat in Glasgow

Box 9.1 captures one of the observations I made while shadowing one particular police patrol, when I rode along with three of the Task Force officers in Glasgow. Given the lack of street violence in evidence during the patrol, the officers focused their attention on intervening in anything they regarded as suspicious as we patrolled some of the most deprived communities in the city.

BOX 9.1: FOOTBALL HOOLIGANS OR STREET ENFORCERS? A NIGHT ON THE TOWN WITH THE TASK FORCE

Dressed in jeans and a hooded top and with a closely shaved haircut, I feel reassured as I look around the unmarked police van and realize that my casual 'cop-like' appearance fits in well with the plainclothes officers. As we weave into Abbey Street, Johnny notices something unusual about a car in front of us. 'Look at that, mate – what's the plate … SE04 …'. As Gary tries to copy down the registration plate, Johnny revs up the unmarked police van and speeds down two narrow streets, takes a left into Weaver Road and tails the car until it finally pulls over to the side. I follow the two young cops as they jump out of the van and approach the car. 'It's police, mate', Gary declares, while holding up the police badge that dangles around his neck, attached to a blue lanyard. The young white guy, who is in his mid-20s, dressed in a tracksuit and a baseball cap, looks slightly taken aback as he scans us. But, at the same time, he shows no sign of resentment. 'What did I do?', he asks. 'Is this your motor?', Gary enquires of him. 'Aye', the young man replies. 'Do you live around here, mate?', Gary asks. 'Aye, just down the road', replies the man. 'We're doing a few car checks tonight, can you step out of the car for a few minutes, mate?', Gary asks – and then quickly adds, 'I can smell a wee bit of cannabis – is

---

that cannabis mate?'. 'Aye, I must admit I did have a couple of joints', replies the man while getting out of the car. 'Any drugs in the car?', Gary asks, to which the man replies 'no'. The two young cops then begin the process of searching the car, but find nothing. 'What do you work at yourself, mate?', asks Johnny. 'I'm a mechanic', the man replies. Following a quick document check and the noting of the guy's personal details in his police log book, Gary announces 'you're OK to go'. The young guy thanks the cops and gets back into his car.

We get back into the van and Johnny drives off. I am puzzled about why this young man had attracted the cops' attention. 'What aroused your suspicion, Johnny?', I ask. 'Well, there were a few things there', Johnny replies. 'First of all he was driving a bit fast and plus he has that look that is popular with a lot of neds and gang members – the tracksuit and the baseball cap.' I ask the guys why they didn't breathalyse him and they explain that you need to be in uniform to do that, or otherwise they could call out back-up from a uniform squad. 'He gave no appearance of being under the influence of alcohol', Gary explains, 'that's why I stuck my head right in the window of the car right away to talk to him – to make sure. There was a smell of cannabis, but no sign of any other drugs'.

As we drive along one of the main roads, Johnny spots a group of five young boys standing on the street corner. He pulls up at the kerb and rolls down the window. 'Alright, lads? It's police, mate, are you just goin' home?' Johnny asks the tallest of the young boys. 'No, just goin' oot', he replies. One of the other boys comes up to the window and immediately spots the Stone Island jacket that Johnny is wearing. 'Nice jacket, big man – are you a football casual?!' 'Aye, you'll need to get one yourself, mate', Johnny replies. 'What are yoos kickin' aboot in this for, anyway?', ask the young boys, pointing to the unmarked police van. 'We're undercover – Gangs Task Force', replies Gary. The two young cops get out of the car and walk round to where the young boys are standing. I follow them and observe their interactions on the street. 'We're just gonna give you a wee search lads, OK?', Johnny asks. 'Aye nae bother big man', one of the boys replies, and the two young cops proceed to search the boys' pockets in turn. Once they are satisfied that the boys have no weapons or drugs in their possession, the officers tell them they are free to go.

As we get inside the van, I hear one of the young lads say to the others, 'he's alright, man – he's cool!'. 'Did you hear that?', Johnny asks once we are back in the van, 'he asked about the Stone Island jacket ... I've had this jacket for years, but I keep it and still wear it because it creates a point of connection with the young lads ... it creates a talking point'. 'Yeah, I've got a jumper too', says Benny, showing me his Stone Island label. When I listen to these officers, I realize that they clearly enjoy their interactions with the young lads out on the street, and therefore position themselves in a way that will encourage these interactions through the clothes they wear.

Suddenly, a young man in a car parked ahead of us arouses the officers' interest, again because of how he is dressed. Johnny pulls the van up and we all get out of the car. They once again show their ID and ask the young man to step out of the car and begin to search him, finding a small piece of cannabis in his left pocket. 'OK, what have we got here ... you know that we can charge you under section 23 of the Misuse of Drugs Act for this?', Gary comments, 'is there anything else that you shouldn't have?'. They continue to search his person, finding only a lottery ticket. 'Och, you shouldn't bother with these things, mate, they're too hard!', the officers joke. I am immediately struck by how these guys can enforce the law and issue cautions one minute, and revert back to small-talk the next; it strikes me that the informal discussion helps to defuse potentially volatile situations on the streets of Glasgow. Johnny takes the radio and, following questioning, relays information about the young man's name, date of birth and postcode. 'OK, we have found an unknown substance in your pocket – for the records, can you tell me what it is?', they ask, and the young man, whose name is Kevin, replies 'cannabis'.

As Johnny continues to fill in a report and liaises with senior officers over the radio, Gary, Benny, and I engage in informal discussion with Kevin. 'It's cold, man', comments Kevin as he tries to keep warm on this bleak January evening. 'Yeah, it's bitter, man', Gary replies. 'Have you had much bother with the polis before, mate?', asks Gary. 'No ... I haven't had a fine or anything for about three years', replies Kevin. Once again, I am struck by the informal way in which these officers engage in conversation with the guys on the street, both in relation to small-talk and also to their previous offences. Once back in the van, Johnny confirms that Kevin will shortly receive a court citation for possession of four or five grams of cannabis. 'He'll probably end up with a fine, but we confirmed that he has seven previous convictions.' We drive on, and my adrenalin begins to pump harder as I wait for our next encounter.

Author's fieldnotes, Glasgow

It has been argued that the police service exists to protect the weakest in society, and that individual officers' ability to carry out this task successfully rests on building good relationships with local citizens, especially young people (Strang, 2005; Reiner, 2010). However, adversarial contact between the police and young people is a common occurrence, and officers often engage in disproportionate targeting of economically marginalized young males. In their research in Scotland, McAra and McVie (2005) find that those youngsters who come under the purview of the police often become part of a suspect population, and that officers are consistently more likely to pick on young men from less affluent backgrounds. Other research has also suggested that the use of stop-and-search strategies has grown in recent years, and that these are applied particularly heavily among young men from deprived social backgrounds (Muncie, 2000; Sharp and Atherton, 2007; Reiner, 2010; Gormally and Deuchar, 2012). Some studies have also claimed that officers often make judgements about the 'respectability' of young people on the basis of how they dress, and associate certain clothing styles with criminal intention (Fine *et al.*, 2003; Garcia, 2005; McAra and McVie, 2005).

The Criminal Justice (Scotland) Act 1980 (consolidated by the Criminal Procedure [Scotland] Act [1995]) gave police statutory powers to stop, search, and detain individuals without arrest, charge, or formal caution if there are 'reasonable grounds to suspect' that they are in possession of offensive weapons or that an offence has been, or is about to be, committed (McAra and McVie, 2005: 10). Further, the Misuse of Drugs Act 1971 gave police similar statutory powers to stop and search those who they suspect of being in possession of illegal drugs. Pennycook (2010) observes that stop-and-search procedures have become a routine part of everyday life for many youngsters in urban communities in Scotland, and that the attitudes of those officers who intercept them often alienate the young people involved. In such cases, young people begin to expect negative interventions and thus approach officers with hostility (Gormally and Deuchar, 2012).

My observations of police patrols in Glasgow both support and contradict these previous findings. While shadowing plainclothes Task Force officers during specialized patrols, there was some evidence that suspicion was most commonly focused on young men living in socially deprived areas of the city. It could be argued that Johnny's observation that the young man in the car had 'that look that is popular with a lot of neds and gang members' demonstrates evidence of prejudicial profiling. In this case, the items of clothing worn by the young man (namely a baseball cap and tracksuit) rendered him more suspect (confirming earlier findings by Quinton *et al.,* 2000; Fine *et al.,* 2003). Later, the officers stopped and searched five young men because they were hanging around in a group on a street corner; and, later still, another young man was intercepted because of his personal appearance. Mead (2002) notes that there is no legal obligation on police officers to seek informed consent before a search, nor to inform an individual that they have the right to refuse to comply (see also Pennycook, 2010). The young men I encountered while out on patrol in Glasgow were often stopped and searched without explanation, consultation, or opportunity to refuse to consent. It could be argued that the searches were based on reasonable suspicion, but that to some extent officers drew on criminal stereotypes (Duran, 2009). On one occasion, although the decision to search was based on profiling of criminal stereotypes, the search turned out to be justifiable as the young man in question was in possession of class B drugs (Gov.UK, 2013).

Although these stop-and-search interventions were arguably unevenly targeted, and motivated to some extent by prejudicial suspicion and class-related profiling, the encounters I observed were not at all adversarial (contradicting the earlier findings of McAra and McVie, 2005). The reasons for this appeared to be associated with the officers' preferred clothing and their collective ability to interact informally with the young men, creating points of connection and minimizing reactivity (Hammersley and Atkinson, 2007). As a participant as well as observer, my own plainclothes 'cop-like' appearance helped me to blend in with the patrol unit and may have assisted in building these relationships (Van Maanen, 1988). Reiner (2010: 195) draws attention to the undercover cop tactic of engaging in subtle forms of deception, and adopting the 'image of a deviant' to gain acceptance on the streets. In some respects, the officers I observed engaged in such deception through deliberately wearing fashion accessories associated with football hooliganism that were regarded as 'hip' and 'cool' by the young men they intercepted. However, although the officers were in plain clothes, they did not attempt to mask their police identity or infiltrate the youth or street culture they were observing. Rather, they used the fashion labels to gain the trust of the young men and enhance the potential for forming positive relationships.

Research suggests that clothing has a powerful impact on how people perceive each other. Johnson (2001) argues that clothes can play an important role in the initial development of social relationships, and can have a greater effect on creating first impressions than personality. He argues that the police uniform often evokes stereotyped notions about an officer's 'status, authority, attitudes and motivations' and can elicit emotions of fear or anger (ibid. 28). The Task Force officers' decision to wear plain clothes created a more relaxed environment. And, as the earlier interview data revealed, their undercover appearance created a sense of kudos in the young men since they assumed that these officers held senior roles in specialist plainclothes branches. The officers' decision to wear brands associated with football hooliganism, combined with their ability to engage in informal small-talk and create supportive and humorous interactions, helped gain the young lads' respect. In some ways, it also seemed as if the morale of the officers was increased through their being accepted and revered by the young men on the streets.

The Task Force officers in Glasgow thus demonstrated a healthy balance between their concerns for social order and for promoting positive relationships within communities. Although the approach of these specialized officers cannot be regarded as representing wider police practice in Glasgow, they appeared to harmonize the tensions between adopting a welfare- and justice-orientation to their work, and assumed the roles of both 'humanitarian peacekeepers' and crime fighters (Hodgson, 2001: 536; Bartie and Jackson, 2011). The random and sometimes prejudicial use of stop-and-search procedures among young males in lower-income neighbourhoods is a continuing source of concern, and reflects the radical perspectives associated with 'hard policing' tactics. However, in the incidents described in Box 9.1 and other incidents I observed in Glasgow, the specialized officers also adopted the liberal democratic model of 'soft policing' through their positive interactions and relationship-building via subtle deception (Button, 2004; Reiner, 2010). They believed that words were more effective than confrontation or coercion, and used innovative approaches to secure trust and initiate rapport (Hodgson, 2001). Thus, unlike in Cincinnati, antagonism was kept to a minimum and the frontline officers managed to carry out their statutory police responsibilities while building valuable human relationships with young people.

I cannot make any universal generalizations about frontline policing practice in Glasgow or about the wider work of the Gangs Task Force, and I recognize that my own presence may have influenced the behaviour of officers. However, my experience of police practice in the Gangs Task Force suggests that the officers use certain tactics to put young people at ease and initiate greater cooperation, in their attempts to build community safety through enforcement. These tactics may help to complement the wider focus on preventive, supportive policing that permeates the policy landscape in Scotland and underpinned the focus of CIRV.

The last four chapters have illustrated that police officers in both Cincinnati and Glasgow led the implementation of CIRV through both enforcement and prevention. But a wide range of other partners played valuable roles in engaging young people through pre-emptive strategies designed to lead them away from violence. In Part 4 I examine the roles adopted by streetworkers, youth workers, and social service partners. I also explore how various approaches were used to prevent youth violence from escalating in Cincinnati and Glasgow and engage young people in the wider services offered by the CIRV initiative.

Part Four

Non-traditional partners
and informal engagement:
The role of street and
community work

4

Chapter 10

Faith, love, and hope: The work of Street Advocates in Cincinnati

We show a 'tough love' to them ... we reach out to them and we say, 'man, you are somebody, you ain't no thug.'

Aaron, Street Advocate

Part 3 documented the cultural reorientation that senior police officers had to embrace to implement the focused deterrence principles underpinning CIRV, and described the tensions between command-level strategy and frontline street practice, particularly in Cincinnati. Nonetheless, the CIRV model focused on the primacy of prevention over detection, with multi-agency working as the cornerstone of violence-reduction (Carnochan and McCluskey, 2010; Reiner, 2010). Part 4 investigates in both cities the organizations that formed non-traditional partnerships with the police to achieve the key strategies and goals. I begin in Cincinnati, where Street Advocates played a major role in deterring violence and creating bridges between the police, social service providers, and the young men on the streets.

Over the years, studies in the USA have found that street outreach interventions can help to reduce youth violence and engage high-risk youth in pro-social activities (Bibb, 1967; Mattick and Kaplan, 1967; Klein, 1971; Needle and Stapleton, 1983; Braga *et al.*, 2001; Kennedy, 2011). Decker *et al.* (2008: 4) assert that street outreach workers can play valuable roles as 'violence interrupters' who curtail disputes before they escalate. To do so, however, street workers must have credibility with young people, so as to question, challenge, and work with them to 'move them on' and change their decision-making processes (Sampson and Themelis, 2009: 130). Building trust and positive relationships with young people is essential. But, as argued by Decker *et al.* (2008: 5), street workers also need to balance the trust that young people place in them with willingness to inform police if there is potential for violence or harm.

Some believe that religion can be a resource for emotional coping, replacing the tendency to use violence and substance abuse to deal with social pressures (Cullen *et al.*, 1999; Agnew, 2006; Giordano *et al.*, 2008). Further, Rohrbaugh and Jessor (1975) found that participation in religious observances helped offenders gain personal control through accessing new social networks and new standards of appropriate conduct. However, while some studies have found evidence that religion can help deter criminal behaviour (Higgens and Albrecht, 1977; Evans *et al.*, 1995; Jang and Johnson, 2001), others find a lack of tangible evidence to support claims of the role of faith-based programmes in preventing recidivism (Volokh, 2011). In his critique of faith-based approaches to youth work, Sercombe (2010) argues that, while it may be legitimate to use spirituality as an engagement tool with youth, the emphasis should not be on proselytising but on listening, assessing, clarifying, and, if required, referring young people on to other sources of support.

Regardless of the mixed views about the nature and impact of spirituality and religion on pro-social development, it is fair to say that the black Christian church continues to exert a strong influence over the behaviour of large numbers of African Americans (Billingsley and Caldwell, 1991; Coleman and Cunningham, 1996). Some researchers argue that the Baptist church is seen as a champion of freedom and a hallmark of black American civilization, and that religious participation affords many people protection, guidance, and support (Lincoln, 1989; Olive, 2003). Anderson (1999: 35) points out how, in disadvantaged neighbourhoods, religious involvement distinguishes families and individuals as being 'decent' rather than 'street'. Giordano *et al.* (2008) argue that Christian observance can become a mechanism for desistance because many of the core themes in the Bible relate directly to offenders' problem areas, notably temptation and forgiveness. Engaging in the types of generative activities inherent in Christian teaching has been found to stimulate rehabilitation and retroflexive reformation, whereby the help-givers are often helped more than the help-receivers (Cressey, 1955; Maruna, 2001; see also Barry, 2006).

During my visits to Cincinnati, I conducted extensive interviews with Street Advocates to identify how they viewed their role in trying to reduce youth violence. I also engaged in participant observation, accompanying Advocates while they built relationships with local people in the city's deprived communities. In this chapter I summarize the central themes from the discussions and observations. In particular, I explore the way the Advocates engaged young people through pre-emptive strategies in neighbourhoods with a history of high homicide rates and gang-related shootings. I examine the role played by spiritual and religious experiences, and the particular importance some Advocates placed on faith-based approaches to reintegrating offenders. I also describe how Advocates prevented violence from escalating and engaged young people in the wider services offered by the CIRV initiative.

Living in, and walking with, the community

Most of the Street Advocates in Cincinnati were reformed offenders (see Chapter 4). They helped other young men to move away from violence through engaging with them on the streets and participating in the call-in sessions at Hamilton County Court. The Advocates generally lived in socially deprived communities where violence and homicides occurred regularly, and they saw themselves as an integral part of the communities they served. This was brought home to me through the participant observation I carried out in Cincinnati. Box 10.1 presents my observations of Street Advocates' work in a deprived community just north of the city's central business district.

> ### Box 10.1: A day in the world of a Street Advocate
>
> As I walk around the offices of the Street Advocates, I notice that there are many images associated with the values that underpin their work and also the cost of the violence on young lives. A large notice declares 'In memory of those we lost' and directly across from it are photographs of the many victims of the violence: young men gunned down at a young age, and women and children caught in the cross-fire or deliberately shot-at by guys who have gone on the rampage. I walk out of the Street Advocates' offices into the blazing sunshine of a mid-May afternoon, accompanied by Aaron – one of the older members of the team. We begin our walk up the road towards a large market which is a focal point in the community. Even though this neighbourhood suffers from widespread violence and is a magnet for drug dealers, many local residents gather at the marketplace every day to buy fresh fruit and vegetables. On the way up to the market, we pass a young African American male, dressed in jeans and a t-shirt and with the fresh face of youth. Aaron acknowledges him by saying 'hey, how you doin' bro'?' and the young man reciprocates. Once we pass the next block, Aaron tells me quietly, 'that guy there is one of the sellers'. I comment on how pleasant it seems in this square where the market is situated. 'Yeah, but around these streets is where a lot of the drug sellers hang out, and the shooters', he replies. His comments bring home to me how immense the contrasts are in this neighbourhood.

We walk up a couple of streets and turn into East Melville Avenue, where I am struck by the large crowd hanging around outside the housing blocks there. One young man is sitting on the edge of the building counting a large bundle of dollar bills. Aaron acknowledges all of the guys sitting around there, and they all seem to know him. They nod at him and shake his hand, and sometimes he stops to say a few words. We walk around into Almond Street and I notice a large mural with the illustration of a revolver and a 'stop the violence' message across it [depicted on the cover of this book]. 'There was a shooting right there in that park, by the basketball nets', Aaron tells me – pointing to the playground ironically just across from the 'stop the violence' sign.

Aaron then takes me into a local shop on the next street, where a young black man is fixing a mobile phone behind the counter. Aaron introduces me and explains that the man is an important member of his network – 'I connect the young men with these guys', the man explains as he continues to work on the phone. Aaron explains to me the importance of these networks: guys who work in local shops or cafés provide him with updates about how local youths are doing, and often act as gatekeepers who facilitate communication between the Advocates and the young offenders. We leave the shop and walk further along East Love Street. 'Hey, how you doin?', Aaron says to men and women of all ages on various corners as we walk along. He introduces me to some, and they shake my hand and acknowledge me with cautious interest.

As we walk back up to the Street Advocates' offices, we pass more local residents and Aaron continues to wave to them, connect with them, and make his presence known on the streets. On the way, he talks to me about the fundamental principles underpinning his approach out on the streets: 'Most of the guys we talked to today out on these streets are selling drugs ... walking around here, it's about relationship-building – so that they'll come to me for help ... We don't walk up to them and say 'quit, quit!', but they know we ain't scared to come to them and give our testimony ... we show a 'tough love' to them ... we reach out to them and we say, "man, you are somebody, you ain't no thug".'

> As our afternoon comes to an end, Aaron takes me into his car and weaves around the streets of this deprived community. As we turn back onto Red Street and begin the descent towards downtown, I notice that the buildings begin to look cleaner with each passing block. A few blocks down, I notice white faces appearing on the streets for the first time. As I say my goodbyes to Aaron and get out of the car at downtown, I see young white men dressed in business suits on their way from work in the city banks. As I gaze skyward, I crane my neck to look at the skyscrapers and realize that I could be in any American city now. But, wherever it is, it is certainly a different world from the one I just left – eight blocks and ten minutes' walk away.
>
> Author's fieldnotes, Cincinnati

The observations captured in Box 10.1 reflect how the 'consequences of persistent urban poverty and joblessness coalesce into acute alienation from mainstream society' (Anderson, 1999: 323). The hopelessness that many inner-city African Americans feel has paved the way for the underground economy to flourish, organized around a 'code of violence and predatory activity' (Anderson, 1999: 325). Although no violence was apparent during the afternoon that I walked around with Aaron, the impact of it was very visible in the photographs of the deceased in the Street Advocates' offices. It was also in the background of the subtle and unobtrusive strategies Aaron used to build relationships and establish networks to facilitate trustful communication with local offenders.

Gambetta (2009: xv) refers to signals as the 'stuff of purposive communication'. Against the backdrop of normality in the local market area where we walked, signals of young men's involvement in street life and the code that goes with it were displayed in the way they were hanging around on street corners. Many observed passers-by with caution and suspicion, and one was counting the assets derived from the alternative economy in front of local residents.

There were stark contrasts between the local anti-violence campaign that led to the construction of the large mural depicted on the cover of this book and the anecdotal evidence of shootings taking place in the adjacent playground. Just as stark were the contrasts between local downtown affluence and uptown poverty, where an urban colour line had been drawn along a class fracture as a result of 'white flight' and the exodus of upwardly mobile black families from the ghetto areas (Wacquant, 2008). In the context of mass unemployment, the growing criminal economy, and high levels of shootings and homicides, Aaron blended in with the community and built credibility with local youths. His own previous involvement with violence, combined with his local history in the community, enabled him to build trust and respect, and to develop relationships with the help of local contacts. He mediated conflict and became a stimulus for what Maruna (2001: 96) describes as the 'looking-glass recovery' process. He believed in the local young men, and strove to empower them to realize that they had enough personal value to adopt alternative identities that could replace the ones associated with crime (Giordano *et al.*, 2008). His aim was to help them become architects of their own futures, as opposed to 'acceptors of limited existences' (Olive, 2003: 39).

Violence interruption, street credibility, and moral reasoning

Like Aaron, other Street Advocates had a close association with the communities where they lived and worked. By interacting informally with local residents and young people, they became privy to insider information that at times enabled them to interrupt the flow of violence:

> A lot of times we get notice that something's gettin' ready to happen and we go in and interrupt. We know that it's an area where there's been shootings and it's gettin' ready to flare back up again because somebody's gettin' ready to retaliate. And we go in and start tryin' to calm things down.
>
> Mickey, Street Advocate

> It's called ... violence interruption. Somebody may call one of us because they know that one of us may have credibility.
>
> Lemar, Street Advocate

The Advocates talked about diffusing potentially violent situations and creating a stabilizing and calming effect. Marcus explained that they often played the role of surrogate father to young offenders, and became positive role models:

> It's like, some of the young guys I know, their mothers are crack heads or their mothers are users – they got nowhere to turn to except the people on the streets. And they gettin' ready to turn into cold-blooded killers. They don't have no respect for nobody and it's just somethin' they see in us.
>
> Marcus, Street Advocate

Some Advocates felt it was important to share their own offending backgrounds to establish credibility among young men on the streets. They believed many of the young men were intrigued when they became aware of the change that had taken place in the Advocates' lives:

> They know what we used to do and they know that we're not doin' that any more and I think it kind of intrigues them … I mean, with these guys and some other guys, it's the same story – like we all have different backgrounds but we were all in the streets doin' negative and now they see us out there tryin' to do somethin' else and … I think that's what makes, that's what draws them to us at the beginning.
>
> Darius, Street Advocate

In the aftermath of a homicide, grief and resentment can fuel new violent rivalries and deadly feuds (Anderson, 1999: 139). Street Advocates therefore looked for opportunities to intervene and interrupt the flow of violence at funerals:

> Like at the funeral we're talkin' about … this guy was about to shoot at another guy [who was] coming to the funeral. 'I'm on my way to pay my respects but yet I really didn't like him', that's what he's sayin', right, and he was in broad daylight about to try and shoot this guy in front of … probably two, three hundred people there … but when I popped up and he seen me, he kinda let it go for now.
>
> Lemar, Street Advocate

During volatile situations like this, Advocates engaged young men in moral reasoning. They made offenders aware of the consequences of their actions while also encouraging them to change the focus of their motivation away from selling drugs and using violence onto more creative and productive pursuits (Maruna, 2001):

> When you tell these guys, 'if you do something wrong, this is what is gonna happen to you … you're out there sellin' drugs, you've got three kids and if they catch you, you're goin' away for 10–15 years, you're gonna do harm to them kids – you're in the penitentiary, you can't help 'em now. Think, think – what you gonna do when you get out?'.
>
> Aaron, Street Advocate

In Chapter 6 I illustrated how senior police officers valued the work of the Advocates and the intelligence they gathered in the community. However, although they passed on useful information about community perceptions and reactions during funerals or at crime scenes, Rashan stressed that Street Advocates did not see themselves as informants but as facilitators and mediators:

> We're not informants ... our mandate ... we are the liaison for the police department and for the city hall 'cause we go in ... we have events where we can gradually bring city councils, city people, and the police back into the community ... as people who are part of the community.
>
> Rashan, Street Advocate

Aaron talked about the need to show offenders 'tough love' (see Box 10.1 above). He endeavoured to support the young men, but also to challenge their ingrained perceptions of the male gender role that focused on the values typically associated with machismo (Rodriguez *et al.*, 2003). During call-in sessions held in Hamilton County Sheriff Court and on the streets, he convinced them that being a man is about more than participating in the street life (Anderson, 1999):

> We reach out to 'em and ... we really let them know, 'you really want to be a real man? It would take a real man to do the right thing – to take responsibility for your kids, your sons, your daughter, or help your mamma.'
>
> Aaron, Street Advocate

'Tough love' was therefore about developing strong relationships with young men on the streets and helping them to adopt alternative identities (Giordano *et al.*, 2008). Some Advocates also expressed the potential for religious development to offer a route to redemption (Maruna, 2001; Nurden, 2010).

Faith-based approaches and testimonies

Some of the older Street Advocates talked at length about how they would openly share their Christian faith with the young men on the streets. Aaron saw this approach as a natural extension of the need to build a fatherly relationship with them and show them friendship and love:

We build a relationship with 'em. You see 'em every day, you pass 'em by so you're building a relationship. We had a young man one time – I called him every day, 'how you doin' today? What's goin' on? What you got goin' on?'. And he was like, it freaked him out – 'why does this man keep callin' me every day?'. And you tell him – 'it's because I love you, man'. And you startle him – this is what a real father does, he probably never had a dad. So now you're tellin' him you love him, man. And all you can tell him is 'believe in the promise that Jesus gave you'.

Aaron, Street Advocate

As Aaron indicated, the Advocates were persistent in their attempts to talk to young offenders on the street and show them love and support. Rashan referred to the Baptist background of many African American families, and how he encouraged young men to re-focus on their core value system to gain peace and renewed hope:

You have many of these young men and women who were raised in traditional Baptist families, religious families. Maybe mom and daddy didn't go to church but you always heard God, you always heard Jesus. You always heard what's right, what's wrong, being raised ... so that value system is there. And it's important because, when people have nowhere else to turn to, whenever everything else appears to be lost, they have nothing left to turn to but God ... to repent and try to find ... some peace somewhere, you know, in order to keep going on.

Rashan, Street Advocate

Another Advocate, Patrice, felt it was very important to encourage offenders to work at their faith and become active Christians. He described the impact this had had on young men and on the church where he was now a minister:

If you can instil in a person a genuine belief in God and faith in God ... The Bible tells me faith without work is ... it's dead ... I've had a whole lot of guys from the programme come over to the church ... right now in our church about half of the adult males, even half of the teenage males are ex-felons. And we went from a congregation of 160–180 to a congregation of almost 300 now in about a two-year span. We've got a male praise dance team, made up of guys – they praise dance, and these guys have collectively about 40 years of incarceration in the whole group – some guys have three to four years, some guys might have 20 and these guys are not wimps ... we've got a couple of weight lifters, guys that are really athletic ... what we do is give them a new gang to hang out with.

Patrice, Street Advocate

Sercombe (2010: 31) identifies the roots of youth work as being associated with evangelism and stimulating religious conversion as a source of transformation. However, in most Western societies, contemporary youth work has moved away from theological justifications for intervention to ones focused on countering issues of injustice and deprivation. While religious motivations continue to be active among some community organizations, Sercombe argues that faith-based interventions cease to be empowering and autonomous if the motivation for service is the faith community's 'ambitions for growth' (Sercombe, 2010: 32). Patrice's approach was based on the strong faith tradition associated with the African American community as a source of perseverance and social transformation (Olive, 2003). He encouraged young men to see alternatives to the forms of 'hegemonic masculinity' associated with machismo, which normalizes violence as a way to gain respect and power on the streets (Connell, 1987; Anderson, 1999; Rodriguez *et al.*, 2003). However, his approach was also motivated by the desire to increase the size of his church congregation. Thus, his practice had a two-fold purpose – to facilitate ethical agency and empowerment while also proselytising (Jeffs and Smith, 2005; Sercombe, 2010).

Some younger Advocates felt that it was less important to look to religion. They preferred to focus on restoring the moral character of the offenders they met by providing social support that enabled them to cope better with social pressures:

I believe in God, I believe in good and evil, that's what I believe in ... I don't believe in religion. I don't believe in organized religion, you know. It's always something right here (points to heart) that tells you what's right and what's not. It's a voice and I follow that voice. And everybody out here, whether they're criminal or they're not, has that voice whether they wanna adhere to it or, or listen to it ... sometimes the overwhelmingness in what you have to do, like I said, child support, paying bills, taking care of the children ... makes you not be able to hear that voice because there's so many things. And I think that if we try to, you know, move some o' that stuff out the way and try to, you know, find some way ... whether it's employment, whether it's education, better schools. We try to get those mental blockages out, then we can, you know, then we can start to progress.

Lester, Street Advocate

Hence, the Street Advocates in Cincinnati sought to enmesh young men in supportive relationships, characterized by unconditional love (Barry, 2006). Maruna (2001: 102) refers to the generative motivations so common among reformed offenders, and how they develop an impulse towards volunteerism, mentoring, and adopting the role of the wounded healer. The data illustrates that the Advocates took on this role to build trust and credibility on the streets (see also Chapter 12 for further illustrations of this). Some older Advocates evangelized and proselytised, while younger Advocates adopted a subtler form of spiritualism (Nurden, 2010; Sercombe, 2010). In such cases, they created opportunities for young people to see their own potential for growth and development within a moral framework, as a first stage towards engaging them in wider social and employment-related opportunities (Nurden, 2010).

Opportunities and challenges of achieving social recognition

Street Advocates were committed to helping young offenders leave the street life behind through directing them towards finding jobs. Romeo talked about how he tended to attract the young men's attention on the streets of Cincinnati by talking to them about the possibility of employment opportunities and handing out relevant literature:

We carry around some literature ... we would start off by sayin', 'what's up, brother, how you doin? ... listen I wanna help you – if you know somebody who's looking for employment'. And so when you're talking about looking for employment ... 'listen, there are some construction programmes that I might be able to get you into. Let's have this conversation'. So you use the literature to spark their interest.

Romeo, Street Advocate

Following on from these initial conversations, the Advocates set up employment training courses for the offenders while also liaising with employers and trying to convince them to give the young men a fresh start. They saw this as enabling them to turn away from offending and be driven by alternative goals:

We offer them the best services that we have available to us which is running this training, which is to try to get them into college … in a lot of cases we talk to employers and try to get them hired … janitorial work or landscaping … we try to help the guys as best we can. We put on our ties and we go and talk to employers … and say, 'look, we got these guys who have records; they want to change their lives around, somebody needs to give them a chance – will you give this guy a chance? I've been mentoring this guy for six months or however long and he's a good guy, I'll vouch for this guy'.

Darius, Street Advocate

Advocates described how the social services dimension of the CIRV initiative enabled young men to be fast-tracked into work training programmes run by organizations such as Cincinnati Works and the Urban League of Cincinnati (see Chapter 6). Although they were not always able to guarantee that the young men would secure permanent jobs, Advocates explained that the training courses provided them with new routines, new priorities, and a sense of hope:

You know, there's some guys that have never worked, period. They don't have a clue what it means to be on time, how to work with others … you know, waking up every day at seven o'clock knowing you gotta be at work by eight. You know, all these things – they have to be taught. So there's a three-week programme that most of the guys have to go through before they will be considered for employment.

Sandra, Street Advocate

On a scale from one to ten [the opportunity to get a job] is about four. But what it is, is a hope shot. There are programmes now for them to get into – that's a ten. I can get them into a job preparation programme … and that programme will begin to de-institutionalize their brain a little bit. Because now they gotta go somewhere every day for 12 days. And so they get up. In that programme they're gonna give 'em a business suit. They're gonna give 'em a resumé [Curriculum Vitae]. They're gonna give 'em a flash drive, an email address. So all of a sudden they're feeling, from this little bit o' stuff … a hope shot.

Romeo, Street Advocate

The Advocates offered the young men social support and liaised with wider agencies so as to lead them into opportunities for training initiatives while fostering in them a desire for lasting accomplishments (Maruna, 2001). Barry (2006: 133) argues that giving offenders 'social recognition' can aid them in making the transition towards criminal desistance. Social recognition is derived from a combination of *expenditure* and *accumulation* of social, economic, cultural, and symbolic capital. Sandra's and Romeo's attempts to provide training opportunities for young offenders were driven by their belief that this would enable the young men to accumulate: job skills, job tenure, and educational attainment (cultural capital); a new sense of status and identity associated with the trappings of business suits and CVs (symbolic capital); new social networks and routines (social capital); and the 'hope shot' associated with being able to convert their new-found qualifications and experience into better employment prospects and money in the future (economic capital) (Robson, 2009). By accumulating capital, offenders can make fledgling attempts at moving towards desistance (McNeill, 2012). In Chapter 12 I show how some of the offenders involved in CIRV programmes benefited from this and could later sustain their criminal desistance by engaging in the expenditure of capital through generative action.

As the CIRV initiative moved across the Atlantic, other types of partnership work started up in the Scottish context. In the next chapter I examine the outreach, education, training, and intensive support initiatives in evidence in Glasgow, and their subtle focus on taking young men on personal and spiritual journeys.

Chapter 11

Sport, youth work, and intensive support: Taking young men on social and spiritual journeys in Glasgow

> *The small changes, the small differences in their life are the ones that make it a little bit more positive.*
>
> Alana, intensive support worker

The last chapter described how the Street Advocates in Cincinnati interrupted the flow of violence on the streets, offered social support, and promoted redemption and agency through evangelism. In Scotland, it is common to find detached youth workers engaging young people in conversation on the streets of most towns and cities. They seek to build relationships with young people and lead them towards positive outcomes (Davies, 2009; Tett, 2010). Where appropriate, they grasp opportunities to encourage youths to reflect on the consequences of their risk-taking and law-breaking (Jeffs and Smith, 2005; Tett, 2010). Detached work is always characterized by informality, conversation, and recognition that the youth worker is only present on the young person's terms (Coburn and Wallace, 2011). Above all, youth workers start from where the young person is, and encourage them to reflect on their experiences, foregrounding their interests (Wood and Hine, 2009). They work with them on the elements of the social contexts that have the most impact on them, support them in negotiating the difficulties created by social exclusion, and help them to be 'actors in their own lives' (Sercombe, 2010: 24).

Youth work in Scotland and the UK has its roots in the charitable and philanthropic practices of nineteenth-century community-based organizations (Davies, 1999; Tett, 2010; Coburn and Wallace, 2011). As I have observed, ethical youth work today should be less about evangelism and proselytising and more about listening, assessing, clarifying and, if required, referring young people on to other sources of support and exploration (Sercombe, 2010). Nurden (2010: 128) argues for a focus on spirituality as opposed to religion, to find ways of working with young people that are 'authentic within contemporary culture'. By learning about themselves, others, and the creation of which they are a part, young people can develop an 'alternative identity construct' that can provide an antidote to some of the negative effects that a post-modern culture has on them (Nurden, 2010: 122).

In Glasgow's version of CIRV, senior police officers and their social service partners recognized that youth outreach work could play a valuable role in challenging oppressive influences that may stimulate violence, by providing support from 'significant others' (Hucklesby, 2009: 253). I therefore conducted interviews with youth workers and members of the community development agencies that engaged with the CIRV programme in Glasgow. I observed how one organization provided young men with intensive support in the community, and gained insight into how these individuals and teams engaged with young offenders – and the perceived impact this engagement had had. In this chapter I outline the main themes and salient issues arising from the interviews and participant observation.

Engagement and motivation through recreational sport

Previous research in Scotland has found that participation in sport has the capacity to increase self-esteem and positive identity, reduce destructive behaviour, and improve socialization skills (Deuchar, 2009a). Football, in particular, can become a catalyst for change, build positive citizenship, and generate social capital (Collins and Kay, 2003; Sandford *et al.*, 2006; Deuchar, 2009a). In Glasgow, I found that football was a popular means of engaging with young men who were involved in street violence. Through detached streetwork and informal conversations in communities, members of CIRV's partner agencies encouraged some of the most disadvantaged, oppressed, and violent young men to get off the streets on a Friday night and instead play in football leagues:

> The football programme ... was the engagement tool ... [we] would go and speak to them about ... you know, 'look guys, give up the gangs and come and get involved'.
>
> Billy, community agency manager

> We worked with the Rebel group and they were all-powerful, if you ever seen the group walking towards you, you thought, 'oh my God' – these boys were all bears ... so we said, 'right yoos are gonnae take part in the football, the street league stuff. It's a team,

so we'll train you for the next ten weeks as a professional team ... we'll get you in the gym' and they're going, 'great, great, that's brilliant'.

Tom, community agency manager

I got about 12 coaching staff in and I said, 'we're gonna book Edgar Academy ... and we're gonna have a football night. Let's get the right guys along' ... that quite literally kicked CIRV off ... I think the competitive sport worked ... because people were in neutral territory, quite literally, on a football pitch.

Peter, community agency manager and coach

Wacquant (2004: 50) writes of the boxing gym as a 'quintessentially masculine space' where the culture is ostensibly egalitarian and members relish the fact that they share membership in the 'same small guild' (ibid. 68). The same could be said of the football pitch; it can become a site for demonstrating and reinforcing traditional working-class masculine values and engendering a sense of community and belonging among disparate groups of young men (Parker, 2001). Peter managed Sidekix, a sport and personal development agency that was a key partner in CIRV. He was also an experienced coach, and encouraged young men to participate in organized football leagues as an alternative to violence. Through the leagues, he brought rival gang members together and initiated a team spirit and opportunities for self-directed communication and collective agency:

Although the Rebels are playing the Torches and they desperately want to beat them ... there's a structure here that we need to adhere to and they need to adhere to. And if I don't adhere to that structure ... I might be removed from the situation. And I won't be able to help my guys any more. So football, football makes you realize things about structure and life very quickly. Because you've also only got five minutes at half time to sort things ... the team focus is, it's the biggest thing.

Peter, community agency manager and coach

Peter believed that the young men who took part in the football leagues gained an incentive to move away from the influence of alcohol and drugs, and to focus instead on improving their health and fitness:

I think the football ... was absolutely the catalyst for them considering other aspects in their life. Because up to that point,

153

their situation was getting up at two o'clock in the afternoon, goin' oot at five o'clock at night ... to get wasted [drunk] and ultimately to get back into the hoose at two. And ... the idea was if you want to compete on a Friday night you need to come so ... I've got you on a Friday night, right ... when I have you I'm gonnae make you physically active and I'm gonnae make you tired and you're gonnae think twice about what you do when you go doon the road, right. But what I'm also gonnae do is in order for you to play on a Friday night which you now value ... I need you to come another night to training. So that might be a Tuesday night or a Wednesday night or even a Thursday night for some, right. So that's two nights of the week where I've got you and I've made you physically active. And being physically active, you know, you start to ask yourself questions. You know, 'I couldnae last there ... is that because of how much I'm smoking, how much I'm eating, how much I'm drinking?'.

Peter, community agency manager and coach

However, some youth work coordinators involved in the CIRV initiative did not agree that football was the right mechanism for engaging young men. Lewis was a manager at FARE, a local youth and community work organization in the east end of Glasgow. He felt that the physical aggression associated with football could stimulate (rather than repress) subsequent street violence:

Using football as a means for getting young people together isn't the way forward in my view. We saw a number of young people ... attend Saturday night football games and probably there was more violence caused by it than the reduction that we hoped the football would allow. And what I mean by that is ... we used to get eight areas together, rival areas ... and you would only need one bad tackle for the consequences of that bad tackle to then happen the following evening. So there was many, many an incident where there were skirmishes between the local youths in local areas and they were obviously at that particular time stopped by the police ... we were causing a lot of the problems. I've no doubt that other organizations that use that tactic of using football as a means of tackling gang issues are causing problems.

Lewis, community agency manager

154

Lewis disagreed with the practice of trying to push rival gang members together to play football. He felt that youth work was about 'giving ownership to young people ... getting their views about what they feel about life' and helping them with the problems they encounter (reflecting principles outlined by Davies, 1999; Wood and Hine, 2009; Sercombe, 2010; and Coburn and Wallace, 2011). He believed in spending time with young people on the streets or during recreational activities and looking for opportunities to open up informal conversation focused on 'getting their thoughts and feelings about various things in the world'. He also believed that outward-bound sport was a stronger means than football of initiating communication among rival gang members, through enabling them to focus on a common goal in the context of a high-risk situation:

> We used a number of different techniques – we used outward-bound sport, which is more about communication. It's about young people having to talk to each other. I'm not saying there's not communication on a football field, of course there is. But communication on a football field is more, 'I'm free ... over here ... pass the ball to me'. But if you go, for example, gorge walking, it's about 'how can I help you up this gorge? Show me where your hand is' ... if you're rock climbing, 'put your life in my hands' ... and I've often seen rival gang members helping each other up the rock face. They weren't the best of mates, but they had a common goal.
>
> Lewis, community agency manager

Male team sports have long been associated with the 'legitimation of male hegemony', characterized by the expression of aggression and even violence (Clayton and Harris, 2009). But Sandford *et al.* (2006) also argue that channelling the masculine culture associated with toughness, individual honour, and physical performance into a disciplined, controlled, and competitive environment leads to physical, psychological, and social benefits. Some agencies in Glasgow tried to instil a commitment to participate in football because they believed that it generated 'pull' factors that enabled young men to move away from street violence (Barry, 2006). For others, achieving these outcomes required a youth-centred ideology and a wider focus on high-adrenalin recreational activities where common goals were established and effective communication was essential.

Spiritual journeys and positive attitudes

Engaging young men in recreational activities was an important means of enabling them to move away from their dependency on alcohol, drugs, and violence. But, building on his earlier views, Lewis also stressed the importance of engaging informally with youngsters on the street at the outset:

> The way we work is if we're at a certain street at a certain time on a certain evening, the following week we're at that same street, same time, that same evening. Anybody who's hanging about a certain street corner will see us at the same time over a number of weeks. And eventually the young people would come to us and ask us what we're doing. Because at the end of the day it's their patch, it's their territory. Once the engagement has started, we then work wi' the community, a bottom-up approach.
>
> Lewis, community agency manager

These views were consistent with the current focus on promoting autonomy and empowerment among young people, outlined in the prevailing Community Learning and Development (CLD) policies and competencies in Scotland (Scottish Executive, 2007; CLD Standards Council for Scotland, 2009). Partnership between youth work and schools was also seen as important, and some youth workers and reformed offenders supported young pupils who were on the margins of participating in violence (Learning and Teaching Scotland [LTS], 2009; Deuchar and Ellis, 2013). Working alongside the police, youth workers, and teachers in secondary schools in the east end and north of Glasgow also encouraged young people to attend self-referral sessions in the Sheriff Court. They were then referred to other initiatives run by the partner agencies in CIRV.

Many young men were directed to initiatives coordinated by Kan Do, a training and development agency that specializes in team-building skills and raising self-esteem. Tom coordinated the workshops run at Kan Do. He talked about how he helped the young clients re-consider their entrenched attitudes about masculinity:

> It's going back to that Scottish thing about 'do not show a weakness, love is a weakness. Do not cry, never cry'. I mean, I've seen boys really desperate to cry but [they] don't cry ... and then they wonder how they burst into violence.
>
> Tom, community agency manager

The faith-based, religious theme projected by Cincinnati streetwork programmes was not as overt in Glasgow. This was due, in part, to the increasingly secularized nature of the west of Scotland and a realization that the context of religion might not always be the best means of engaging young people who are involved in violence (see Chapter 8 for other details). However, Graham was a reformed murderer who contributed to the self-referral sessions and the Kan Do programme (for further details about Graham's past, see Chapter 5). As a Christian, he drew on his faith when he spoke to young men, and found that, after some initial embarrassment, some of the boys responded positively to his messages:

> They could handle being intoxicated with drugs, they could handle breaking their mother's heart ... they could handle that, but the minute I would say to them, 'my life changed because Jesus Christ came into my life', they couldnae handle that. They didnae know how to react to it. Some of them got embarrassed. But I would confront it in the class, and I would say, 'it's amazing how we're embarrassed by God but we're not embarrassed because I've taken somebody's life. There's something wrong there' ... (but) some of the boys would say, you know, 'can you pray things get different, that things become different for me?'. And I would say, 'yeah, I will pray about that.'
>
> Graham, reformed offender and CIRV volunteer

Although some authors (for instance Hay and Nye, 1998) define spirituality as an awareness of God, spiritual development can also be defined more in terms of gaining a 'heightened awareness of oneself and others' (Nurden, 2010: 122). It can be seen as a means of 'getting in touch with the deeper parts of life' and growing in experience, understanding, and response (ibid. 123). Tom talked about Graham's input into the personal development courses he ran for young men. He valued the way Graham challenged the youngsters' instinctive reaction to view him as a hero and also their narrow views about masculinity:

> Graham dropped in all the time and worked with the groups ... when he first came in, it was sad in many ways because the boys, when they started to hear Graham's story – what he'd done, that he had committed murder ... he was a hero to them at first through the murder ... and he went, 'don't applaud me – don't applaud what I've done ... I'll tell you a real man – a real man is somebody that's got a family, gets up at six o'clock in the morning

and goes to his work every day in life, hail, rain or snow. That's a
tough guy – that's a man …'.

Tom, community agency manager

During the ten-week personal development courses offered by Kan Do, there
was a subtle, underlying focus on spirituality in its broadest sense, rather than
the narrower focus on religion that was common in Cincinnati. Following on
from the discussions that Graham facilitated, Tom and his colleague Colin
encouraged the young men to think about how to change their lives and build
agency and initiative:

We build up the self-esteem, looking at what they can do rather
than what they can't do.

Colin, community agency manager

During the ten-week programme there's very much a focus on
confidence, self-esteem … we used to encourage them because
you're dealing with real clever, switched-on guys … and we talk
about entrepreneurs … 'OK, you're lookin' for a job, why not start
your own business? Don't expect to be led … take the initiative …
take responsibility in your life … go and get it, your dream – what
is your dream?'.

Tom, community agency manager

After three weeks on the course, Tom could often see an increase in confidence
and self-belief among the young men involved:

I always felt after about three weeks you seen a big, big change
in people because they started to think about themselves – they
started to think about, 'I could dae that job – I could go for that'.
I was quite surprised, the impact in that time.

Tom, community agency manager

Lee (1999) identified four possible spiritual journeys, namely *inward* journeys
(self), *outward* journeys (others), *downward* journeys (environment), and
upward journeys (God). The Kan Do team helped the young men to engage in
inward and *outward* journeys. Through their conversations, they encouraged
them to take a wider view of masculinity that focused on earning a living
and supporting a family. They appealed to them to use their initiative to
fulfil personal goals and develop social credibility (Maruna, 2001; Barry,
2006). Meanwhile Graham encouraged the youngsters to take *inward* and
downward journeys, re-considering their responses to his own testimonies of

violence and reflecting more on the impact of that violence on families and communities. But he also took groups of young men on *upward* spiritual journeys in which he helped them to become more comfortable about exploring and talking about God and turning towards prayer. Tom noticed changes in the young men's spiritual development throughout the ten-week programmes:

> When he spoke about God, I've never seen the room so ... uncomfortable in my life ... but it's amazing – once they settled into it, they came out wi' great things about God, Jesus ... it was incredible – he brought God into these guys and stirred them ... it was interesting afterwards, when you were driving people about and they were ... they started talking about God and Jesus and different religions ... through Graham, through working wi' us, we showed them a bit of light.
>
> Tom, community agency manager

Changing social networks and providing intensive support

Once the young men had completed the ten-week development courses at Kan Do, many were encouraged to go to the Bambury Centre, a community regeneration centre in the heart of Glasgow's east end. Through a competitive tendering process, the Centre had managed to secure funding to create paid community-based work placements for the young participants in CIRV. Billy coordinated the placements and said they were specifically geared towards those who had a history of engaging in moderate-to-serious levels of violence and crime:

> The kind of jobs we got was like landscaping jobs, football coaching jobs, caretaker jobs ... youth workers, and a whole range of jobs like that ... young people came from all parts of the east end of Glasgow ... young people who had been seen within their community hanging about street corners ... crime levels in terms of conviction rates varied ... there were some that were fairly minor – caught carrying knives and been done for disorder and breach o' the peace, to quite a high majority wi' quite high tariffs in terms of, you know, attempted murder ... the jobs were for 26 weeks, they were seven pounds an hour, full-time, 30 hours a week.
>
> Billy, community agency manager

Billy talked about how participating in the work placements enabled the boys to change their social networks and broke down territorial barriers between rival gangs:

> They started to get a few quid in their pocket and a bit of independence about them and they started goin' into the town for a pint instead of hanging aboot the street corners ... and their social networks changed for the better in a lot of cases ... we had guys from different gangs workin' in teams, guys who [had] stabbed each other ... workin' together and goin' into toon at night and drinkin' together.
>
> Billy, community agency manager

For those at the more extreme end of serious offending, intensive support was also offered via Includem, a charitable organization that works exclusively with the most troubled and vulnerable young people and provides flexible services 24 hours a day. Those young men referred to the organization were appointed a one-to-one worker who provided support both to them and their families. There was also a helpline they could call at any time, any day of the week, if they felt in need of additional support. Alana, an intensive support worker at Includem, described how the organization filled a gap that could not be addressed by the other social service agencies:

> Social work were basically swamped and unable to spend the time and build the relationships with these young people that they drastically needed to influence any kind of change ... it's about recognizing that these young people have often been let down by services that they've been in before or they've fallen through the net and are coming to us.
>
> Alana, intensive support worker

Alana observed that young men were often referred to Includem following the self-referral sessions at the Sheriff Court. But members of the Gangs Task Force also liaised with the organization; officers who charged young people for street violence at the weekend would often pass on their details to Includem to prevent their behaviour from escalating. They also informed key workers if any of their existing clients had drifted back into offending:

> We had to recognize that enforcement was part of policing ... [but] often it was from these enforcements that we took the referrals. So,

on the back of that we would go in and say, you know, 'you've seen what happens – the option here is to stop it happening again'. And the police were very good at letting us know ... if it was young people we were already working with.

Alana, intensive support worker

Personal workers met with young people in their care three times a week, but not in a formal environment such as an office. They conducted meetings in informal, community settings, at times and places that suited the young people:

The majority of the contacts are dealt with in a very relaxed, comfortable environment. So it's not about bringing them into the office ... I mean, I consider my car my office, 'cause it's a matter of picking them up from wherever they are, whether it's home or out with their friends, doing a contact in the community and that could be sitting in the car park or McDonald's, it could be the leisure centre ... just depending what we're covering that day, and then returning them to wherever they want to be.

Alana, intensive support worker

During early meetings, personal workers would focus on building positive relationships based on 'respect, honesty and care' (Includem, 2010: 11). But they would also challenge their young clients, and collaborate with them to agree the focus of the intervention. They would work with the young men to set goals and specify the support they needed to overcome social barriers. The young men would then participate in one or more themed modules where they began to explore the impact of their current behaviour on themselves and others, and to become aware of, and confident in, the 'possibility of a different life' (Includem, 2010: 18). Tailored, flexible interventions were created to suit individual needs, and workers held coaching conversations with youngsters, to enable them to connect what they had learned to real life, embed new ways of thinking, and continue to progress towards positive outcomes (ibid.). Key workers were persistent in trying to help the young men referred to them through CIRV, even when things did not go to plan and they slipped back into offending. Box 11.1 sets out my observations while accompanying Alana during a meeting with one of the young men in her care.

BOX 11.1: INTENSIVE SUPPORT IN THE COMMUNITY – AN AFTERNOON OUT WITH INCLUDEM

As we drive into the local neighbourhood where Gavin lives, Alana explains that this 18-year-old man has not participated in gang violence for almost a year. However, he picked up a new charge for robbery and assault four months ago, and his court hearing is still to take place. But Gavin seems to have been moving in the right direction, gradually leaving his old offending lifestyle behind over the past few months: 'I will write a report for the court, to let them know that Gavin has been working with me and how well he has been doing', Alana explains, 'so that might make a difference. Because he hasn't picked up any charges for all these months, he was due to be finished with us but Gavin has said that he wants to continue, so that's a good sign. He'll be moving on to a new worker next week, who will help him in his transition phase while he's applying for training schemes and for jobs'. She then explains that Gavin is also due in court on Monday for a minor offence he was involved in in the early part of last year.

We park outside Gavin's house, and his mum shouts out of the window and indicates that he is not there. Alana calls his mum on her phone and she explains that Gavin is at his gran's house. His mum asks if we can give her a lift round there, and within minutes she appears at the front door and then hurries over to the car. As she settles into the passenger seat, Alana introduces me to her. As we make the five-minute journey to Gavin's gran's, I can sense that the young mother is anxious about the court hearing on Monday. 'He's got court on Monday – will you be able to take him there?' Alana explains that she will collect Gavin and take him to court, and the mother seems happy with this. 'He just needs to get by this, and hopefully he'll be OK', the mum says anxiously.

We arrive at Gavin's gran's house and watch as the door opens. Dressed in a grey tracksuit and trainers, Gavin comes out of the house and climbs into the car beside us, while saying a few words to his mum in passing. Alana asks how he is doing. 'Alright, are you comin' to court wi' me on Monday?', he asks. 'Yes, I'll come and pick you up at ten o'clock so you need to be ready for me. I'll drop you off but then I need to go away', Alana replies. 'Who'll take me home?', Gavin asks. 'Darren, one of the other workers will come and get you', explains Alana. Gavin seems happy with this arrangement and asks

Alana if they can go to the golf range today for their meeting. 'Yes, that's fine – I know you like it there', Alana replies with a smile.

We arrive at the golf range five minutes later and Gavin collects the golf clubs while Alana pays for the balls. We walk up the stairs and arrive at the range, where Gavin begins to hit some balls while we talk to him informally. 'Gavin's been doing really well', Alana comments to me, 'and he could have finished with us next week but he wanted to stay on longer'. 'That's good, Gavin', I say to the boy as he takes a firm, steady swipe at another ball. Each ball that he hits seems to lunge into the air with a loud crack under the strength of Gavin's golf swing, and some of the balls disappear into the trees, never to be seen again. 'See, this is good', Alana comments as she turns towards me, 'it gets rid of a lot of energy for him'.

After the golf, we go to the café … I ask Gavin how he first got involved in Includem. Gavin and Alana explain that one of Gavin's friends had been referred to Includem, and Gavin then contacted the organization himself because he felt that he needed support as well. 'I watched some of my pals gettin' battered, and gettin' the jail', Gavin explains as he continues to send text messages on his phone while drinking his hot chocolate, 'and I decided I wanted out'. When Alana goes to the toilet, I ask him how he finds working with her. 'Aye, she's great – you can tell Alana anything', he explains. Once Alana returns, I ask Gavin how he feels about going to court for the assault and robbery. 'That's the thing I'm really scared of', he mutters slowly, 'but if you fly with the crows you get shot with the crows', he adds philosophically.

As we drive back round to Gavin's gran's house to drop him off, Alana asks him how he is getting on with his mum. 'Alright, I haven't seen her in ages', Gavin replies, even though I remember that he had spoken to her just before he got into the car with us earlier this afternoon. 'Well, be ready for me on Monday morning … and call me on Saturday if you feel rubbish, ok?', Alana tells him. Gavin nods his head and gets out of the car. As we pull out of the street, Alana explains to me that Gavin used to call the helpline a lot at the weekends, but not any more. 'If you say to young people – "phone us if you need help", they won't do it. But if you say, "call me if you feel rubbish", they might.' I comment on the way in which Gavin appeared not to be engaging with his mother. 'Yes, his mother's on methadone and has mental health problems as well – so there are a lot of complications. But he's been with us for nine months ... He will move to the transition support team and have reduced levels of contact.' As we drive away, I look back at Gavin as he makes his way into his gran's house. It strikes me that this young man has clearly benefited from the social and moral support that has come his way via Includem, and I hope that his life continues to remain crime-free.

Author's fieldnotes, Glasgow

Trotter (2008: 222) argues that 'pro-social modelling' involves practitioners exhibiting pro-social values, comments, and actions and confronting pro-criminal values during their work with offenders. Praise should be used to affirm crime-free periods and workers should reward clients by giving them their time, providing positive evidence, and reducing the frequency of contact. The support session described in Box 11.1 illustrates that Alana used these strategies extensively. By meeting with Gavin informally and taking him on a relaxed outing to the golf range, Alana built a support structure around him and encouraged him to engage in positive leisure pursuits (Includem, 2010). She looked for opportunities to reinforce his positive progress through praise, and offered him support and care. Alana believed in the 'transformative power of positive, respectful relationships' that were established through regular and purposeful contact with both Gavin and his mother (Includem, 2010: 13). During our interview, Alana described how she also encouraged clients such as Gavin to reflect on their social networks and make informed choices based on an awareness of how these networks impact on their offending lifestyles:

It is about saying, 'well, you know, there's a difference between having these attachments and being involved in crime'. And that's where we want to put, you know, the line in the sand and say, 'you can still have these friends, you can still have these relationships ... but you need to make a conscious decision now whether you're gonna spend the rest of your life involved in crime or not'.

Alana, intensive support worker

Previous research by Khan and Hill (2007) found that young people often develop positive relationships with Includem workers and mentors. These authors emphasize the workers' listening skills and their ability to build trust and respect, to actively help the young people in their care and give good advice. The observational data in Box 11.1 echo this evidence. Gavin valued the support Alana offered him, and felt he could talk to her about anything.

Alana had good listening skills; she showed empathy towards Gavin's previous lifestyle and the challenges in his family while also rewarding his current, non-offending behaviour (Trotter, 2008). She offered to help him by taking him to court, writing letters of support for his impending trial, and making herself available to him at weekends via the out-of-hours telephone helpline, while encouraging reduced frequency of contact (Trotter, 2008). The respect Gavin had developed for Includem was evident in his decision to continue to seek transitional help beyond his intensive support period. Alana also noticed the subtle changes that took place in the lives of other young clients she worked with:

> The small changes, the small differences in their life are the ones that make it a little bit more positive. You don't know what would have gone on if those changes hadn't been made. The small changes are really often forgotten about.
>
> Alana, intensive support worker

The outreach, education, training, and intensive support initiatives linked to the Glasgow CIRV project were characterized by opposing and contradictory ideological approaches. On the one hand, a conservative ideology directed young men away from anti-social behaviour and took them on subtle spiritual journeys, with differential association at the centre and Christian values at the periphery (Maruna, 2001; Giordano *et al.*, 2008). On the other, a socialist ideology motivated the community agencies to alleviate disadvantage by guiding young men back into employment and providing holistic forms of social care and intensive, pro-social, support for high-level offenders. Agencies sought to target specific groups of young men who were deemed to be at risk and provided them with leisure-oriented activities, work-related skills development, and the beginnings of positive, respectful relationships to promote social transformation (Trotter, 2008; Coburn and Wallace, 2011).

The focus on violence-prevention among young men therefore brought together a wide range of social service partnerships, on both sides of the Atlantic. The impact of the work is illustrated by the impressive reductions in violence seen in both Cincinnati and Glasgow (VRU, 2011; Engel *et al.,* 2013). However, at a more personal level, I wanted to dig underneath the statistics further and examine the journeys the young men had travelled – as both clients and volunteers – as they moved towards desistance. I also wanted to understand the journey that CIRV itself had gone on as it became embedded in wider policy and practice. These journeys are the focus of the final part of this book.

Part Five

5

Journeys, insights, and
continuing applications

Chapter 12

Journeys towards desistance in Cincinnati and Glasgow

I was caught in that wee bit of thinkin', 'how are some of these young boys not seein' it? I'm no' really gettin' results' ... forgettin' that I'm a result ... what I'm givin' away, I'm keepin'.

Jack, reformed offender and CIRV volunteer, Glasgow

In Part 3 I outlined how police departments in Cincinnati and Glasgow had shifted their strategic focus, towards violence-prevention through multi-agency partnership work, and I signalled the challenges remaining in frontline practice. In Part 4 I explored the role of non-traditional partners such as youth and outreach street workers and members of community agencies. I indicated how they reached out and engaged with young men in Cincinnati and Glasgow as part of the violence-prevention strategies of CIRV. Evaluative reports have recorded the encouraging reductions in violent youth crime in both cities. But these reports fail to tell us *why* and *how* criminal desistance has occurred among CIRV participants, if at all, and the role the related initiatives may have played in stimulating it. This chapter attempts to fill that gap by examining the individual stories of some of the clients and volunteers.

Bottoms *et al.* (2004: 370) point out that the principle meaning of the verb 'to desist' is to '"cease, stop (or) forebear" ... with a related sub-sense of "refrain, abstain"'. They argue that, while the first two words of the principle meaning imply permanence, the third does not and neither does the sub-sense. So desistance should not be seen so much as an 'event or state' but rather a 'process or an on-going work in progress' (McNeill and Maruna, 2008: 225) that is often characterized by setback, hope, and despair (McNeill, 2009). Many criminologists believe that desistance journeys are hazardous and fraught, and that desisting offenders often oscillate between periods of offending and long gaps in-between (Haigh, 2009; Soothill and Francis, 2009). Others have suggested that there is a difference between primary and secondary desistance. For instance, McNeill (2009: 26) describes primary desistance as a 'lull or crime-free gap in a criminal career', whereas secondary desistance occurs when offenders experience a fundamental change in self-identity, assume the role of a 'changed person', and adopt new and transformed roles in life (McNeill and Maruna, 2008: 226).

Some authors have drawn attention to the 'age–crime curve', which illustrates that crime (and street violence in particular) is a 'young person's game' and that most offenders desist in their early 20s (McNeill and Maruna, 2008: 227, and see also Matza, 1964; Farrington, 1997; Bottoms *et al.*, 2004). But while some believe that desistance is fundamentally a biological process, others have argued that changing social bonds and subjective narrative constructions also play a role (McNeill, 2003). Referring to social control theory, Laub and Sampson (2001) argue that strong social bonds to institutions can bring about increased conformity and thus stimulate desistance. A central element in the process of desistance is the 'knifing off' of offenders from their immediate environment through introducing them to new social contexts that bring increased structure and routine (Laub and Sampson, 2003: 145). Further, some have argued that desistance is best understood in the context of human relationships, and that social bonds can generate social capital that leads to increased participation and inclusion in wider society (Barry, 2006; Huebner *et al.*, 2007; McNeill and Maruna, 2008; McNeill, 2009). Simply put, desistance may be prompted by someone believing in offenders and offering moral support to them during their attempts to reconstruct their identities (McNeill, 2004: 429; McNeill and Maruna, 2008).

Maruna (2001) refers to the generative motivations so common among offenders. The process of desisting from crime is often accompanied by an impulse to draw on a 'damaged past' to help protect the future interests of others (McNeill, 2004: 432). Maruna argues that 'help-givers are often helped more than help-receivers', through a process of 'retroflexive reformation' (ibid. 124, and see also Chapter 10). Desistance is thus about finding a way to make good a troubled past by making a positive contribution to families or communities now (McNeill, 2009). Maruna found that the self-narratives of former offenders who had moved towards secondary desistance were often 'care-oriented, other-centred and focused on promoting the next generation' and that many former offenders adopted identities associated with 'wounded healers' (McNeill and Maruna, 2008: 232). By turning their negative experiences into 'cautionary tales or hopeful stories of redemption' that they share with younger men, reforming offenders engage in a process of identity change and move along on their journeys towards secondary desistance (ibid. 232).

Part 2 looked at the issues that led young men into violence on both sides of the Atlantic. In the case of Glasgow, young men's experiences of criminal justice sanctions were often devoid of concern for rehabilitation and care. These sanctions were not embedded in an understanding of what it is that stimulates desistance. In this chapter I return to some of the young men's lives in both Glasgow and Cincinnati and identify which situational contexts and structural influences enabled them to move towards desistance (Laub and Sampson, 2003). In boxes 12.1–12.5, I summarize the young men's journeys and the role played by CIRV in supporting them, as either clients or volunteers. As before, the occasional use of direct quotations from interview transcripts helps to illuminate their experiences. Each case study is followed by a short discussion in the light of relevant themes from the literature.

> ## BOX 12.1: DONNY'S JOURNEY
>
> As illustrated in Chapter 5, Donny had a history of participating in gang violence and selling drugs. He first became involved in CIRV when he was encouraged to attend a self-referral session in Glasgow Sheriff Court by his school teachers and local community police officers. Through a subsequent case-management process, he was referred to the Kan Do self-development programme as a means of building his self-esteem and confidence (for further details on Kan Do, see Chapter 11). Donny was apprehensive at first, since he was aware that rival gang members he used to fight with would also be taking part in the programme. However, after a few weeks Donny made friends with some of the other young men through playing football and engaging in recreational activities. During his time on the programme, he was asked to speak to younger boys in a local school about his experiences of being stabbed in a gang fight, and to discourage them from participating in violence. Later, he was referred to Includem and was appointed an intensive support worker who helped him to continue to stay away from gang violence and selling drugs. Donny valued the support his key worker gave him, and felt he could confide in her – even when he slipped back into selling drugs as a means of gaining money when jobs were hard to come by: 'You could speak to the Includem worker about anything, really. You can tell them you've just sold a bag of weed (cannabis) or somethin', whatever. And they won't grass you in or anythin' ... they'd just try and gie you a wee bit of advice to try and stop'. Donny had already decided to move away from gang violence by the time he was referred to CIRV as a client, because he had seen his best friend stabbed and suffer severe injuries. He was also trying hard to stay away from using and selling drugs. He felt that CIRV gave him the extra impetus

to try to maintain the changes he had made: 'It was thinkin' about all the stuff and that, that helped me gie up. I think basically Includem gave me like an extra push.'

Donny's journey illustrates that desistance is, indeed, not an event but a 'work in progress' (McNeill and Maruna, 2008: 225). Although he had moved away from gangs and street violence, he was still selling drugs and had not reached a stage that might be described as secondary desistance by the time he was participating in CIRV. However, by sharing his experiences of gang violence in schools, Donny began to engage in generative pursuits and the expenditure of social and emotional capital (Barry, 2006). He drew on his own past to create cautionary tales, with the aim of protecting the interests of other young people (Maruna, 2001; McNeill, 2004; McNeill and Maruna, 2008). At the same time, Donny benefited from the support he received from Includem. He gained a feeling of trust and moral support through his relationship with his key worker and knew that he could confide in her while he oscillated between periods of offending and the lulls between them (Haigh, 2009; Soothill and Francis, 2009). The combination of having a trusting relationship, seeing the impact of violence on his close friend, and taking on generative responsibilities enabled him to begin to reconstruct his identity as a permanent desister (Barry, 2006; McNeill and Maruna, 2008).

Box 12.2: Jack's journey

As Chapter 5 illustrated, Jack experienced persistent feelings of emotional isolation and fear during his childhood and adolescence, which led him to become involved in violent offending. By the time he reached his 30s, he was residing in a homeless unit in Glasgow but just wanted to be a good father. The new responsibility he had gained from being a parent had encouraged him to reflect on his life: 'I looked into my daughter's eyes, and I knew that it had to stop or I would damage this little girl with the way I was living'. Around the same time, he received a phone call from a friend who worked in prisons, who told him about the CIRV project. Jack felt that the phone call came just at the right time, since he had been contemplating the idea of trying to help others that had suffered from the same kind of trauma that he had: 'Right at that time, I was thinkin' about, how can I put a bit back – how can I use my experience to help others? ... I wanted to help people from addictive, traumatic backgrounds into a better way of living using my own experience'. Jack met with senior police officers attached to the programme, who persuaded him to share his experiences at the self-referral sessions. Although he was nervous, he stood up in the Sheriff Court on several occasions and tried to convince other young men to move away from violence. He subsequently began working closely with the police and other CIRV partners and became a regular member of the voluntary team.

Later, Jack participated in the Kan Do programme along with a group of younger men who had been involved in violence. He then contributed to workshops that supported youngsters to move away from gangs and violence. But, where Graham had attempted to take young men on journeys shaped by Christianity (as described in Chapter 11), Jack believed that a more indirect approach worked best. He took youngsters on more subtle spiritual journeys, where they gained a deeper understanding of themselves and each other: 'I think you've got to slip it in ... it's the whole non-judgemental, non-critical approach ... God gave you a brain for a reason, right, so you need to use everyday language to describe spiritual things 'cos if you just say "hand it all over to Jesus, blah, blah, blah", they're gonna just say, "get that to f***", cause they're still full of all that bravado and worried about what their pals think of them.'

Jack completed some informal mentoring training, but was unable to work with young men on a one-to-one basis because his criminal record prevented him from gaining a clean disclosure certificate that would allow him to work intensively with vulnerable young adults. However, he continued to help implement workshops and felt that it helped to motivate and inspire other young men to leave violence behind. More importantly, he also felt that working with other young men in this way helped him personally to move further away from his old lifestyle: 'I've done this voluntary for two and a half years and it's just moved me further and further away from that way of life ... I was caught in that wee bit of thinkin', "how are some of these young boys not seein' it? I'm no' really gettin' results" ... forgettin' that I'm a result ... what I'm givin' away, I'm keepin.'

In a similar way to Donny, Jack had begun a desistence journey prior to becoming involved with CIRV, and becoming a father was a further major turning point. But Jack's experiences as a volunteer in CIRV led to a fundamental change in his self-identity (Maruna, 2001). Drawing on the lessons of his damaged past, he was able to create opportunities for other young men to see their own potential for growth and development within a moral framework (Giordano *et al.*, 2008; Nurden, 2010). Barry (2006) argues that taking on responsibility for helping others and providing them with social, emotional, and cultural capital can lead to the social recognition needed to stimulate secondary desistance. The experiences of Jack confirm this. He recognized that what he was 'giving away' he was 'keeping'. Jack's involvement in other-centred pursuits had a therapeutic power that enabled him to engage in more lasting desistance and change, while also helping others to do the same (Maruna, 2001; McNeill, 2012).

BOX 12.3: JIM, ROBBIE, AND DEL'S JOURNEYS

In Chapter 5 I described how Jim, Robbie, and Del progressed from gang violence onto selling drugs within their local community. Later, they began participating in football leagues in Glasgow arranged by Sidekix (see Chapter 11 for more details on this organization). In turn, they were encouraged by the coaches to come along to the self-referral sessions and learn more about the CIRV programme. Because they were older than the other clients and had already started moving away from violence, Jim, Robbie, and Del were encouraged to become paid mentors to other young men who were referred to CIRV. They took part in the Kan Do personal development programme together, helping to deliver workshops. Although they had sold drugs occasionally prior to becoming involved in the programme, supporting other young men brought a sense of responsibility and the motivation to move even further away from crime: 'The progress you seen from when you met these boys was second to none, it was really good. They had a purpose, they had somebody ... it was as if they had another pal they could talk to ... you're basically tryin' to help them oot through the phone calls, and the feelin' I got was success ... it was brilliant, 'cause you'd helped somebody, basically, to better themselves.' Jim explained that he, Robbie, and Del began to discipline themselves to stay away from drugs and to avoid violence at all costs, because they had become role models to young boys: 'You're tryin' to stable yoursel'. You don't want to turn up and try and help somebody when you're havin' drug issues.'

Over a period of six months, the three young men helped more than 180 youngsters by running workshops, answering phone calls, coaching football sessions, and engaging in informal mentoring. They also participated in several self-development and training courses that helped to increase their own confidence. All three hoped that their involvement would lead to permanent employment as mentors. But they were ultimately disappointed when the funding for CIRV ended and they were left without any prospects. In turn, they felt that the young lads in their care were also let down: 'We just got dropped, so [the boys] just get dropped as well, basically ... they've built up confidence to speak to you and then everythin' just gets dropped and that's taken away from them.' After the funding ended and the three men lost their jobs, they struggled to find other employment because of their criminal records. They ultimately became desperate and felt compelled to gravitate back into crime: 'I was stable at one point, when I was goin' home, takin' money home to the missus and the wean and providin' for them ... I'm no' even workin' at the moment ... I've been in and oot of labourin' jobs [but] never had a permanent contract ... I've even had to sell drugs to try and make some money ... that's the only thing you can fall back on to try and get money, you know what I mean?'

Jim, Robbie, and Del's story again shows that some young men oscillate between offending and non-offending before moving towards permanent desistance (Barry, 2006; McNeill and Maruna, 2008; Haigh, 2009; Soothill and Francis, 2009). For these three young men, the opportunity to take responsibility for helping others led to a fundamental identity change and a motivation to stay away from drugs and violence. But in addition to gaining generative impulses, they were motivated by the status they gained from being able to provide for their families. Paid employment in CIRV renewed their identities as help-givers and family men (Laub and Sampson, 2003). However, when the structure of the CIRV programme disappeared and they struggled to find other work, the frustrations they felt lured them back into crime. They felt let down and stigmatized by the way their criminal records followed them around. Thus, even though these young men had begun to believe they had found a new script for the future, their time with CIRV merely represented a prolonged lull in their offending lifestyles (Laub and Sampson, 2003; McNeill, 2009).

BOX 12.4: KEENAN AND LEMAR'S JOURNEYS

As I touched-on briefly in Chapter 4, Keenan became involved in street violence in Cincinnati as a teenager, following the death of his father. When he was in his 20s he was sentenced to life imprisonment for robbery, drug charges, and manslaughter. When he was in prison he phoned his grandmother, who managed to revive some fundamental Christian values within Keenan that would change his life forever: 'I called grandma and ... she said, "your mamma told me you've been shootin' that stuff, boy ... you know we're not gonna get you out but what you need to do is sit down and call on Jesus, boy". ... I lay down and I pulled a little blanket over my head, crying, and I found myself talkin' to God.' When Keenan awoke the next morning, he had a hunger to read the Bible. He became a born-again Christian while still in prison and, on his release, took up prison ministry. He subsequently joined the team of Street Advocates within CIRV and became active in sharing his story with younger men (see Chapter 10 for further details of Street Advocates' work). Keenan gained a great deal from acting as a mentor to these young men, using an evangelistic approach to encourage them to keep persevering in their journey towards desistance. As a result, he too continued to stay away from crime and saw himself as one of the 'success stories' to emerge from CIRV.

Lemar was released from prison in 2009, having served a three-year sentence for drug possession and gun crime in Cincinnati (see Chapter 4 for other details about Lemar's life). As one of his friends had just gone through the CIRV programme and recommended it to him, Lemar contacted the Street Advocate team and offered to volunteer. He quickly found that many of the young men on the streets who were involved in violence had a healthy respect for him and were prepared to listen to his advice because of the credibility he had as a reformed offender (see also Chapter 10). Lemar went on to become a permanent, paid member of the Street Advocate team. He interacted regularly with young men on the streets, and liaised with service providers on the CIRV team to try to get them on training courses and work placements. He gained opportunities to support other young men through personal mentoring, which in turn enabled him to transform his whole outlook and devote his life to helping others: 'There was a guy that used to live in the streets and he used to sell drugs. He ended up using drugs to support his habit and he ended up burglarizing and robbing, doing all types of mad things and I got him and he's been clean for six months. He's been employed ... he's started to box and train ... he's just proud of life and he said he's never been happier ... just to be part of that and actually taking a

> a little credit, that's a great feeling for me, doing something positive … giving back.'

As discussed in Chapter 10, some believe that religion can provide a resource for emotional coping, replacing the tendency to resort to violence and substance abuse as emotional reactions to social pressures (Cullen *et al.*, 1999; Agnew, 2006; Giordano *et al.*, 2008). Drawing on his family's traditional cultural associations with the black American church, Keenan's conversion became a defining moment for him (Lincoln, 1989; Olive, 2003). The combined impact of becoming a Christian and Street Advocate enabled him to become other-centred and take on generative commitments (McNeill and Whyte, 2007). He looked to evangelism as a catalyst for change, to reach out to young men and encourage them to adopt alternative identities. Like many of the other volunteers I talked to, helping others enabled him to continue to walk the desistance path himself and to create an alternative identity construct as a 'success story'. Although Lemar did not use religious evangelism as a means of reaching out to young men, he nevertheless established credibility on the streets as a 'wounded healer' (Maruna, 2001: 102). His own desistance journey was also motivated by a desire to 'give back' his time and effort to support social transformation in others (Olive, 2003).

BOX 12.5: KIEREN'S JOURNEY

As outlined in Chapter 5, Kieren was involved in gang violence and the hyper-volatile world of street crime during his young adult life in the east end of Glasgow. He eventually served a three-and-a-half-year prison sentence for a firearms charge. Following his release, he became involved in the CIRV programme and participated in the Sidekix football leagues (see Chapter 11 for further details on Sidekix). He became a voluntary football coach and encouraged a group of young gang members from his community to sign up to CIRV. Kieren gradually became an informal mentor to these young men and also ran workshops focusing on issues such as anti-violence, conflict resolution, and anger management. At the same time, senior officers and members of the CIRV service delivery team encouraged Kieren to contribute to other training programmes. Kieren shared his own life experiences and encouraged young men to change the way they responded to the pressures around them: 'I was just developing my own sort of wee ideas on programmes when I was teachin' the kids … talkin' to them about my experiences and my own personal views and how they should go about life and how they could change their attitudes towards school and towards their parents and towards life in general.' Kieren subsequently gained an employment contract to deliver sessional coaching and youth work linked to the CIRV programme. He also accompanied senior officers and social service partners as they knocked on doors in the east end of Glasgow and encouraged young men to sign up for CIRV.

Having a paid contract enabled Kieren to gain confidence, self-esteem, and a sense of independence that he had long sought-after. Having become a father, this was particularly important to him: 'You could provide for your son, you had pride in yourself as a dad because you could take your son oot, you could dae a bit of shoppin' ... you could pay your bills ... it gave you a bit of self-belief.' He also gained renewed confidence from the mentoring work he was doing with the young men. He built positive relationships through football and helped them to move away from drugs, crime, and violence through role-play activities during workshops. At the same time, he continued to gain confidence thanks to having Peter as a mentor within Sidekix, and being able to share his personal challenges with him.

Thus, the presence of a strong role model, the confidence he gained from having a job, and the renewed sense of responsibility he had from being a father enabled him to distance himself even further from crime: 'It was resilience and just reflecting ... I was able to express myself to Peter, tell Peter exactly what happened ... and what gave me that strong belief and commitment was a taste of work ... and I've got a son so I could't go back to sellin' drugs or a life of crime.' Through the role-play work he developed with the young men on the programme, Kieren's long-term interest in acting began to deepen. Through personal contacts in the CIRV programme, he was introduced to a leading film director who invited him to audition for his new film. Kieren was delighted when he was offered the leading part, in which he played a young Glasgow father who is given one final opportunity to stay out of jail through a community payback scheme.

Coaching and mentoring other young men enabled Kieren to adopt a transformed role in life, in which his own damaged past helped him to support and protect others (Maruna, 2001; McNeill and Maruna, 2008). Further, he expressed his interest in acting by using it as a tool to enable others to reflect on social pressures in more adaptive ways, rather than through violence (Agnew, 2006). As in the other case studies I have explored, Kieren's adoption of the 'wounded healer' role was therefore an important means of enabling him to stay away from crime (Maruna, 2001: 102). However, his new responsibilities as a young father also played a vital role. Maruna (2001) argues that the generative commitments associated with parenthood fill a void, making criminality too risky (Barry, 2006; McNeill and Whyte, 2007). Kieren's overwhelming concern for supporting his son meant that the structure and rewards associated with paid employment provided much-needed stability, confidence, and pride. Combined with the moral support he received from Peter, Kieren's involvement as a paid team member in CIRV enabled him to adopt a new identity as a hard worker, a good provider, and – most important of all – a desister (Laub and Sampson, 2003).

Changed lives, changed identities – but uncertain futures

Laub and Sampson (2003: 145) argue that offenders move away from crime due to individual choices and situational contexts, but that 'structural influences linked to important institutions' help to sustain desistance. The process of desistance thus operates simultaneously at different levels and across different contextual environments (ibid.). The biographical case studies in this chapter illustrate this. They provide an insight into how individual and social contextual issues interacted in the lives of the young men I met, and how institutions (including those associated with CIRV) supported their desistance journeys. The young men moved away from violence and crime as a result of the interplay between trigger events, institutional influences, social bonds, and narrative changes in personal and social identities (McNeill, 2012). But some encountered challenges that halted their journey and rendered uncertain their prospects for sustaining their progress to secondary desistance.

Trigger events were unique to the individuals concerned, but were typically characterized by taking on new responsibilities and personal commitments or experiencing emotional transitions. For instance, both Kieren and Jack became fathers and this stimulated a desire to change their criminal identities because of their new commitment to take care of, and provide for, their children. Keenan experienced a religious conversion and a new commitment to his faith that inspired him to change. And Donny experienced the emotional trauma of seeing his friend become a victim of violence, which motivated him to reconsider his own lifestyle.

Following these initial decisions to change, participants made fledgling attempts to move towards desistance. Each of them came into contact with positive institutional influences through CIRV, whether they engaged with the programme as clients, volunteers, or both. These structural environments and the supportive human relationships within them provided a 'knifing off' effect that enabled them to move further away from their past and towards sustained periods of desistance (Laub and Sampson, 2003: 145). For instance, Donny's relationship with his keyworker was influential, and Kieren, Jim, Robbie, and Del all gained moral support from their football coach. In some cases, paid employment enabled the young men to take further action towards desistance because they were proud to be able to provide for their families. In addition, all of them engaged in generative action within CIRV programmes. These experiences served as catalysts for longer periods of sustained change. Sharing cautionary tales in schools, on the streets, or in workshops influenced the young men to change their identities through taking on the role of the 'wounded healer' (Maruna, 2001: 102).

However, several of the young men's stories confirm McNeill's (2009) earlier observations that the process of desistance is a work in progress, characterized by setback and periods of re-offending. Maruna and Farrall (2004) summarize how journeys towards desistance, stimulated by the type of agency that CIRV brought about, need to be reinforced through social 'delabeling':

> ... a lull can turn into secondary desistance when two things happen. First, the person finds a source of agency and communion in non-criminal activities. They find some sort of 'calling' – be it parenthood, painting, coaching, chess or what Sennet (2003) calls 'craft love' – through which they find meaning and purpose outside of crime ... The second part of our desistance formula, like that of Lemert's deviance theory, involves societal reaction. The desisting person's change in behaviour is sometimes recognized by others and reflected back to him in a 'delabeling process'.
>
> Maruna and Farrall, 2004: 28, cited in McNeill, 2012: 26–7

The young men in Glasgow and Cincinnati came across social and structural barriers that thwarted this 'delabeling' process. As some interviewees were keen to stress, they faced obstacles when seeking employment beyond the confines of CIRV, and so sustained attempts to desist were threatened by social reactions (McNeill, 2012):

I mean if, if you don't have a job, you can't find a job ... you're feeling bad, this and that. I need something to make me feel better. So I go buy some heroin, I go buy some cocaine or I smoke some weed. You know, that's the population. It's an endless cycle.

Romeo, Street Advocate and reformed offender, Cincinnati

The downside was ... I think out of the 60 we took on, I think 12 of them got kept on wi' the employers they went to ... and I actually believe if there's nae job opportunities, we're wastin' our time ... there's got to be an end-product.

Billy, community agency manager, Glasgow

You know what it's like when you climb a ladder and it's taken you further ... you actually fall back further because everyone's let you down again.

Colin, community agency manager, Glasgow

Even if the personal role models were able to believe in the young men, society was not. Some faced new uphill struggles in their attempts to stay away from offending lifestyles because they could not get permanent jobs. Once the funding from CIRV disappeared, or their involvement with the programme ended, some young men found themselves back in a place that was characterized by setbacks and temptations (Bottoms and Shapland, 2011, and see also McNeill, 2012).

Chapter 13

Focused deterrence: Continuing journeys and new applications

The legacy of CIRV is that it fully contributed to a kind of 'sea change' in thinking.

Scott, senior police officer, Glasgow

Writing *Gangs, Marginalised Youth and Social Capital* (Deuchar, 2009a) made me aware of the enormous challenges faced by young people in deprived communities in Glasgow. However, my experience of writing this book has been even more profound. I was inspired to write it by the encouraging figures reporting the violence-reduction that had resulted from CIRV's implementation in Cincinnati and Glasgow. In this book I have attempted to unravel the story behind these statistics, describe the positive issues associated with CIRV, and set out the challenges that remain. I have examined the causes, nature, and impact of the street violence the initiative was designed to address, and the cultural shift that took place within the police departments in both cities to accommodate the new interventions. I have explored the role of Street Advocates, youth workers, and community service organizations in enabling marginalized and oppressed young men to become reintegrated and socially included. Most importantly, I have described how CIRV supported young people in moving towards desistance from crime.

Along the way, I have been shocked and saddened by the experiences of young men such as Arcus, Delory, Jermaine, Rufus, and Wesley in Cincinnati and those of Cammy, Dean, Jordan, Ross, Sean, and Shuggie in Glasgow. But I have also been inspired by reformed offenders including Aaron, Darius, Keenan, and Lemar and by Jack and Kieran, while feeling concerned about what the future might hold for young men like Jim, Del, and Robbie. While impressed by the work of senior officers and staff such as Tony, Joe, Josh and Dave in Cincinnati and Kenny, Ally, Iain, Kate, and Richard in Glasgow, I have been critical of some of the frontline practice I saw in Cincinnati although encouraged about what I found in Glasgow. And, in both cities, the presence of positive role models in the shape of Street Advocates, youth workers, and reformed offenders has given me much hope.

Wacquant's (2009b: 289–90) analysis of what Bourdieu called the 'left hand' and 'right hand' of the State illustrates how the slanting of national activity from the social to the penal arm represented a form of 're-masculinization'. It brought a transition from the kindly 'nanny state' of the Fordist–Keynesian era to the strict 'daddy state' of neoliberalism (ibid. 290). With this transition came a focus on workfare, where employment opportunities were too precarious and ill-paid to offer a true platform for economic autonomy. In addition, it brought a focus on 'prisonfare', where the policy stream responded to social disorder by boosting the deployment of the police and other criminal justice agencies in punitive roles. My interviews with young men in both Cincinnati and Glasgow illustrated the impact of this: many failed to secure meaningful employment and were given no opportunities for rehabilitation or after-care following periods of incarceration. These experiences illustrate the limitations of a punitive, criminalizing approach to youth crime and violence (Barry, 2011).

I believe that the CIRV initiative was an attempt to reverse the process of 're-masculinization' of State responses. The renewed strategic ideology in the CPD and the former Strathclyde Police was focused on re-engaging urban outcasts by rejecting the exclusive focus on the crime-fighting model of police practice. It combined a continuing emphasis on enforcement with a wider focus on social welfare and community involvement, with violence-prevention at its core (Spergel, 1995; Braga, 2008; Wacquant, 2008; Kennedy, 2009, 2011). However, there were tensions in terms of the internal differentiations associated with police culture, particularly in Cincinnati, where the individual dispositions of some officers in the specialized enforcement unit conflicted with the policing *field* at command level and the professional belief system or *habitus* that CIRV had brought about (Bourdieu, 1990).

In both cities, police officers forged non-traditional partnerships through the multi-agency collaboration that characterized CIRV. In Cinncinnati, Street Advocates enacted the role of 'Superman', publicizing their ex-gang member identities and drawing on their damaged pasts to save the lives of others (McHugh, 2013). They mentored young men and directed them towards training programmes and temporary work placements, which they believed would enable them to accumulate social, economic, cultural, and symbolic capital (Barry, 2006; Robson, 2009). By contrast, in Glasgow, youth and community workers and volunteers resisted the tendency to publicize and celebrate their former gang or offending identities, where they may have existed. Their subtle, unobtrusive approaches were more akin to the role of 'Clark Kent' than they were to that of 'Superman' (McHugh, 2013).

CIRV complemented and supported young offenders' journeys towards desistance in several ways. It provided them with positive institutional influences, supportive human relationships, and an opportunity to take on generative activities. These combined influences stimulated both fledgling and more sustained desistance attempts among the young men (as in Laub and Sampson, 2003). However, some of the youngsters were unable to secure employment after their time with CIRV due to their criminal records, so their attempts at desistance were jeopardized by social and structural barriers (McNeill, 2012). Several found themselves again surrounded by obstacles and temptations, and struggling to embark on renewed desistance journeys (as also illustrated by Bottoms and Shapland, 2011).

Beyond my own journey, and those of clients, volunteers, officers, and social service partners in CIRV, the initiative itself continues to travel on. Following the success of CIRV in Cincinnati, the focused deterrence strategies underpinning it have continued in other cities and other states. In Glasgow, although the funded period of CIRV ended in 2011, its legacy also lives on and the principles underpinning it have continued to be applied in wider contexts. In the remainder of this final chapter, I discuss the wide-ranging ways in which the focus on prevention, intervention, and inter-agency collaboration is increasingly being applied more broadly across the USA, Scotland and the UK.

Focused deterrence across multiple American contexts

Following the successful implementation of CIRV in Cincinnati, the National Network for Safe Communities was launched in New York City in 2009. The Network is an alliance of cities dedicated to 'advancing proven strategies to combat violent crime, reduce incarceration and rebuild relations between law enforcement and distressed communities' (National Network for Safe Communities [NNSC], 2013). It brings together the jurisdictions around America that are currently implementing a group violence-reduction strategy, a drug intervention strategy, or both. It recognizes that there is too much violence in America, that the impact of drug markets is unacceptable, and that intolerable tensions can still arise between law enforcement agencies and local communities (Kennedy, 2011). Those who have been implementing focused deterrence strategies for many years are now being joined by new sites in the Network, and there is a shared focus on collaboration, evaluation, and sustainability. All of the projects attached to the Network are aimed at identifying core offenders, forming partnerships between law enforcement, service providers, and community representatives, and communicating a credible moral community message against violence. They also project a plausible law enforcement message about the consequences of further violence, and provide a genuine offer of help for those who want to change (Kennedy, 2011; NNSC, 2013).

The projects associated with the Network have consistently led to positive results. In 2007, a 'pulling levers' focused deterrence strategy was implemented to reduce crime and disorder problems associated with an illegal drug market operating in Rockford, Illinois. Evaluations suggest that since its inception it has led to a statistically significant 22 per cent reduction in non-violent offences and a non-statistically significant reduction in violent offences in the target neighbourhood (Braga and Weisburd, 2012b). Similar strategies were implemented in Nashville, Tennessee in 2008 to reduce crime and disorder problems associated with an illegal drug market in the McFerrin Park neighbourhood. The Drug Market Intervention (DMI) strategy, modelled on the earlier High Point intervention implemented in North Carolina, provided direct threat of law enforcement sanctions against dealers. It brought about powerful informal social control via local families and community participants, and offered services to those who wished to leave the drug trade behind. The intervention led to a statistically significant 55.5 per cent reduction in illegal drug possession offences in the neighbourhood (Braga and Weisburd, 2012b). Similarly impressive results have been achieved by the new Operation Ceasefire strategy implemented in Newark, New Jersey. The project used trained street outreach staff, public education campaigns, and community mobilization to prevent shootings (Skogan *et al.,* 2008). It combined the threat of federal prosecutions with offering violent offenders alternative options via the implementation of offender notification meetings, as in Cincinnati (Braga and Weisburd, 2012b).

The Network strategies are now being deployed in more than 50 communities across the USA, including Los Angeles, Chicago, Stockton, and Indianapolis (NNSC, 2013). The strategies have gone state-wide in California, with support from the Governor's office and private foundations. Several cities in Ohio, including Dayton and Canton, have implemented strategies based on the Cincinnati initiative and have recorded subsequent reduced levels of violence in their neighbourhoods (Kennedy, 2011). Thus, the common-sense strategies associated with focused deterrence are beginning to have a national influence on driving down crime in the USA. Kennedy (2011: 271) cites the views of Jeffrey Rosen, a law professor at George Washington University, Washington DC. Rosen has observed that the 'relative simplicity of the solutions ... is at the core of their radical potential'. And these simple solutions are also continuing to have an impact on the other side of the Atlantic.

Current strategies for justice and policing in Scotland

The principles underpinning CIRV in Glasgow (see Chapter 5) started out against the backdrop of an increasing policy focus within the Scottish justice system on the proactive prevention of crime. Thanks to the insights gained from CIRV's implementation, the emphasis on violence-prevention has become stronger. The Police and Fire Reform (Scotland) Act 2012 has led, from 2013, to the creation of a new single police service, Police Scotland. The policing principles underpinning the new service recognize that reactive or response tactics involving enforcement will always be needed, but also the pressing need to counterbalance this with a strong focus on prevention. Within Police Scotland inconsistencies in national systems and procedures are being harmonized, while the local discretion of Divisional Commanders to deal with local issues continues to be upheld (ACPOS, 2012). A single force ensures equal access to national and specialist services such as violence-reduction teams, and the work of the Gangs Task Force (now renamed the Alcohol and Violence Task Force) has now gone nationwide under the force's new Licensing and Violence Reduction Division (LVRD). One senior officer with responsibility for implementing the work of the LVRD nation-wide described how the single force now takes a consistent approach to nominal offender management through tasking, enforcement, intervention, and prevention:

> With every Divisional Commander in the new Scottish divisions, we've asked them to implement a tasking process that involves nominals. They probably don't have gang issues but they will have nominals who commit violence ... so they'll have a dedicated tasking process with their partners to do that ... [so] we'll identify the key areas for violence in Scotland. First of all, we'll do the enforcement part – we can deal wi' all that stuff. But then the team that are doing preventions and interventions ... will look at a longer-term approach so that if we have to move about to different areas ... it's almost a legacy behind there that we don't just leave it till it rises again. So ... we do the nominal management through the tasking process, we go through for the enforcement, then we look at prevention/intervention and that assets-based legacy so it doesnae reappear again ...
>
> Brian, senior police officer, Glasgow

Against the backdrop of this focused and consistent approach to policing violence, the Scottish Government's new strategy for justice in Scotland sets out an ambitious agenda of programme-based interventions. These seek to transform the justice system and promote information-sharing and partnership work to create 'flourishing communities' (Scottish Government, 2012: 5). Taking account of the Christie (2011) report on the future delivery of public services, the Government strategy stresses the need for a 'decisive shift towards prevention' of crime. It also draws attention to the need for 'greater integration of public services at local level driven by better partnership, collaboration and effective local delivery' (ibid. 13). In terms of youth violence, the Government strategy is centred around the following key priorities:

- working with families and children at the earliest stage in their lives to divert those most at risk away from crime
- pursuing a public health approach to tackling violence, intervening before the first indications of violence appear, and ensuring that those already involved in violence are given the appropriate help they need to desist
- supporting the Violence Reduction Unit in developing innovative practice and investing in creative programmes such as the No Knives, Better Lives youth engagement initiative which supports young people to prevent and deter knife-carrying and use
- reducing the harmful impact of drug and alcohol use by investing in prevention, treatment, and support services for young people
- diverting young people from statutory measures, prosecution, and custody through early intervention and robust community alternatives
- reducing reoffending rates by improving the commissioning and performance of rehabilitation services.

Scottish Government, 2012: 44–5

One particular feature of the strategy has been the introduction of a whole-system approach to preventing and reducing offending by young people. This approach involves putting in place a 'streamlined and consistent planning, assessment and decision-making process for young people involved in offending' (Scottish Government, 2013: 1). It works across all systems and agencies, and brings together Government policy frameworks into one holistic approach that provides multiple ways of keeping young people away from criminal justice processes (Scottish Government, 2011a, 2013).

First, a focus on early and effective intervention (EEI) means that police reports for low-level offending are diverted from the Children's Reporter or

Procurator Fiscal to multi-agency services providers that share information and agree on an appropriate response. Although previously focused only on young people under the age of 16, intervention has now been extended to include 16–17 year-olds. Second, where cases are referred to the Fiscal, diversionary programmes are offered as an alternative to prosecution and may include a focus on drug and alcohol misuse, conflict resolution, and alternatives to offending. And third, for those under-18s who have missed opportunities for EEI or diversion and who are now in court, help can be offered including bail support as an alternative to remand. At all stages the approach requires the exchange of relevant and sensitive information between the Crown Office, Procurator Fiscal Service, service providers, and statutory and voluntary organizations (Scottish Government, 2011a, 2013).

The legacy of CIRV and One Glasgow

The principles underpinning the Scottish Government's justice strategy have been applied in Glasgow, enabling the CIRV philosophy to live on. The One Glasgow project is a collaboration between Police Scotland, Glasgow City Council, NHS Greater Glasgow and Clyde, Glasgow Housing Association, Department of Work and Pensions, Job Centre Plus, and the Scottish Fire and Rescue Service. The project's priority areas include early intervention and a proactive approach to violence-prevention for children aged 0–8 and their families. Early years and early intervention initiatives are targeted at the most vulnerable individuals and are focused on improving social functioning (GCPP, 2011). The programme also seeks to reduce offending among 12–25 year-olds. By adopting the whole-system approach, One Glasgow implements rigorous case-management, targets those who are on the periphery of offending, and encourages inter-agency collaboration to ensure sustained action. It also provides pre-release support for young offenders moving from prison back into their communities (GCPP, 2011).

One senior officer involved in One Glasgow argued that the national focus on violence-prevention illustrates the influence CIRV has had:

> Everyone's thinking has moved on – police, criminal justice partners, everyone's saying 'right, what do we do to prevent offending in the first place, or preventing re-offending? What can we do to remove pathways into crime?'. Everyone's having that discussion. A lot of people, a lot of services have caught up with CIRV ... everyone uses language that CIRV was using in 2008 ... co-ordination, partnership working, tailor-made intervention, mentoring, or peer support. In actual fact, if you were to put a lot

of what you see now today under a microscope you can actually see, 'that's kinda like CIRV'. The legacy of CIRV is that it fully contributed to a kind of 'sea change' in thinking.

Scott, senior police officer, Glasgow

Scott described the main focus of One Glasgow and how the police have been proactive in bringing about a focus on preventing youth offending:

One Glasgow is a Glasgow City-led programme to remove duplication among a whole range of services and deliver better improvements in service and better outcomes. It's [focusing on] 0–8 years, which is being led by Social Work Services, [but also on] reducing offending [among] 12–25 year-olds … the police on behalf of the City of Glasgow and the whole range of partners … deliver the reducing offending and re-offending [programmes] … we will deal with those who offend but we actually want to have fewer people offending in the first place.

Scott, senior officer, Glasgow

Implementing One Glasgow has thus become a natural extension of the work that was going on in CIRV. Following the ending of the Scottish Government funding in 2011 and the loss of some of the partner agencies, as described in Chapter 11, CIRV became subsumed into the work of One Glasgow. The remaining members of the team focused on EEI through running workshops and organizing briefing sessions for schools in communities where youth violence was an issue. The team implemented the principles underpinning the CIRV self-referral sessions:

We took the call-in model and we took it to the secondary and primary schools here in the east end [of Glasgow] … you'll get the full range, the full spectrum of kids. You've got the kids who are not involved in it at all. [But] if they hear the message, that's gonna reinforce that they have made the right decision. You will get those who are on the periphery or know somebody who's involved in it. That will hopefully make them draw back from that periphery edge that they're on, or it'll maybe, it'll empower them to have the conversation wi' somebody else that they know that's involved in it … and share information. But sort of pull them back from the brink. Those that are involved in it, it's very clear – 'do you know what these are, these are the actual consequences, both short-term and longer-term, if I do this'. So pretty much like a call-in. I spoke first, Jack [reformed offender] spoke, the mother of the victim spoke, the school spoke, and then I kinda washed up at the end.

Scott, senior police officer, Glasgow

In addition to the sessions in schools, young people in the east end of Glasgow who were on the periphery of street-oriented violence were encouraged to participate in workshops. They worked alongside local community police officers to share personal perspectives, build trust, and establish positive relationships. The sessions enabled young people to better understand the role of the police and the reasons underpinning stop-and-search campaigns, as well as helping local police understand the emotions and priorities of youth (Deuchar *et al.*, 2012).

These initiatives in Glasgow may be replicated in other parts of Scotland, depending on local needs and the discretion of Divisional Commanders in the police. Senior managers in Police Scotland empower Divisional Commanders to make decisions about how best to intervene on, and prevent, local issues related to youth violence. On some occasions, they may turn to strategies associated with POP and focused deterrence to implement community 'listening events' (Durie *et al.*, 2004). As one senior officer observed:

> People that are accountable in this structure are the Chief Constable and the Divisional Commanders – they're accountable for reducing the violence … one of the things [the Divisional Commander] was working on … it wasn't a call-in, it was almost like a briefing session where you get everybody into the community. It's not as brutal as a call-in where you get victims, mums and stuff talking about homicide and things … it's almost like that chat through the community – 'let's see what we can do to make communities better'. But again, if I try and introduce a CIRV model in Clackmannan, do they have that issue there? Do they have the violence at that level? Do they have that peer group pressure? … I don't know that they do. So it would have to be dependent on that.
>
> Brian, senior police officer, Glasgow

One Scottish academic I interviewed had been involved in analysing the quantitative impact of CIRV in Glasgow. He believed that using the same model in wider UK locations should only be done with great caution, due to the different nature of violence, the different ethnic makeup of gangs, and the different policing traditions of other settings. However, when I interviewed American criminologist David Kennedy, he argued that CIRV was based on an operating framework that could be applied in any setting:

This is not a programme but it's an operating framework and that framework has been implemented in ways with differing detail in many different places. Part of people's error in looking at Boston or CIRV or any of these others is to think it's a programme – it's not a programme. It's a way of approaching a problem with a simple but defined strategic orientation. People tend to look at a lot of the details other than implementation and say 'oh, this is a different programme'. No it's not a different programme. Everybody does law enforcement a little bit differently. Everybody does social services differently, everybody organizes their community piece differently. None of that matters, what matters is the basic logic that's being brought to bear on the problem.

David Kennedy, American criminologist

In the summer of 2011, inner-city riots exploded in several London boroughs and in other towns and cities across England. In the immediate aftermath, the UK Prime Minister called for a report into the influence of street gangs. Since one in five of those arrested in connection with the riots in London was a known gang member, a group of senior ministers consulted with international experts, senior police officers, and local authority officials, as well as talking to young people themselves. One outcome of this consultation was a decision to bring about an integrated service response, focused on prevention, and emphasize pathways out of crime (Home Office, 2011). The strategies used in the USA and Glasgow were again of interest.

The 2011 summer riots: New solutions to old problems

Following the riots, the UK Home Secretary held an international forum bringing together experts from across the world on issues of youth and gang violence. Delegates included the Chief of Los Angeles Police Department, Director of the Ceasefire project in Illinois, a former Police Chief in Cincinnati, the Director of the Violence Reduction Unit in Scotland, and Dr Robin Engel, Associate Professor of Criminal Justice at the University of Cincinnati. Invited guests also included those who had experience of successfully implementing anti-violence initiatives in France, Spain, Germany, Austria, Sweden, and England. The objective of the forum was to identify international best practice on tackling youth violence, and particularly gang-related violence, as well as to agree on future principles and strategies (Home Office, 2011).

In the final report, the Home Office (2011) set out detailed plans for tackling youth violence in England in the period 2011–15. In summary, the plans were centred around the following principles:

- **providing support to local areas** to tackle youth and gang violence: for example, an 'Ending Gang and Youth Violence' Team would work with a virtual network of more than a hundred advisers to provide practical advice and support to local areas with serious issues of youth violence; a sum of £10 million was allocated to support the most vulnerable communities in improving the way in which local services work with at-risk young people; and an additional £1.2 million would be used to improve services for youth
- **preventing young people becoming involved in violence** in the first place, by creating a new emphasis on early intervention: for instance, more health visitors would be recruited and £18 million would be invested in specialist services to identify and support domestic violence victims and their children; new improvements to the education offered to excluded pupils were to be made, to reduce the risk of their involvement in violence; and more support would be offered to parents worried about their children's behaviour by working with a range of family service providers to develop new advice and guidance on gangs and violence
- **providing pathways out of violence for young people**: for example, intensive family intervention work would be delivered, and a new set of diversion schemes would be introduced for young offenders at the point of arrest; better local guidance would be provided to those young people who present at Accident and Emergency wards because they have been affected by violence; and new offending behaviour programmes would be launched for young people in secure accommodation and for those released from custody
- **initiating punishment and enforcement** to suppress the violence of those who refuse to exit violent lifestyles: for instance, mandatory sentences would be implemented for those found using a knife
- **initiating wider partnership working** to join up the ways in which different local areas respond to youth violence: one example of this was to encourage wider data-sharing between agencies and promote multi-agency approaches to service delivery.

Home Office, 2011: 8–9

Thus, although the UK Government's strategy includes punitive approaches to youth justice, there is also an emphasis on prevention, partnership working, and the need to provide pathways out of crime. The Home Office has shown an intense interest in CIRV and some small-scale pilot strategies have already been implemented. Iain, a now-retired Scottish senior officer who had been closely involved with the Glasgow version of CIRV was instrumental in applying its principles successfully in the borough of Enfield in London. In spite of the differences in the type of violent offenders and cultural issues to be found there, the initiative nonetheless created an impact:

> The borough of Enfield is in the north-east [of London]. It's a huge borough, 300,000 of a population and with a gang problem round about the south corridor and to the east of the borough. They had a multi-agency approach already in place ... run by the council, with key services – police, social work, that kind of thing. They already had services in place so they really just wanted some method of identifying and engaging with the young people. So I was asked to set up and run a call-in session. The call-in session [we delivered] in Glasgow ... is a perfect fit for there but you change the speakers. It has to be local people, people that can engage with the people that they have. Glasgow's gang problem was very much west of Scotland, working class – in Enfield, it was very much black, African, Turkish, Somalian – a different ethnic base for the gangs – the same territorial issues, the same respect issues with a drugs element ... so it was really identifying the appropriate speakers with the right ethnic backgrounds to get the right message across to them ... it was easy if you knew what you were doing. I already had the knowledge of Cincinnati and Glasgow and, with assistance, using their local knowledge and identifying the right type of speaker and looking at the target audience, yeah – it worked.
>
> Iain, (retired) senior police officer, Glasgow

The 'operating framework' that David Kennedy referred to during our interview is now increasingly being applied in numerous contexts on both sides of the Atlantic. As Kennedy has argued elsewhere, those taking forward the principles underpinning the operating framework will never agree on everything. But they agree on enough to continue to make the framework successful:

> It's not everything. Everybody doesn't want all of the same things. The community wants every single gang member to turn his life around; that's probably never going to happen. The cops want every single gang member to stop doing every single crime; that's probably not going to happen. The gang members want the cops to leave them alone; they're not going to get it. But they agree on enough to completely change the way we're doing things. Here's

what everybody agrees on ... the killing's wrong ... it's got to stop ... [and] nobody should go to prison who doesn't have to. We have to stop locking everybody up ... everybody who wants help should get it, as much as we can.

Kennedy, 2011: 282–3

Final reflections

It has reduced group member-involved homicides ... so in that aspect it's been successful. If you look at it from ... the services standpoint where they're trying to get these folks jobs and employment and get them out of the life, it's been an abject disaster ... you're saying basically 'here's a job training thing' ... I can train you in the world, but if I can't get you a job then it doesn't do you any good whatsoever.

Dave, senior police officer, Cincinnati

It's a greater risk out on the street, but there's a greater reward and some of these guys are used to bringing in a lot of money and to tell them that they can get a job, but it's flippin' hamburgers at a fast-food restaurant for a minimum wage, there's no hook to bringing them in. Because they've got more status on the street.

John, senior police officer, Cincinnati

The public sector has a long way to go ... [there was] a young guy who volunteered as a bin man, you know – refuse collector. And they were happy to have him as a volunteer, but he did well and turned up every day. But then when he applied for a job, his criminal record got in the way of him being employed ... I think what we have to do is enable the public sector to be a bit braver about this ... because, of course, the alternative is that these guys have no way of making a living and so just return to something less productive which ultimately will be more harmful for society.

Paul, Scottish academic

These words from the research participants underline the fundamental challenges associated with initiatives such as CIRV. This book has illustrated the strong potential of multi-agency, focused deterrence strategies to support young men's journeys towards criminal desistance. But it has also drawn attention to the social and structural barriers that arise when reformed offenders seek meaningful and fulfilling employment opportunities beyond the confines of these strategies. Sustained desistance attempts can be jeopardized by such barriers (McNeill, 2012). My analysis has illustrated that CIRV complemented offenders' journeys towards desistance in several ways, and particularly through its focus on stimulating generativity. McNeill and Maruna (2008) argue that facilitating generativity should be at the heart of effective practice with offenders, and that prison does a great job of *hindering* generativity because of its unique ability to 'separate individuals from their social responsibilities and civic duties' (ibid. 233). Further, McNeill (2004) argues that we must avoid sending out the message that offenders are fundamentally 'bad' or beyond redemption, since such messages may become self-fulfilling (McNeill, 2004). Rather, we need case-management processes, embedded within an understanding of the desistance process, that enable ex-offenders to give something back to other people and communities and to re-define themselves as care-givers. Those involved in CIRV managed to assist young men in many ways to achieve these goals. But our wider penal institutions, public sector organizations, employers, and society in general need to do likewise.

The principles that underpinned CIRV are increasingly becoming mainstreamed in the USA, Scotland, and the UK generally. There is a strong focus on preventing youth violence through problem-oriented, focused policing and greater integration of public services. I hope that these strategies reach out and transform the lives of those young men who still cannot find jobs, who are socially excluded and engulfed in violence and the street codes that stimulate it. We need to continue to gather a robust evidence-base that demonstrates the potential of these initiatives to heal communities, re-engage the oppressed, and save lives. To make that happen, we also need strong and trusting partnerships between police officers, service providers, employers, and academics. As I know from experience, this takes time, energy, and lots of perseverance.

Looking back across the pages of this book, I know that my own perseverance has paid off. I have explored, analysed, and actively participated in police practice and the wider strategies that complement it. By becoming a marginal native, I have built reciprocity and gained insights into the positive aspects of police practice and social service provision, as well as identifying some of the challenges. I hope that the insights I have offered will help support the police and their public service partners in positive ways, as they continue with the challenging job of building safe, inclusive, and flourishing communities.

References

ABC News (2012) 'Cincinnati police chief promises more crackdowns on gangs'. 30 March. Online. www.wcpo.com/dpp/news/local_news/cincinnati-police-chief-promises-more-crackdows-on-gangs (accessed 17 May 2013).

Agnew, R. (1992) 'Foundation for a general strain theory of crime and delinquency'. *Criminology*, 30, 47–87.

—— (2006) *Pressurised into Crime: An overview of general strain theory*. Los Angeles: Roxbury.

Aldridge, J., Medina, J., and Ralphs, R. (2008) 'Dangers and problems of doing gang research in the UK'. In Van Gemert, F., Petersen, D., and Lien, I.L. (eds) *Street Gangs, Migration and Ethnicity*. Collumpton: Willan.

Aldridge, J., Ralphs, R., and Medina, J. (2011) 'Collateral damage: Territory and policing in an English gang city'. In Goldson, B. (ed.) *Youth in Crisis: 'Gangs', territoriality and violence*. London: Routledge.

Alpert, G.P., MacDonald, J.M., and Dunham, R.G. (2005) 'Police suspicion and discretionary decision making during citizen stops'. *Criminology*, 4, 407–34.

Alvarez, R. (2009) *The Wire: Truth be told*. New York: Grove Press/HBO.

Anderson, E. (1999) *Code of the Street*. New York: W.W. Norton and Co.

Anderson, S., Kinsey, R., Loader, I., and Smith, C. (1994) *Cautionary Tales: Young people, crime and policing in Edinburgh*. Aldershot: Ashgate Publishing Limited.

Association of Chief Police Officers in Scotland (ACPOS) (2011) *ACPOS Youth Strategy 2011–2014*. Glasgow: ACPOS.

—— (2012) 'First Chief Constable of the new Police Service of Scotland appointed'. Online. http://acpos.police.uk/News%20Items/News26_09_12b.html (accessed 15 May 2013).

Bandes, S.A. (2011) 'And all the pieces matter: Thoughts on *The Wire* and the criminal justice system'. *Ohio State Journal of Criminal Law*, 8 (2), University of Miami Legal Studies Research Paper No. 2011–19. Online. http://ssrn.com/abstract=1687250 (accessed 25 March 2013).

Bannister, J., Pickering, J., Batchelor, S., Kintrea, K., and McVie, S. (2010) *Troublesome Youth Groups, Gangs and Knife Carrying in Scotland*. Edinburgh: Scottish Government.

Barry, M. (2006) *Youth Offending in Transition: The search for social recognition*. London: Routledge.

—— (2011) 'Explaining youth custody in Scotland: The new crisis of containment and convergence'. *Howard Journal of Criminal Justice*, 50 (2), 153–70.

Bartie, A., and Jackson, L.A. (2011) 'Youth crime and preventive policing in post-war Scotland (c.1945–71)'. *Twentieth Century British History*, 22 (1), 79–102.

Battin-Pearson, S.R., Hill, K.G., Abbott, R.D., Catalano, R.F., and Hawkins, J.D. (1998) 'The contribution of gang membership to delinquency beyond delinquent friends'. *Criminology*, 36, 93–116.

Bauman, Z. (2012) *Liquid Modernity*. Cambridge: Polity Press.

Bayley, D.H., and Mendelsohn, H. (1969) *Minorities and the Police*. New York: The Free Press.

Bayley, D.H., and Nixon, C. (2010) 'The changing environment for policing, 1985–2008' (New Perspectives in Policing series). Cambridge, MA: Harvard Kennedy School and NIJ.

Bennett, T., and Holloway, K. (2004) 'Gang membership, drugs and crime in the UK'. *British Journal of Criminology*, 44 (3), 305–23.

Bereswill, M. (2011) 'Inside out: Transitions from prison to everyday life: A qualitative longitudinal approach'. In Farrall, S., Hough, M., Maruna, S., and Sparks, R. (eds) *Escape Routes: Contemporary Perspectives on Life after Punishment*. Abingdon: Routledge.

Bernard, T.J., and Engel, R.S. (2001) 'Conceptualising criminal justice theory'. *Justice Quarterly*, 18, 1–30.

Bibb, M. (1967) 'Gang related services of mobilization for youth'. In Klein, M. (ed.) *Juvenile Gangs in Context: Theory, research and action*. New Jersey: Prentice Hall.

Billingsley, A., and Caldwell, C.H. (1991) 'The church, the family and the school in the African American community'. *Journal of Negro Education*, 60 (3), 427–40.

Black, D. (1980) *The Manners and Customs of Police*. New York: Academic Press.

Bottoms, A., and Shapland, J. (2011) 'Steps towards desistance amongst male young adult recidivists'. In Farrall, S., Sparks, R., Hough, M., and Maruna, S. (eds) *Escape Routes: Contemporary perspectives on life after punishment*. London, UK: Routledge.

Bottoms, A., Shapland, J., Costellos, A., Holmes, D., and Muir, G. (2004) 'Towards desistance: Theoretical underpinnings for an empirical study'. *Howard Journal of Criminal Justice*, 43 (4), 368–89.

Bourdieu, P. (1990) *In Other Words: Essay towards a reflexive sociology*. Cambridge: Polity Press.

Bradshaw, P. (2005) 'Terrors and young teams: Youth gangs and delinquency in Edinburgh'. In Decker, S.H., and Weerman, F.M. (eds) *European Street Gangs and Troublesome Youth Groups*. Lanham: Altamira Press.

Braga, A. (2001) 'The effects of hot spots policing on crime'. *Annals of the American Academy*, 578, 104–25.

—— (2008) 'Pulling levers focused deterrence strategies and the prevention of gun homicide'. *Journal of Criminal Justice*, 36, 332–43.

Braga, A., Kennedy, D., Waring, E., and Piehl, A. (2001) 'Problem-oriented policing, deterrence, and youth violence: An evaluation of Boston's Operation Ceasefire'. *Journal of Research in Crime and Delinquency*, 38, 195–225.

Braga, A., and Weisburd, D. (2012a) 'The effects of focused deterrence strategies on crime: A systematic review and meta-analysis of the empirical evidence'. *Journal of Research in Crime and Delinquency*, 49 (3), 323–58.

—— (2012b) *The Effects of 'Pulling Levers' Focused Deterrence Strategies on Crime*. Oslo: The Campbell Collaboration.

Braga, A., Weisburd, D.L., Waring, E.J., Mazerolle, L.G., Spelman, W., and Gajewski, F. (1999) 'Problem-oriented policing in violent crime places: A randomized controlled experiment'. *Criminology*, 37, 541–80.

Bullock, K., and Tilley, N. (2002) *Gangs, Shootings and Violent Incidents in Manchester: Developing a crime reduction strategy*, Crime Reduction Research Series Paper 13. London: Home Office.

—— (2003) *Crime Reduction and Problem-oriented Policing*. Cullompton: Willan.

Burke, R.H. (2004) 'Introduction'. In Burke, R.H. (ed.) *Hard Cop, Soft Cop: Dilemmas and debates in contemporary policing*. Cullompton: Willan.

Button, M. (2004) '"Softly, softly": Private security and the policing of corporate space'. In Burke, R.H. (ed.) *Hard Cop, Soft Cop: Dilemmas and debates in contemporary policing*. Cullompton: Willan.

Campbell, B. (1993) *Goliath: Britain's dangerous places*. London: Methuen.

Carnochan, J., and McCluskey, K. (2010) 'Violence, culture and policing in Scotland'. In Donnelly, D., and Scott, K. (eds) *Policing Scotland*. 2nd ed. Abingdon: Willan.

Carr, P.J., Napolitano, L., and Keating, J. (2007) 'We never call the cops and here is why: A qualitative examination of legal cynicism in three Philadelphia neighbourhoods'. *Criminology*, 45 (2), 445–80.

Centre for Social Justice (2009) *Dying to Belong: An in-depth review of street gangs in Britain*. London: Centre for Social Justice.

Chan, J.B.L. (1997) *Changing Police Culture: Policing in a multicultural society*. Cambridge: Cambridge University Press.

Chare, N. (2011) 'Policing technology: Listening to cop culture in *The Wire*'. *Journal for Cultural Research*, 15 (1), 15–33.

Christie, C. (2011) *Commission on the Future Delivery of Public Services*. Edinburgh: Scottish Government.

Clarke, C. (2006) 'Proactive policing: Standing on the shoulders of community-based policing'. *Police Practice and Research*, 7 (1), 3–17.

Clayton, B., and Harris, J. (2009) 'Sport and metrosexual identity: Sports media and emergent sexualities'. In Harris, J., and Parker, A. (eds) *Sport and Social Identities*. Hampshire: Palgrave Macmillan.

Cloward, R., and Ohlin, L. (1960) *Delinquency and Opportunity: A theory of delinquent gangs*. New York: The Free Press.

Coburn, A., and Wallace, D. (2011) *Youth Work in Communities and Schools*. Edinburgh: Dunedin.

Cohen, A.K. (1955) *Delinquent Boys: The culture of the gang*. New York: The Free Press.

Coleman, G., and Cunningham, P. (1996) *African American Stories of Triumph over Adversity: Joy cometh in the morning*. Westport, CT: Bergin and Garvey.

Collins, M., and Kay, T. (2003) *Sport and Social Exclusion*. London: Routledge.

Community Learning and Development (CLD) Standards Council for Scotland (2009) *The Competences for Community Learning and Development*. Glasgow: CLD Standards Council.

Connell, R.W. (1987) *Gender and Power*. Cambridge: Polity Press.

Corsaro, N., Hunt, E.D., Hipple, N.K., and McGarrell, E.F. (2012) 'The impact of drug market pulling levers policing on neighborhood violence'. *Criminology and Public Policy*, 11, 167–99.

Crawford, A. (2009) 'Criminalizing sociability through anti-social behaviour legislation: Dispersal powers, young people and the police'. *Youth Justice*, 9 (1), 5–26.

Cressey, D.R. (1955) 'Changing criminals: The application of the theory of differential association'. *American Journal of Sociology*, 61 (2), 116–20.

Cullen, F.T., and Gendreau, P. (2000) 'Assessing correctional rehabilitation: Policy, practice and prospects'. In Horney, J. (ed.) *Policies, Processes and Decisions of the Criminal Justice System*. Washington DC: National Institute of Justice.

Cullen, F.T., Wright J.P., and Chamlin, M.B. (1999) 'Social support and social reform: A progressive crime control agenda'. *Crime and Delinquency*, 45 (2), 188–207.

Curry, G.D., Decker, S.H., and Egley, A., Jr. (2002) 'Gang involvement and delinquency in a middle school population'. *Justice Quarterly*, 19, 275–92.

Daily Record (2013) 'Gangs of Britain: New series sees Kemp Brothers uncover the past and present of Britain's criminal underbelly'. 20 April. Online. www.dailyrecord.co.uk/news/crime/gangs-britain-new-series-sees-1842306 (accessed 20 May 2013).

Davies, B. (1999) *From Thatcherism to New Labour: A history of the Youth Service in England, Volume 2: 1979–1999*. Leicester: Youth Work Press.

—— (2009) 'Defined by history: Youth work in the UK'. In Verschelden, G., Coussée, F., Van de Walle, T., and Williamson, H. (eds) *The History of Youth Work in Europe and its Relevance for Youth Policy Today*. Strasbourg: Council of Europe Publishing.

Decker, S. (2007) 'Expand the use of police gang units'. *Criminology and Public Policy*, 6 (4), 729–34.

Decker, S., Bynum, T.S. McDevitt, J., Farrell, A., and Varano, S. (2008) *Street Outreach Workers: Best practices and lessons learned*. Boston, MA: Northeastern University.

Decker, S., and Van Winkle, B. (1996) *Life in the Gang: Family, friends, and violence*. New York: Cambridge University Press.

DeJong, C., Mastrofski, S., and Parks, R. (2001) 'Patrol officers and problem solving: An application of expectancy theory'. *Justice Quarterly*, 18: 31–61.

Deuchar, R. (2009a) *Gangs, Marginalised Youth and Social Capital*. Stoke on Trent: Trentham.

—— (2009b) 'United front can help youngsters escape violence'. *The Herald*, 17 February.

—— (2010a) 'Brave new approach to ending gang violence'. *The Scotsman*, 5 April.

—— (2010b) '"It's just pure harassment ... as if it's a crime to walk in the street": Anti-social behaviour, youth justice and citizenship – the reality for young men in the east end of Glasgow'. *Youth Justice*, 10 (3), 258–74.

—— (2011) '"People look at us, the way we dress, and they think we're gangsters": Bonds, bridges, gangs and refugees – a qualitative study of inter-cultural social capital in Glasgow'. *Journal of Refugee Studies*, 24 (4), 672–89.

—— (2012) 'The impact of curfews and electronic monitoring on the social strains, support and capital experienced by youth gang members and offenders in the West of Scotland'. *Criminology and Criminal Justice*, 12 (2), 113–28.

Deuchar, R., and Ellis, J. (2013) '"It's helped me with my anger and I'm realising where I go in life": The impact of a Scottish youth work/schools intervention on young people's responses to social strain and engagement with anti-social behaviour and gang culture'. *Research in Post-Compulsory Education – Special Issue: Reclaiming the Disengaged?*, 18 (1–2), 98–114.

Deuchar, R., and Holligan, C. (2010) 'Gangs, sectarianism and social capital: A qualitative study of young people in Scotland'. *Sociology*, 44 (1), 13–30.

Deuchar, R., Miller, J., and Hunter, I. (2012) *The Impact of the 'Space Unlimited' Integration Project*. Paisley: University of the West of Scotland.

Dolowitz, D., and Marsh, D. (2000) 'Learning from abroad: The role of policy transfer in contemporary policy-making'. *Governance*, 13, 5–24.

Donnelly, D. (2010) 'Policing the Scottish community'. In Donnelly, D. and Scott, K. (eds) *Policing Scotland*. 2nd ed. Abingdon: Willan.

Donnelly, D., and Scott, K. (2010) 'Introduction: policing Scotland'. In Donnelly, D., and Scott, K. (eds) *Policing Scotland*. 2nd ed. Abingdon: Willan.

Donnelly, P.D. (2013) 'An overview of research on violence reduction at the University of St Andrew's'. *Scottish Institute for Policing Research Annual Report*. Dundee: SIPR.

Donnelly, P.D., and Tombs, J. (2008) 'An unusual day in court'. *British Medical Journal*, 337 (a2959), 1419

Donohue, J.J., and Levitt, S.D. (2001) 'The impact of legalized abortion on crime'. *Quarterly Journal of Economics*, 116 (2), 379–420.

Du Bois, W.E.B. (1953) *The Souls of Black Folk*. New York: The Modern Library.

Duran, R.J. (2009) 'Legitimated oppression: Inner-city Mexican American experiences with police gang enforcement'. *Journal of Contemporary Ethnography*, 38 (2), 143–68.

Durie, R., Wyatt, K., and Stuteley, H. (2004) 'Community regeneration and complexity'. In Kernick, D. (ed.) *Complexity and Healthcare Organisation: A view from the street*. London: Radcliffe Medical Press.

Durkheim, E. (1897/1952) *Suicide*. London: Routledge.

—— (1938) *The Rules of Sociological Method*. New York: The Free Press.

Dyson, M.E. (ed.) (1996) *Between God and Gangsta Rap: Bearing witness to black culture*. New York: Oxford University Press.

Earle, R. (2011) 'Boys and zone stories: Perspectives from a young men's prison'. *Criminology and Criminal Justice*, 11 (2), 129–43.

Eck, J.E., and Maguire, E. (2000) 'Have changes in policing reduced violent crime? An assessment of the evidence'. In Blumstein, A., and Wallman, J. (eds) *The Crime Drop in America*. Cambridge, UK: Cambridge University Press.

Eck, J.E., and Rothman, J. (2006) 'Police–community conflict and crime prevention in Cincinnati, Ohio: The collaborative agreement'. In Bailey, J. (ed.) *Public Security and Police Reform in the Americas*. Pittsburgh, PA: University of Pittsburgh Press.

Eck, J.E., and Spelman, W. (1987) *Problem-Solving: Problem-oriented policing in Newport News*. Washington, DC: Police Executive Research Forum.

Emerson, R.M., Fretz, R., and Shaw, L. (1995) *Writing Ethnographic Fieldnotes*. Chicago: University of Chicago Press.

Engel, R.S. (2003) 'Explaining suspects' resistance and disrespect toward police'. *Journal of Criminal Justice*, 31, 475–92.

Engel, R.S., and Johnson, R. (2006) 'Toward a better understanding of racial and ethnic disparities in search and seizure rates'. *Journal of Criminal Justice*, 34, 605–17.

Engel, R.S., Skubak-Tillyer, M., and Corsaro, N. (2013) 'Reducing gang violence using focused deterrence: Evaluating the Cincinnati Initiative to Reduce Violence (CIRV)'. *Justice Quarterly*, 30 (3), 403–39.

Engel, R.S., and Swartz, K. (2013) 'Race, crime, and policing'. In Bucerius, S.M., and Tonry, M. (eds) *Oxford Handbook on Ethnicity, Crime, and Immigration*. New York: Oxford Press.

Engel, R.S., and Whalen, J.L. (2010) 'Police academic partnerships: Ending the dialogue of the deaf, the Cincinnati experience'. *Police Practice and Research*, 11, 105–16.

Esbensen, F-A., and Huizinga, D. (1993) 'Gangs, drugs and delinquency in a survey of urban youth'. *Criminology*, 31 (4), 565–89.

Evans, D., Cullen, F.T., Dunaway, G., and Burton, V. (1995) 'Religion and crime reexamined: The impact of religion, secular controls and social ecology on adult criminality'. *Criminology*, 33, 195–224.

Fagan, J., and Davies, G. (2000) 'Crime in public housing: Two-way diffusion effects in surrounding neighbourhoods'. In Goldsmith, V., McGuire, P.G., Mollenkopf, J.H., and Ross, T.A. (eds) *Analysing Crime Patterns: Frontiers of practice*. Thousand Oaks, CA: Sage.

Farrington, D.P. (1997) 'Human development and criminal careers'. In Maguire, M., Morgan, R., and Reiner, R. (eds) *The Oxford Handbook of Criminology*. 2nd ed. Oxford: Clarendon.

Fine, G. (1993) 'Ten lies of ethnography'. *Journal of Contemporary Ethnography*, 22 (5), 267–94.

Fine, M., Freudenberg, N., Payne, Y., Perkins, T., Smith, K., and Wanzer, K. (2003) 'Anything can happen with police around: Urban youth evaluate strategies of surveillance in public places'. *Journal of Social Issues*, 59, 141–58.

Fiori-Khayat, C. (2008) 'Ethnicity and juvenile street gangs in France'. In Van Gemert, F., Peterson, D., and Lien, I.L. (eds) *Street Gangs, Migration and Ethnicity*. Portland: Willan.

Fraser, A., Burman, M., Batchelor, S., and McVie, S. (2010) *Youth Violence in Scotland: Literature review*. Online. www.scotland.gov.uk/Resource/Doc/326952/0105428.pdf (accessed 7 December 2012).

Freire, P. (1972) *Pedagogy of the Oppressed*. Harmondsworth: Penguin.

Gambetta, D. (2009) *Codes of the Underworld: How criminals communicate*. New Jersey: Princeton University Press.

Garcia, V. (2005) 'Constructing the "other" within police culture: An analysis of a deviant unit within the police organization'. *Police Practice and Research*, 6 (1), 65–80.

General Register Office for Scotland (2011) *Information about Scotland's People*. Online. www.gro-scotland.gov.uk/index.html (accessed 20 October 2012).

Gillen, J. (2009) 'The cooperation of narrative in an entrepreneurial city: An analysis of Cincinnati, Ohio, in turmoil'. *Geografiska Annaler Series B: Human Geography*, 91 (2), 107–22.

Giordano, P.C., Longmore, M.A., Schroeder, R.D., and Sefrin, P.M. (2008) 'A life-course perspective on spirituality and desistance from crime'. *Criminology*, 46 (1), 99–132.

Glasgow Community and Safety Services (2008) 'Community Initiative to Reduce Violence (CIRV): Oversight group strategy paper'. Glasgow: GCSS.

—— (2012) *Youth Disorder: Quarter 3: 2011/2012 Comparison*. Glasgow: GCSS.

Glasgow Community Planning Partnership (GCPP) (2011) *One Glasgow*. Glasgow: GCPP.

Gold, R. (1958) 'Roles in sociological field observation'. *Social Forces*, 36, 217–23.

Goldstein, H. (1979) 'Improving policing: A problem-oriented approach'. *Crime and Delinquency*, 25, 236–58.

—— (1990) *Problem-oriented Policing*. New York: McGraw-Hill.

Goldstein, J. (1960) 'Police discretion not to invoke the criminal process: Low-visibility decisions in the administration of justice'. *Yale Law Journal*, 69, 543–89.

—— (1963) 'Police discretion: The ideal versus the real'. *Public Administration Review*, 23, 140–8.

—— (1977) *Policing a Free Society*. Cambridge, MA: Ballinger.

Gormally, S., and Deuchar, R. (2012) 'Young people, the police and anti-social behaviour management in the west of Scotland'. *International Journal on School Disaffection*, 9 (1), 51–66.

Gould, J.B. and Mastrofski, S. (2004) 'Suspect searches: Assessing police behavior under the constitution'. *Criminology and Public Policy*, 3, 316–62.

Gov.UK (2013) 'Drugs penalties'. Online. www.gov.uk/penalties-drug-possession-dealing (accessed 14 May 2013).

Graham, W. (2012) '"Pulling levers" in Scotland to tackle gangs and violent crime: A comparative analysis of international criminal justice policy transfer'. Presented at the American Society of Criminology Conference, Chicago, November.

Greenberg, B., Elliott, C.V., Kraft, L.P., and Proctor, H.S. (1975) *Felony Investigation Decision Model – An analysis of investigative elements of information*. Menlo Park, CA: Stanford Research Institute.

Greenwood, P.W., Chaiken, J., Petersilia, M., and Prusoff, L. (1975) *Criminal Investigation Process, III: Observations and analysis*. Santa Monica, CA: Rand Corporation.

Gutierrez Riviera, L. (2010) 'Discipline or punish? Youth gangs' responses to "zero tolerance" policies in Honduras'. *Bulletin of Latin American Research*, 29 (4), 492–504.

Hagedorn, J. (1998) *People and Folks: Gangs, crime and the underclass in a Rustbelt city*. 2nd ed. Chicago: Lakeview Press.

—— (2008) *A World of Gangs: Armed young men and gangsta culture*. Minneapolis: University of Minnesota Press.

Haigh, Y. (2009) 'Desistance from crime: Reflections on the transitional experiences of young people with a history of offending'. *Journal of Youth Studies*, 12 (3), 307–22.

Hallsworth, S. (2011) 'Gangland Britain? Realities, fantasies and industry'. In Goldson, B. (ed.) *Youth in Crisis: Gangs, territoriality and violence*. London: Routledge.

Hallsworth, S., and Young, T. (2008) 'Gang talk and gang talkers: A critique'. *Crime Media Culture*, 4 (2), 175–95.

Halpin, T. (2010) 'Crime investigation in Scotland'. In Donnelly, D. and Scott, K. (eds) *Policing Scotland*. 2nd ed. Abingdon: Willan.

Hammersley, M. (2006) 'Ethnography: Problems and prospects'. *Ethnography and Education*, 1 (1), 3–14.

Hammersley, M., and Atkinson, P. (2007) *Ethnography: Principles in practice*. London: Routledge.

Hay, D., and Nye, R. (1998) *The Spirit of the Child*. London: HarperCollins.

Herbert, S. (2001) '"Hard charger" or "station queen"? Policing and the masculinist state'. *Gender, Place and Culture*, 8 (1), 55–71.

Higgins, P.C., and Albrecht, G.L. (1977) 'Hellfire and delinquency revisited'. *Social Forces*, 55, 952–8.

Hodgson, J.F. (2001) 'Police violence in Canada and USA: Analysis and management'. *Policing: An International Journal of Police Strategies and Management*, 24 (4), 520–49.

Holligan, C., and Deuchar, R. (2009) 'Territorialities in Scotland: Perceptions of young people in Glasgow'. *Journal of Youth Studies*, 12 (6), 727–42.

Home Office (2011) *Ending Gang and Youth Violence: A cross-government report including further evidence and good practice case studies*. London: Stationery Office.

Hucklesby, A. (2009) 'Understanding offenders' compliance: A case study of electronically monitored curfew orders'. *Journal of Law and Society*, 36 (2), 248–71.

Huebner, B.M., Varano, S.P., and Bynum, T.S. (2007) 'Gangs, guns and drugs: Recidivism among serious, young offenders'. *Criminology and Public Policy*, 6 (2), 187–222.

Huff, C.R. (1998) 'Comparing the criminal behavior of youth gangs and at-risk youths'. *National Institute of Justice Research Brief*, October.

Includem (2010) *Includem's Framework of Intervention*. Glasgow: Includem.

Jang, S.J., and Johnson, B.R. (2001) 'Neighbourhood disorder, individual religiosity and adolescent use of illicit drugs: A test of multilevel hypotheses'. *Criminology*, 39, 109–44.

Jankowski, M.S. (1991) *Islands in the Street: Gangs and American urban society*. Los Angeles: University of California Press.

Jeffs, T., and Smith, M. (2005) *Informal Education: Conversation, democracy and learning*. Nottingham: Educational Heretics Press.

Joe, D., and Robinson, N. (1980) 'Chinatown's immigrant gangs'. *Criminology*, 18 (3), 337–45.

Johnson, R.R. (2001) 'The psychological influence of the police uniform'. *The Law Enforcement Bulletin*, 70 (3), 27–32.

Karmen, A. (2004) 'Zero tolerance in New York City: Hard questions for a get-tough policy'. In Burke, R.H. (ed.) *Hard Cop, Soft Cop: Dilemmas and debates in contemporary policing*. Cullompton: Willan.

Karp, S., and Stenmark, H. (2011) 'Learning to be a police officer: Tradition and change in the training and professional lives of police officers'. *Police Practice and Research: An International Journal*, 12 (1), 4–15.

Katz, C.M., and Webb, V.J. (2006) *Policing Gangs in America*. New York: Cambridge University Press.

Kelling, G.L., Pate, A.M., Dieckman, D., and Brown, C.E. (1974) *The Kansas City Preventive Patrol Experiment: Summary report*. Washington, DC: The Police Foundation.

Kelling, G.L., Pate, A.M, Ferrara, A., Utne, M., and Brown, C.E. (1981) *Newark Foot Patrol Experiment*. Washington, DC: Police Foundation.

Kennedy, D.M. (1997) 'Pulling levers: Chronic offenders, high-crime settings and a theory of prevention'. *Valparaiso University Law Review*, 31 (2), 449–84.

—— (2009) *Deterrence and Crime Prevention: Reconsidering the prospect of sanction*. New York: Routledge.

—— (2011) *Don't Shoot: One man, a street fellowship, and the end of violence in inner-city America*. New York: Bloomsbury.

Kennedy, D.M. and Braga, A. (1998) 'Homicide in Minneapolis: Research for problem-solving'. *Homicide Studies*, 2, 263–90.

Kennedy, R. (1997) *Race, Crime, and the Law*. New York: Pantheon Books.

Khan, F., and Hill, M. (2007) *Evaluation of Includem's Intensive Support Services*. Glasgow: Includem.

Kintrea, K., Bannister, J., and Pickering, J. (2011) '"It's just an area – everybody represents it": exploring young people's territorial behaviour in British cities'. In Goldson, B. (ed.) *Youth in Crisis? 'Gangs', territoriality and violence*. London: Routledge.

Kintrea, K., Bannister, J., Pickering, J., Suruki, N., and Reid, M. (2008) *Young People and Territoriality in British Cities*. York: Joseph Rowntree Foundation.

Klein, M. (1971) *Street Gangs and Street Workers*. New Jersey: Prentice Hall.

—— (2008) 'Foreword'. In Van Gemert, F., Petersen, D., and Lien, I.L. (eds) *Street Gangs, Migration and Ethnicity*. Collumpton: Willan.

Klein, M., Weerman, F.M., and Thornberry, T.P. (2006) 'Street gang violence in Europe'. *European Journal of Criminology*, 3 (4), 413–37.

Klepal, D. and Andrews, C. (2001) 'Stories of 15 black men killed by police since 1995'. *Cincinnati Enquirer*, 15 April.

Krug, E.G., Dahlberg, L.L., Mercy, J.A., Zwi, A.B., and Lozano, R. (2002) *World Report on Violence and Health*. Geneva: World Health Organization.

Kupers, T.A. (2005) 'Toxic masculinity as a barrier to mental health treatment in prisons'. *Journal of Clinical Psychology*, 61 (6), 713–24.

LaFave, W. (1962) 'The police and nonenforcment of the law – Part I'. *Wisconsin Law Review*, 240, 104–37.

Lammy, D. (2011) *Out of the Ashes: Britain after the riots*. London: Guardian Books.

Laub, J.H., and Sampson, R.J. (2001) 'Understanding desistance from crime'. In Tonry, M.H. and Norris, N. (eds) *Crime and Justice: An annual review of research*. Chicago: University of Chicago Press.

Laub, J.H., and Sampson, R.J. (2003) *Shared Beginnings, Divergent Lives: Delinquent boys to age 70*. Cambridge, MA: Harvard University Press.

Learning and Teaching Scotland (LTS) (2009) *Bridging the Gap: Improving outcomes for Scotland's young people through school and youth work partnerships*. Glasgow: LTS.

Lee, J. (1999) *Spiritual Development*. London: United Reform Church.

Levitt, S.D. (2004) 'Understanding why crime fell in the 1990s: Four factors that explain the decline and six that do not'. *Journal of Economic Perspectives*, 18 (1), 163–90.

Leyland, A.H. (2006) 'Homicides involving knives and other sharp objects in Scotland, 1981–2003'. *Journal of Public Health*, 28 (2), 145–7.

Leyland, A.H., and Dundas, R. (2010) 'The social patterning of deaths due to assault in Scotland, 1980–2005: Population-based study'. *Journal of Epidemiology and Community Health*, 64, 432–9.

Lilly, J.R., Cullen, F.T., and Ball, R.A. (2011) *Criminological Theory: Contexts and consequences*. Los Angeles: Sage.

Lincoln, C.E. (1989) 'The Black church and black self-determination'. Paper presented at the Association of Black Foundation Executives, Kansas City, MO, April.

Lindsay, R. (2012) 'Glasgow, the most violent and depraved city in all of Europe'. *Beyond Highbrow – Robert Lindsay*. Online. http://robertlindsay.wordpress.com/2012/08/07/glascow-the-most-violent-and-depraved-city-in-all-of-europe/ (accessed 25 October 2012).

Local 12 News (2010) 'Dozens arrested in local gang roundup'. 22 February. Online. http://tinyurl.com/q5ugazv (accessed 28 August 2013).

Loeber, R., Kalb, L., and Huizinga, D. (2001) 'Juvenile delinquency and serious injury victimization'. *Juvenile Justice Bulletin*. Office of Juvenile Justice and Delinquency Prevention. Washington DC: US Department of Justice, Office of Justice Programs.

Loftin, C., and McDowell, D. (1982) 'The police, crime, and economic theory: An assessment'. *American Sociological Review, 47*, 393–401.

MacDonald, R., Webster, C., Shildrick, T., and Simpson, M. (2011) 'Paths of exclusion, inclusion and desistance'. In Farrall, S., Hough, M., Maruna, S., and Sparks, R. (eds) *Escape Routes: Contemporary perspectives on life after punishment*. London: Routledge.

Maruna, S. (2001) *Making Good: How ex-convicts reform and rebuild their lives*. Washington DC: American Psychological Association.

Maruna, S., and Farrall, S. (2004) 'Desistance from crime: A theoretical reformulation'. *Kolner Zeitschrift fur Soziologie und Sozialpsychologie, 43*, 171–94.

Mastrofski, S., Snipes, J.B., Parks, R.B., and Maxwell, C.D. (2000) 'The helping hand of the law: Police control of citizens on request'. *Criminology, 38*, 307–42.

Mastrofski, S., Snipes, J., and Supina, A. (1996) 'Compliance on demand: The public's response to specific police requests'. *Journal of Research in Crime and Delinquency, 33*, 269–305.

Mattick, H., and Kaplan, N.S. (1967) 'Stake animals, loud-talking leadership in do-nothing and do-something situations'. In Klein, M.W., and Myerhoff , B.G. (eds) *Juvenile Gangs in Context: Theory, research and action*. New Jersey: Prentice Hall.

Matza, D. (1964) *Delinquency and Drift*. New Jersey: Prentice-Hall.

—— (1969) *Becoming Deviant*. New Jersey: Prentice-Hall.

May, L. (2009) 'Cincinnati Works to share model for poverty reduction across U.S.'. *Business Courier*, 4 May. Online. www.bizjournals.com/cincinnati/stories/2009/05/04/story3.html?page=all (accessed 14 May 2013).

McAra, L., and McVie, S. (2005) 'The usual suspects?: Street-life, young people and the police'. *Criminal Justice, 5* (5), 5–36.

McDowell, L. (2003) *Redundant Masculinities?: Employment change and white working class youth*. Oxford: Blackwell.

McGloin, J.M. (2009) 'Delinquency balance: Revisiting peer influence'. *Criminology, 47*, 439–77.

McHugh, R. (2013) 'Ex-gang members in gang intervention practice: Superman, Clark Kent and Nietzsche'. Paper presented at the BERA/TAG Symposium *Street Violence, State Violence, Symbolic Violence: How does youth and community work respond?*, University of the West of Scotland, Hamilton, May.

McNeill, F. (2003) 'Desistance-focused probation practice'. In Hong Chui, W., and Nellis, M. (eds) *Moving Probation Forward: Evidence, arguments and practice.* Harlow: Pearson Longman.

—— (2004) 'Desistance, rehabilitation and correctionalism: Developments and prospects in Scotland', *The Howard Journal*, 43 (4), 420–36.

—— (2009) 'What works and what's just?'. *European Journal of Probation*, 1 (1), 21–40.

—— (2012) 'Four forms of "offender rehabilitation": Towards an interdisciplinary perspective'. *Legal and Criminological Psychology*, 17 (1), 18–36.

McNeill, F., and Maruna, S. (2008) 'Desistance, generativity and social work with offenders'. In McIvor, G., and Raynor, P. (eds) *Developments in Social Work With Offenders.* London: Jessica Kingsley.

McNeill, F., and Whyte, B. (2007) *Reducing Reoffending: Social work and community justice in Scotland.* Cullompton: Willan.

Mead, D. (2002) 'Informed consent to police searches in England and Wales: A critical re-appraisal in the light of the Human Rights Act'. *Criminal Law Review*, 791–804.

Mecklenborg, J. (2012) 'What's the story behind Cincinnati's 50-year population decline?'. *UrbanCincy*, 26 July. Online. www.urbancincy.com/2012/07/whats-the-full-story-behind-cincinnatis-50-year-population-decline/ (accessed 7 May 2013).

Meltzer, H., Doos, L., Vostanis, P., Ford, T., and Goodman, R. (2009) 'The mental health of children who witness domestic violence'. *Child and Family Social Work*, 14, 491–501.

Merton, R. (1938) 'Social structure and anomie'. *American Sociological Review*, 3, 372–682.

Messerschmidt, J. (1993) *Masculinities and Crime: Critique and reconceptualisation of theory.* Lanham, MD: Rowman and Littlefield.

Miller, D. (2008) *The Comfort of Things.* Cambridge: Polity Press.

Mittell, J. (2009) 'All in the game: *The Wire*, serial storytelling and procedural logic'. In Harrigan, P., and Wardrip-Fruin, N. (eds) *Third Person: Authoring and exploring vast narratives.* Cambridge, MA: MIT Press.

Muir Jr., W.K. (1977) *Police: Streetcorner politicians.* Chicago: University of Chicago Press.

Muncie, J. (2000) 'Youth victimization'. *Criminal Justice Matters*, 41 (1), 20–1.

—— (2009) *Youth and Crime.* 3rd ed. London: Sage.

National Advisory Commission on Civil Disorders (1968) *The National Advisory Commission on Civil Disorders (The Kerner Report).* New York: Bantam Books.

National Network for Safe Communities (NNSC) (2013) homepage mission statement. Online. www.nnscommunities.org

National Research Council (2004) *Fairness and Effectiveness in Policing: The evidence.* Washington, DC: National Academies Press.

Needle, J.A., and Stapleton, W.V. (1983) *Police Handling of Youth Gangs.* Washington DC: US Department of Justice. Online. www.ncjrs.gov/App/Publications/abstract.aspx?Id=88927 (accessed 14 May 2013).

Nelson, I. (2010) 'A night on the slash'. *The Sun*, 25 August. Online. www.thesun. co.uk/sol/homepage/news/scottishnews/3110586/A-night-on-the-slash-in-Scotland.html (accessed 17 May 2013).

Newburn, T. (2013) *Criminology*. 2nd ed. Oxon: Routledge.

Nicholson, J. (2010) 'Young people and the police in Scotland'. In Donnelly, D., and Scott, K. (eds) *Policing Scotland*. 2nd ed. Abingdon: Willan.

Novak, K. J., Frank, J., Smith, B.W., and Engel, R.S. (2002) 'Revisiting the decision to arrest: Comparing beat and community officers'. *Crime and Delinquency*, 48 (1), 70–98.

Nurden, H. (2010) 'Working with faith'. In Jeffs, T., and Smith, M.K. (eds) *Youth Work Practice*. Hampshire: Palgrave Macmillan.

Olive, E. (2003) 'The African American child and positive youth development'. In Villaruel, F.A., Perkins, D.F., Borden, L.M., and Keith, J.G. (eds) *Community Youth Development: Programs, policies and practice*. Thousand Oaks, CA: Sage.

Ozer, M.M., and Engel, R.S. (2012) 'Revisiting the use of propensity score matching to understand the relationship between gang membership and violent victimization: A cautionary note'. *Justice Quarterly*, 29 (1), 105–24.

Papachristos, A., Meares, T., and Fagan, J. (2007) 'Attention felons: Evaluating Project Safe Neighborhood in Chicago'. *Journal of Empirical Legal Studies*, 4, 223–72.

Parker, A. (2001) 'Soccer, servitude and sub-cultural identity: Football traineeship and masculine construction'. *Soccer and Society*, 2 (1), 59–80.

Parks, R.B., Mastrofski, S.D., DeJong, C., and Gray, M.K. (1999) 'How officers spend their time with the community'. *Justice Quarterly*, 16, 483–518.

Patrick, J. (1973) *A Glasgow Gang Observed*. London: Eyre Methuen.

—— (2013) 'Preface to the 2013 edition'. In Patrick, J. *A Glasgow Gang Observed*. Glasgow: Neil Wilson Publishing.

Pennycook, J.D. (2010) 'Police powers and human rights in Scotland'. In Scott, K., and Donnelly, D. (eds) *Policing Scotland*. Devon: Willan.

Pitts, J. (2007) *Reluctant Gangsters: Youth gangs in Waltham Forest*. Bedfordshire: University of Bedfordshire.

—— (2008) *Reluctant Gangsters: The changing face of youth crime*. Cullompton: Willan.

—— (2011) 'Mercenary territory: Are youth gangs really a problem?'. In Goldson, B. (ed.) *Youth in Crisis: 'Gangs', territoriality and violence*. London: Routledge.

Puffer, J.A. (1912) *The Boy and his Gang*. Chicago: Houghton Mifflin Company.

Quinton, P., Bland, N., and Miller, J. (2000) *Police Stops, Decision-Making and Practice*. London: Home Office Policing and Reducing Crime Unit – Research, Development and Statistics Directorate.

Ralphs, R., Medina, J., and Aldridge, J. (2009) 'Who needs enemies with friends like these? The importance of place for young people living in known gangs areas'. *Journal of Youth Studies*, 12 (5), 483–500.

Reid, R. (2011) 'Behind closed doors: Slowing the cycle of reoffending'. *Holyrood*, 25 April. Online. www.holyrood.com/2011/04/behind-closed-doors/ (accessed 21 July 2013)

Reiner, R. (2010) *The Politics of the Police*. Oxford: Oxford University Press.

Reiss, A.J., Jr. (1971) *The Police and the Public*. New Haven, CT: Yale University Press.

Riksheim, E.C., and Chermak, S.M. (1993) 'Causes of police behavior revisited'. *Journal of Criminal Justice,* 21, 353–82.

Robson. K. (2009) 'Teenage time use as investment in cultural capital'. In Robson, K., and Sanders, C. (eds) *Quantifying Theory: Pierre Bourdieu.* London: Springer.

Rodriguez, M.C., Morrobel, D., and Villaruel, F.A. (2003) 'Research realities and a vision of success for Latino youth development'. In Villaruel, F.A., Perkins, D.F., Borden, L.M., and Keith, J.G. (eds) *Community Youth Development: Programs, policies and practice.* Thousand Oaks, CA: Sage.

Rohrbaugh, J., and Jessor, R. (1975) 'Religiosity in youth: A personal control against deviant behavior'. *Journal of Personality,* 43 (1), 136–55.

Rose, N. (2000) 'Government and control'. *British Journal of Criminology,* 40 (2), 321–39.

Rosenfeld, R., Bray, T.M., and Egley, A. (1999) 'Facilitating violence: A comparison of gang-motivated, gang-affiliated, and non-gang youth homicides'. *Journal of Quantitative Criminology,* 15, 495–516.

Rosich, K.J. (2007) *Race, Ethnicity and the Criminal Justice System.* Washington DC: American Sociological Association.

Sampson, A., and Themelis, S. (2009) 'Working in the community with young people who offend'. *Journal of Youth Studies,* 12 (2), 121–37.

Sandford, R.A., Armour, K.M., and Warmington, P.C. (2006) 'Re-engaging disaffected youth through physical activity programmes'. *British Educational Research Journal,* 32 (2), 251–71.

Scalia, J. (2001) 'The impact of change in federal law and policy on the sentencing of, and time served in prison by, drug defendants convicted in US district courts'. *Federal Sentencing Reporter,* 14, 152–8.

Schulhofer, S.T., Tyler, T.R., and Huq, A.Z. (2011) 'American policing at a crossroads: Unsustainable policies and the procedural justice alternative'. *Journal of Criminal Law and Criminology,* 101 (2), 335–75.

Scottish Executive (2002) *Scotland's Action Programme to Reduce Youth Crime.* Edinburgh: Scottish Executive.

—— (2006) *Getting it Right for Every Child: Implementation plan.* Edinburgh: Scottish Executive.

—— (2007) *Moving Forward: A strategy for improving young people's chances through youth work.* Edinburgh: Scottish Executive.

Scottish Government (2007) *Revised Figures for Homicides in Scotland in 2005/06.* Edinburgh: Scottish Government.

—— (2008a) *Equally Well: Report of the ministerial task group on health inequalities.* Edinburgh: Scottish Government.

—— (2008b) *Preventing Offending by Young People: A framework for action.* Edinburgh: Scottish Government.

—— (2008c) *Scotland Performs: National outcomes.* Edinburgh: Scottish Government. Online. www.scotland.gov.uk/About/scotPerforms/outcomes (accessed 14 May 2013).

—— (2011a) *Diversion from Prosecution Toolkit: Diverting young people from prosecution.* Edinburgh: Scottish Government.

—— (2011b) *Homicide in Scotland 2010–11.* Edinburgh: Scottish Government. Online. www.scccj.org.uk/wp-content/uploads/2011/08/0124207_homicide_scotland_10-11.pdf (accessed 8 May 2013).

—— (2011c) *Reintegration and Transitions: Guidance for local authorities, community planning partnerships and service providers.* Edinburgh: Scottish Government. Online. www.scotland.gov.uk/Resource/Doc/359104/0121332.pdf (accessed 10 January 2013).

—— (2011d) *2010/11 Scottish Crime and Justice Survey: Main findings.* Edinburgh: Scottish Government. Online. www.scotland.gov.uk/Resource/Doc/361684/0122316.pdf (accessed 31 October 2012).

—— (2012) *The Strategy for Justice in Scotland.* Edinburgh: Scottish Government.

—— (2013) *Whole System Approach.* Edinburgh: Scottish Government. Online. www.scotland.gov.uk/Topics/Justice/crimes/youth-justice/reoffending (accessed 15 May 2013).

Scottish Parliament (2012) *Police and Fire Reform (Scotland) Act 2012.* Edinburgh: Scottish Parliament.

Seabrook, J. (2009) 'Don't shoot: A radical approach to the problem of gang violence'. *New Yorker,* 22 June.

Sercombe, H. (2010) *Youth Work Ethics.* London: Sage.

Sharp, D. and Atherton, S. (2007) 'To serve and protect? The experiences of policing in the community of young people from black and other ethnic minority groups'. *British Journal of Criminology,* 47 (5), 746–63.

Shaw, C.R., and McKay, H.D. (1942) *Juvenile Delinquency and Urban Areas.* Chicago: University of Chicago Press.

Sherman, L.W., Gartin, P.R., and Buerger, M.E. (1989) 'Hot spots of predatory crime: Routine activities and the criminology of place'. *Criminology,* 27, 27–55.

Skogan, W. (2006) *Police and Community in Chicago: A tale of three cities.* New York: Oxford University Press, Inc.

Skogan, W., Hartnett, S., Bump, N., and Dubois, J. (2008) *Evaluation of Ceasefire-Chicago.* Evanston, IL: Northwest University, Institute for Policy Research.

Skolnick, J.H. (1966) *Justice Without Trial: Law enforcement in democratic society.* New York: Wiley.

Skolnick, J.H., and Bayley, D.H. (1986) *The New Blue Line: Police innovation in six American cities.* New York: Free Press.

Soothill, K., and Francis, B. (2009) 'When do ex-offenders become like non-offenders?'. *The Howard Journal,* 48 (4), 373–87.

Spelman, W. and Brown, D.K. (1984) *Calling the Police: Citizen Reporting of Serious Crime.* Washington DC: Police Executive Research Forum.

Spergel, I. (1995) *The Youth Gang Program: A community approach.* New York: Oxford University Press.

Sprinkle, J.E. (2006) 'Domestic violence, gun ownership, and parental educational attainment: How do they affect the aggressive beliefs and behaviors of children?'. *Child and Adolescent Social Work Journal,* 24 (2), 133–51.

Squires, P. (2008) 'Introduction: Why "anti-social behaviour"? Debating ASBOs'. In Squires, P. (ed.) *ASBO Nation: The criminalisation of nuisance.* Bristol: Policy Press.

Staley, S. (2001) 'Ground zero in urban decline'. *Reason,* November. Online. http://reason.com/archives/2001/11/01/ground-zero-in-urban-decline (registration required) (accessed 28 August 2013).

Stelfox, P. (1998) 'Policing lower levels of organized crime in England and Wales'. *The Howard Journal of Criminal Justice,* 37 (4), 393–404.

Stradling, D. (2003) *Cincinnati: From river city to highway metropolis*. Charleston, SC: Arcadia.

Strang, D. (2005) 'Policing youth in Scotland: A police perspective'. In Scott, K., and Donnelly, D. (eds) *Policing Scotland*. Devon: Willan.

Strauss A., and Corbin J.M. (1990) *Basics of Qualitative Research: Grounded theory procedures and techniques*. London: Sage.

Sutherland, E.H. (1947) *Principles of Criminology*. 4th ed. Philadelphia: J.B. Lippincott.

Suttles, G.D. (1968) *The Social Order of the Slum: Ethnicity and territory in the inner city*. Chicago: University of Chicago Press.

Sykes, G.M. (1958) 'The pains of imprisonment'. In Sykes, G.M. (ed.) *The Society of Captives: The study of a maximum security prison*. Princeton, NJ: Princeton University Press.

Taylor, T.J., Peterson, D., Esbensen, F-A., and Freng, A. (2007) 'Gang membership as a risk factor for adolescent violent victimization'. *Journal of Research in Crime and Delinquency*, 44, 351–80.

Tett, L. (2010) *Community Education, Learning and Development*. 3rd ed. Edinburgh: Dunedin.

Thornberry, T.P., Krohn, M.D., Lizotte, A.J., Smith, C., and Tobin, K. (2003) *Gang and Delinquency in Developmental Perspective*. New York: Cambridge University Press.

Thornton, P. (2003) *Casuals: Football, fighting and fashion – the story of the terrace cult*. Lancashire: Milo Books.

Thrasher, F.M. (1927) *The Gang: A study of 1,313 gangs in Chicago*. Chicago: University of Chicago Press.

Tilley, N. (2008) 'Modern approaches to policing: Community, problem-oriented and intelligence-led'. In Newburn, T. (ed.) *Handbook of Policing*. 2nd ed. Collumpton: Willan.

Tonry, M.H. (2011) *Punishing Race: A continuing American dilemma*. New York: Oxford Press.

Trojanowicz, R.C., and Bucqueroux, B. (1994) *Community Policing: How to get started*. Cincinnati, OH: Anderson.

Trotter, C. (2008) 'Pro-social modeling'. In McIvor, G. and Raynor, P. (eds) *Developments in Social Work with Offenders*. London: Jessica Kingsley.

UK Office for National Statistics (2013) *Crime in England and Wales, Year Ending September 2012*. Online. www.ons.gov.uk/ons/dcp171778_296191.pdf (accessed 5 March 2013).

United Nations Office on Drugs and Crime (UNODC) (2012) *UNODC Homicide Statistics*. Online. www.unodc.org/unodc/en/data-and-analysis/homicide.html (accessed 15 September 2012).

US Department of Justice Federal Bureau of Investigation (2013) *US Crime rate per 100,000 population, 1960–2010*. Online. www.ucrdatatool.gov/Search/Crime/Crime.cfm (accessed 1 September 2012).

Van Gemert, F. and Fleisher, M.S. (2005) 'In the grip of the group'. In Decker, S. and Weerman, F.M. (eds) *European Street Gangs and Troublesome Youth Groups*. Lanham: Altamira Press.

Van Gemert, F., Lien, I.L., and Peterson, D. (2008) 'Introduction'. In Van Gemert, F., Peterson, D., and Lien, I.L. (eds) *Street Gangs, Migration and Ethnicity*. Portland, OR: Willan Publishing.

Van Maanen, J. (1978) 'The asshole'. In Manning, P.J., and Van Maanen J. (eds) *Policing: A view from the street*. California: Goodyear Publishing Co.

—— (1988) *Tales of the Field: On writing ethnography*. Chicago: University of Chicago Press.

Venketesh, S. (2008) *Gang Leader for a Day: A rogue sociologist crosses the line*. London: Penguin.

Violence Reduction Unit (VRU) (2011) *The Violence Must Stop: Glasgow's Community Initiative to Reduce Violence, Second Year Report*. Glasgow: VRU.

Volokh, A. (2011) 'Do faith-based prisons work?'. *Alabama Law Review*, 63: 1–43.

Wacquant, L. (1992) 'Towards a social praxeology: The structure and logic of Bourdieu's sociology'. In Bourdieu, P., and Wacquant, L. (eds) *An Invitation to Reflexive Sociology*. Chicago: University of Chicago Press.

—— (2004) *Body and Soul: Notebooks of an apprentice boxer*. New York: Oxford University Press.

—— (2008) *Urban Outcasts: A comparative sociology of advanced marginality*. Cambridge: Polity Press.

—— (2009a) *Prisons of Poverty*. Minneapolis: University of Minnesota Press.

—— (2009b) *Punishing the Poor: The neoliberal government of social insecurity*. London: Duke University Press.

Waiton, S. (2001) *Scared of the Kids?: Curfews, crime and the regulation of young people*. Sheffield: Sheffield Hallam University Press.

Waiton, S. (2008) *The Politics of Anti-Social Behaviour: Amoral panics*. London: Routledge.

Walker, S. (1977) *Critical History of Police Reform*. Lexington, MA: D.C. Heath.

—— (2001) *Police Accountability: The role of citizen oversight*. Belmont, CA: Wadsworth.

Warren, P.Y., and Tomaskovic-Devey, D. (2009) 'Racial profiling and searches: Did the politics of racial profiling change police behavior?'. *Criminology and Public Policy*, 8, 343–69.

Webb, V.J., and Marshall, C.E. (1995) 'The relative importance of race and ethnicity on citizen attitudes towards the police'. *American Journal of Police*, 14 (2), 45–66.

Weisburd, D., and Eck, J.E. (2004) 'What can the police do to reduce crime, disorder and fear?'. *Annals of the American Academy of Social and Political Sciences*, 593, 42–65.

Weisburd, D., and Green, L. (1995) 'Policing drug hot spots: The Jersey City drug market analysis experiment'. *Justice Quarterly*, 12, 711–35.

Weisburd, D., and Lum, C. (2005) 'The diffusion of computerized crime mapping in policing: Linking research and practice'. *Police Practice and Research*, 6, 419–34.

Weitzer, R. (2000) 'White, black or blue cops? Race and citizen assessments of police officers'. *Journal of Criminal Justice*, 28, 313–24.

Westley, W. A. (1970) *Violence and the police: A sociological study of law, custom, and morality*. Cambridge, MA: MIT Press.

Westmarland, L. (2008) 'Police cultures'. In Newman, T. (ed.) *Handbook of Policing*. 2nd ed. Devon: Willan.

Whyte, W.F. (1943) *Street Corner Society*. Chicago: University of Chicago Press.

Wilson, J.Q. (1968) *Varieties of Police Behavior: The management of law and order in eight communities*. Cambridge, MA: Harvard University Press.

Wilson, J.Q. and Kelling, G.L. (1982) 'Broken windows: The police and neighborhood safety'. *The Atlantic Monthly*, 249, 22–31.

Wood, J., and Hine, J. (2009) *Work with Young People: Theory for policy and practice*. London: Sage.

Wortely, S., and Tanner, J. (2008) 'Respect, friendship and racial injustice: Justifying gang membership in a Canadian city'. In Van Gemert, F., Peterson, D., and Lien, I.L (eds) *Street Gangs, Migration and Ethnicity*. Portland: Willan Publishing.

Yablonsky, L. (1967) *The Violent Gang*. Middlesex: Pelican.

Young, J. (2007) *The Vertigo of Late Modernity*. London: Sage.

Young, T., Fitzgerald, M., Hallsworth, S., and Joseph, I. (2007) *Groups, Gangs and Weapons*. London: Youth Justice Board.

Index